AGILE SOFTWARE DEVELOPMENT

Alistair Cockburn

Addison-Wesley

Boston • San Francisco • New York • Toronto • Montreal
London • Munich • Paris • Madrid
Capetown • Sydney • Tokyo • Singapore • Mexico City

Many of the designations used by manufacturers and sellers to distinguish their products are claimed as trademarks. Where those designations appear in this book, and Addison-Wesley, Inc., was aware of a trademark claim, the designations have been printed with initial capital letters or in all capitals.

The author and publisher have taken care in the preparation of this book, but make no expressed or implied warranty of any kind and assume no responsibility for errors or omissions. No liability is assumed for incidental or consequential damages in connection with or arising out of the use of the information or programs contained herein.

The publisher offers discounts on this book when ordered in quantity for special sales. For more information, please contact:

Pearson Education Corporate Sales Division
201 W. 103rd Street
Indianapolis, IN 46290
(800) 428-5331
corpsales@pearsoned.com

Visit AW on the Web: www.awprofessional.com

Additional copyright information appears on page xxv.

For information on obtaining permission for use of material from this work, please submit a written request to:

Pearson Education, Inc.
Rights and Contracts Department
75 Arlington Street, Suite 300
Boston, MA 02116
Fax: (617) 848-7047

Text printed on recycled and acid-free paper.
ISBN 0201699699
3 4 5 6 7 8 MA   05 04 03 02
3rd Printing   July 2002

AGILE SOFTWARE DEVELOPMENT

The Agile Software Development Series

Alistair Cockburn and Jim Highsmith, Series Editors
For more information check out http://www.aw.com/cseng/

Agile software development centers on four values identified in the
Agile Alliance's Manifesto:

- Individuals and interactions over processes and tools
- Working software over comprehensive documentation
- Customer collaboration over contract negotiation
- Responding to change over following a plan

The development of Agile software requires innovation and responsiveness, based on generating
and sharing knowledge within a development team and with the customer. Agile software
developers draw on the strengths of customers, users, and developers, finding just enough
process to balance quality and agility.

The books in **The Agile Software Development Series** focus on sharing the experiences of
such Agile developers. Individual books address individual techniques (such as Use Cases),
group techniques (such as collaborative decision making), and proven solutions to different
problems from a variety of organizational cultures. The result is a core of Agile best practices
that will enrich your experience and improve your work.

Titles in the Series:

Alistair Cockburn, *Surviving Object-Oriented Projects*, ISBN 0-201-49834-0

Alistair Cockburn, *Writing Effective Use Cases*, ISBN 0-201-70225-8

Lars Mathiassen, Jan Pries-Heje, and Ojelanki Ngwenyama, *Improving Software
Organizations: From Principles to Practice*, ISBN 0-201-75820-2

Alistair Cockburn, *Agile Software Development*, ISBN 0-201-69969-9

Jim Highsmith, *Agile Software Development Ecosystems*, ISBN 0-201-76043-6

To Aidan and Eve

CONTENTS

LIST OF FIGURES

LIST OF STORIES

CHAPTER 3 COMMUNICATING, COOPERATING TEAMS . . . 75

PREFACE

Is software development an art, a craft, science, engineering, or something else entirely? Does it even matter?

Yes, it does matter, and it matters to you. Your actions and their results will differ depending on which of those is more correct.

The main thing is this: You want your software out soon and defect free, but more than that, you need a way to examine how your team is doing along the way.

PURPOSE

It is time to reexamine the notions underlying software development.

The trouble is that as we look at projects, *what* we notice is constrained by what we know to notice. We learn to distinguish distinct and separable things in the extremely rich stream of experience flowing over us, and we pull those things out of the stream for examination. To the extent that we lack various key distinctions, we overlook things that are right in front of us.

We anchor the distinctions in our memories with words and use those words to reflect on our experiences. To the extent that we lack words to anchor the distinctions, we lack the ability to pull our memories into our conversations and the ability to construct meaningful strategies for dealing with the future.

In other words, to reexamine the notions that underlie software development, we have to reconsider the distinctions that we use to slice up our experience and the words we use to anchor our memories.

This is, of course, a tall order for any book. It means that some of the earlier parts of this book will be rather abstract. I see no way around it, though.

The last time people constructed a vocabulary for software development was in the late 1960s, when they coined the phrase *software engineering*, as both a wish and a direction for the future.

It is significant that at the same time the programming-should-be-engineering pronouncement was made, Gerald Weinberg was writing *The Psychology of Computer Programming*. In that book, software development doesn't look very much like an engineering discipline at all. It appears to be something very human-centric and communication-centric. Of the two, Weinberg's observations match what people have reported in the succeeding 30 years, and *software engineering* remains a wishful term.

In this book, I will

- Build distinctions and vocabulary for talking about software development
- Use that vocabulary to examine and anchor critical aspects of software projects that have been pushed to the sidelines too often
- Work through the ideas and principles of methodologies as "rules of behavior"
- Merge our need for these rules of behavior with the idea that each project is unique, and derive effective and self-evolving rules

I hope that after reading this book, you will be able to use the new vocabulary to look around at your project, notice things you didn't notice before, and express those observations. As you gain facility, you should be able to

- Discuss Extreme Programming, the Capability Maturity Model, the Personal Software Process, or your favorite process
- Determine when each process is more or less applicable
- Understand people who have differing opinions, abilities, and experience

AUDIENCE

Each person coming to this book does so with a different experience level, reading style, and role. Here's how you might read the book to use it to your greatest advantage: by experience, by reading style, or by role.

BY EXPERIENCE

This book is written for the more experienced audience. The book does not contain procedures to follow to develop software; in fact, core to the book is the concept that every technique has limitations. Therefore, it is impossible to name one best and correct way to develop software. Ideally, the book helps you reach that understanding and then leads you to constructive ideas about how to deal with this real-world situation.

If you are an intermediate practitioner who has experience with software-development projects, and if you are now looking for the boundaries for the rules you have learned, you will find the following topics most helpful:

- What sorts of methodologies fit what sorts of projects
- Indices for selecting the appropriate methodology category for a project
- The principles behind agile methodologies

Being an intermediate practitioner, you will recognize that you must add your own judgement when applying these ideas.

If you are an advanced practitioner, you already know that all recommendations vary in applicability. You may be looking for words to help you express that. You will find those words where the following topics are presented:

- Managing the incompleteness of communication
- Continuous methodology reinvention
- The manifesto for agile software development

A few topics should be new even to advanced software developers: the vocabulary for describing methodologies and the technique for just-in-time methodology tuning.

BY READING STYLE

The earlier chapters are more abstract than the later chapters.

If you enjoy abstract material, read the book from beginning to end, watching the play of abstract topics to see the resolution of the impossible questions through the course of the book.

If you want concrete materials in your hands as quickly as possible, you may want to skip over the early chapters on the first read and start with Chapter 4, "Methodologies." Return to the sections about "Cooperative Games" and "Convection Currents of Information" to get the key parts of the new vocabulary. Dip into the introduction and the chapters about individuals and teams to fill in the gaps.

By Role

People who sponsor software development can get from this book an understanding of how various organizational, behavioral, and funding structures affect the rate at which they receive value from their development teams. Project sponsors may pay less attention to the details of methodology construction than people who are directly involved in the projects. They should still understand the consequences of certain sorts of methodology decisions.

Team leads and project managers can see how seating, teaming, and individuality affect their project's outcome. They can also learn what sorts of interventions are more likely to have better or worse consequences. They will need to understand the construction and consequences of their methodology and how to evolve their methodology—making it as light as possible, but still sufficient.

Process and methodology designers can examine and argue with my choice of terms and principles for methodology design. The ensuing discussions should prove useful for the field.

Software developers should come to know this material simply as part of being in the profession. In the normal progression from newcomers to leaders, they will have to notice what works and doesn't work on their projects. They will also have to learn how to adjust their environment to become more effective. "Our methodology" really means "the conventions we follow around here," and so it becomes every professional's responsibility to understand the basics of methodology construction.

Organization of the Book

The book is designed to set up two nearly impossible questions at the beginning and derive answers for those questions by the end of the book:

- If communication is fundamentally impossible, how can people on a project manage to do it?
- If all people and all projects are different, how can we create any rules for productive projects?

To achieve that design, I wrote the book a bit in the "whodunit" style of a mystery. I start with the broadest and most philosophical discussions: "What is communication?" and "What is software development?"

The discussion moves through still fairly abstract topics such as "What are the characteristics of a human?" and "What affects the movement of ideas within a team?"

Eventually, it gets into more concrete territory with "What are the elements and principles of methodologies?" This is a good place for you to start if you are after concrete material early on.

Finally, the discussion gets to the most concrete matter: "What does a light, sufficient, self-evolving methodology look like?" and "How does a group create a custom and agile methodology in time to do the project any good?"

The two appendixes contain supporting material. The first contains the "Agile Software Development Manifesto," signed by 17 very experienced software developers and methodologists.

The second appendix contains extracts from three pieces of writing that are not as widely read as they should be. I include them because they are core to the topics described in the book.

HERITAGE OF THE IDEAS IN THIS BOOK

The ideas in this book are based on 25 years of development experience and 10 years of investigating projects directly.

The IBM Consulting Group asked me to design its first object-oriented methodology in 1991. I looked rather helplessly at the conflicting "methodology" books at the time. My boss, Kathy Ulisse, and I decided that I should debrief project teams to better understand how they really worked. What an eye-opener! The words they used had almost no overlap with the words in the books.

The interviews keep being so valuable that I still visit projects with sufficiently interesting success stories to find out what they encountered, learned, and recommend. The crucial question I ask before the interview is, "And would you like to work the same way again?" When people describe their experiences in words that don't fit my vocabulary, it indicates new areas in which I lack distinctions and words.

The reason for writing this book now is that the words and distinctions finally are correlating with descriptions of project life and project results. They are proving more valuable for diagnosis and intervention than any of the tools that I used previously.

The ideas in this book have been through dozens of development teams, eight methodology designs, and a number of successful projects on which I participated.

AGILITY

I am not the only person who is using these ideas:

- Kent Beck and Ward Cunningham worked through the late 1980s on what became called *Extreme Programming* (XP) in the late 1990s.
- Jim Highsmith studied the language and business use of complex adaptive systems in the mid-1990s and wrote about the application of that language to software development in his *Adaptive Software Development*.
- Ken Schwaber and Jeff Sutherland were constructing the Scrum method of development at about the same time, and many project leaders made similar attempts to describe similar ideas through the same years.

When a group of us met in February 2001 to discuss our differences and similarities, we found we had a surprising number of things in common. We selected the word *agile* to describe our intent and wrote the Agile Software Development Manifesto (Appendix A).

We are still formulating the principles that we share and are finding many other people who could have been at that meeting if they had known about it or if their schedules had permitted their presence.

Core to *agile* software development is the use of light-but-sufficient rules of project behavior and the use of human- and communication-oriented rules.

Agility implies maneuverability, a characteristic that is more important now than ever. Deploying software to the Web has intensified software competition further than before. Staying in business involves not only getting software out and reducing defects but tracking continually moving user and marketplace demands. Winning in business increasingly involves winning at the software-development game. Winning at the game depends on understanding the game being played.

The best description I have found for *agility* in business comes from Goldman (1997):

"Agility is dynamic, context-specific, aggressively change-embracing, and growth-oriented. It is not about improving efficiency, cutting costs, or battening down the business hatches to ride out fearsome competitive 'storms.' It is about succeeding and about winning: about succeeding in emerging competitive arenas, and about winning profits, market share, and customers in the very center of the competitive storms many companies now fear."

THE AGILE SOFTWARE DEVELOPMENT SERIES

Among the people concerned with *agility* in software development over the last decade, Jim Highsmith and I found so much in common that we joined efforts to bring to press an Agile Software Development Series based around relatively light, effective, human-powered software-development techniques.

We base the series on these two core ideas:

• Different projects need different processes or methodologies.

• Focusing on skills, communication, and community allows the project to be more effective and more agile than focusing on processes.

The series has these three main tracks:

• Techniques to improve the effectiveness of a person who is doing a particular sort of job. This might be a person who is designing a user interface, gathering requirements, planning a project, designing, or testing. Whoever is performing such a job will want to know how the best people in the world do their jobs. *Writing Effective Use Cases* (Cockburn 2001c) and *GUIs with Glue* (Hohmann, forthcoming) are two individual technique books.

- Techniques to improve the effectiveness of a group of people. These might include techniques for team building, project retrospectives, decision making, and the like. *Improving Software Organizations* (Mathiassen 2002) and *Surviving Object-Oriented Projects* (Cockburn 1998) are two group technique books.
- Examples of particular, successful agile methodologies. Whoever is selecting a base methodology to tailor will want to find one that has already been used successfully in a similar situation. Modifying an existing methodology is easier than creating a new one and is more effective than using one that was designed for a different situation. *Crystal Clear* (Cockburn, forthcoming) is a sample methodology book. We look forward to identifying other examples to publish.

Two books anchor the Agile Software Development Series:

- This one expresses the thoughts about *agile* software development using my favorite vocabulary: that of software development as a cooperative game, methodology as conventions about coordination, and families of methodologies.
- The second book is Highsmith's forthcoming one, *Agile Software Development Ecosystems*. It extends the discussion about problems in software development, common principles in the diverse recommendations of the people who signed the Agile Software Development Manifesto, and common agile practices. Highsmith's previous book, *Adaptive Software Development*, expresses his thoughts about software development using his favorite vocabulary, that of complex adaptive systems.

You can find more about Crystal, Adaptive, and other agile methodologies on the Web. Specific sites and topics are included in the References at the back. A starter set includes these sites:

- www.CrystalMethodologies.org
- www.AdaptiveSD.com
- www.AgileAlliance.org
- My home site, members.aol.com/acockburn

THANKS TO SPECIFIC PEOPLE

Ralph Hodgson has this amazing library of obscure and interesting books. More astounding, though, is how he manages to have in his briefcase just that obscure book I happen to need to read next: Vinoed's *Sketches of Thought* and Wenger and Lave's *Situated Learning*, among others. The interesting and obscure books you find in the References chapter probably came from Ralph's library.

Luke Hohmann tutored me about Karl Weick and Elliot Soloway. Jim Highsmith taught me that "emergent behavior" is a *characteristic* of the rules and not just "lucky." Each spent a disproportionate amount of time influencing the sequencing of topics and accuracy of references, commenting on nearly every page.

Jason Yip beautifully skewered my first attempt to describe information dissemination as gas dispersion. He wrote, "Kim is passing information. Information is green gas. Kim is passing green gas . . ." Yikes! You can guess that those sentences changed!

Bo Leuf came up with the wonderful wordplay of *argh-minutes* (in lieu of *erg-seconds*) as the unit of measure for frustrating communications sessions. He also was kind enough to double-check some of my assertions. For example, he wrote to some Israelis to check my contention that in Israel, "politeness in conversation is considered more of an insult than a compliment." That produced an exciting e-mail exchange, which included (from Israelis): "Definitely wrong on this one, your author. . . . We always say hello and shake hands after not seeing for a few days. . . .

I think your author is mistaking a very little tolerance for mistakes at work for a lack of politeness." Another wrote, "Regarding your being flamed. There is no way out of it, no matter what you say. According to me, Israelis would demand of you to have your own opinion and to stand behind it. And of course they have their own (at least one :-)." Benny Sadeh offered the word I finally used, "frankness."

Martin Fowler contributed the handy concept of "visibility" to the methodology discussion, in addition to helping with constructive comments and being very gentle where he thought something was terrible.

Other energetic reviewers I would like to recognize and thank (in first-name alphabetical order) are Alan Harriman, Allen Galleman, Andrea Branca, Andy Sen, Bill Caputo, Charles Herbaut, Charlie Toland, Chris Lopez, Debbie Utley, Glenn Vanderburg, Hirohide Yazaki, James Hanrahan, Jeff Miller, Jeff Patton, Jesper Kornerup, Jim Sawyer, John Brewer, John Cook, Keith Damon, Laurence Archer, Michael Van Hilst, Nick Fortescue, Patrick Manion, Phil Goodwin, Richard Pfeiffer, Ron Holiday, Russ Rufer, Scott Jackson, Ted Young, Tom DeMarco, and Tracy Bialik.

The Silicon Valley Patterns Group took the trouble to dissect the draft as a group, for which I doubly thank them.

The Salt Lake production team of Elizabeth Wilcox, Cathy Gilmore, John Roberts, and Malia Howland did a fantastic job of turning the manuscript into a final book in an unreasonably short period of time.

All these people did their best to see that I fixed the weak parts and kept the good parts. If I had another few years to keep reworking the book, I might even have been able to get it to the point that they would have accepted it.

In the absence of those extra years, I thank them for their efforts and apologize for not being able to fix all the awkward spots.

Thank goodness the Beans & Brews coffee shop finally started playing jazz and rock again. I lost several months of writing to heavy metal and country music. Thanks to the Salt Lake Roasting Company for staying open until midnight.

To save us some future embarrassment, my name is pronounced "Cō-burn," with a long *o*.

ADDITIONAL COPYRIGHT INFORMATION

INTRODUCTION

Unknowable and Incommunicable

This introductory chapter sets up two questions: "Can you ever know what you are experiencing, and can you ever communicate it?" The short answer, "No, you can't," creates the basic dilemma that this book addresses.

If you can't know what you are experiencing, how can you reflect on projects, and how can you form recommendations for doing better? Both spending time on irrelevant factors and overlooking important factors will hurt you. This inescapable problem faces every person who is trying to work better: methodologist, researcher, and practitioner alike.

Knowing that perfect communications are impossible relieves you of trying to reach that perfection. Instead, you learn to manage the incompleteness of communication. Rather than try to make the requirements document or the design model comprehensible to everyone, you stop when the document is sufficient to the purpose of the intended audience. "Managing the incompleteness of communications" is core to mastering agile software development.

After setting up the two questions, this chapter introduces the idea of operating at different levels of expertise. A novice listens differently than an expert does and asks for different guidance. This third section discusses the importance of understanding the listening levels of the people who are involved in the project.

The final section relates the abstract concepts to everyday life.

This is the most abstract chapter in the book. If you don't enjoy abstract topics, then skim it for now and return to it after reading some of the later, more concrete chapters.

Unknowable and Incommunicable

THE PROBLEM WITH PARSING EXPERIENCE

THE WINE LABEL

A good guest, I gave the hostess my bottle of wine as I arrived, and I watched with curiosity as she put it into the refrigerator.

When she pulled it out at dinnertime, she said, "This will go well with the fish."

"But that's red wine," I finally offered.

"It's white," she said.

"It's red," I insisted, pointing to the label.

"Of course not. It's red. It says so right here. . ." she started to read the label out loud. ". . .Oh! It's red! Why did I put it into the refrigerator?"

We laughed and spent time recalling each attempt we had made to check our respective views of the "truth." How on earth, she asked, could she have looked at the bottle so many times and not noticed that it was a red wine?

People who report on software development projects also make mistakes of observation that get passed along as "facts." Requirements writers are not exempt, either. They observe their user community and produce documents that they think contain only "requirements" but that often contain mistakes of observation as well.

CONFLICTING PARSING PATTERNS

When we live through an experience, we *parse* it, to use the linguistic term. We chop the experience into separate, meaningful chunks that we store for later retrieval. The human mind does this whether we want it to or not.

There are many, and many different, patterns we can use to chop experience into pieces. Each pattern produces a unique perception of the experience.

STEAK TASTING

When I was first going out to restaurants, I worked at distinguishing and enjoying the *taste* of steaks. One day, someone told me that it is not the taste but the *texture* that differentiates steaks.

That single idea invalidated what I had thought about steaks up to then and set up a new parsing pattern for the future.

Each parsing pattern leaves small, unresolved gaps in the result. When we parse according to any one pattern and later put our pieces back together, we get a distorted, simplified, incomplete result. We only hope that it is "close enough" to be useful in the ways we use the recollection.

When two people use different parsing patterns, the resulting, differently shaped thoughts give them quite different vocabularies for describing the same events and different results when the pieces are put back together (all distorted, simplified, and incomplete). Thus, one person might describe steaks based on taste, and another might describe them based on texture. Neither description is complete; worse than that, the two people can't share results with each other.

Let's look at this idea in two separate contexts, first with a visual example and then as it applies to software development.

For the visual example, look at how I put together a shape made entirely from circle arcs (Figure i-1).

Figure i-1 One arc and an arc pair.

From these and some small circles I put together the next shape, which looks a bit like an owl's face (Figure i-2). At this point, notice that I have biased your future perception of these shapes. One of the points in this discussion is the bias created by my giving you the name of the shape early on.

Figure i-2 Arcs forming a face.

Putting two owl heads together produces pictures that might look like lima beans, faces, an apple core, or some other shape that you choose to name (Figure i-3).

Figure i-3 Apple cores?

Finally, I build the picture I had in mind (Figure i-4). What do *you* see in it? How do you parse it into distinguishable sections? Do you see eye shades, embryos, or lima beans? Do you see two yin-yang shapes?

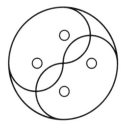

Figure i-4 Complex circle.

Actually, I had in mind two overlapping yin-yang shapes (Figure i-5). Nothing in my intention had to do with arcs, owls, apple cores, or embryos. All of those were secondary effects, artifacts that showed up when I combined the two *yin* and *yang* icons, one mirrored and rotated from the other, and parsed the picture according to a different pattern.

The point of my presenting the images in a different order is to illustrate three things:

- Any complex shape can be parsed according to different patterns.
- Our perception about "what is there" proceeds in different directions depending on how we separate elements.
- What we notice is biased by the vocabulary we start with.

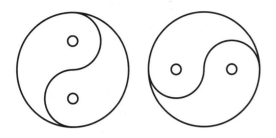

Figure i-5 Yin and yang.

In software development, each person uses his own pattern to parse the experience of being on a project. Each person also falls prey to common errors.

A person might have the notion that humidity is a critical success factor in software development. This person would consequently spend a great deal of effort on measuring and controlling the humidity on projects. A person who is really convinced that humidity is key would not notice for a long time that no great correlation exists between humidity and project outcome. Since I don't have humidity in my project parsing pattern, I couldn't tell you what the humidity was in each of my projects, how it varied over time, or how it might have correlated with project outcome.

A person might believe that following a defined process is crucial to project success. This person would consequently spend a great deal of effort measuring and controlling adherence to the process. A person really convinced that process is key would not notice for a long time the absence of correlation between following a process and the project outcome.

Just as bad as focusing on something irrelevant is omitting something crucial in the parsing pattern. Suppose, for a moment, that a scientist who is doing geomagnetic experiments in a building is unaware that the walls of the building contain iron. Not only will he get anomalous results, but he will not understand where they came from or how to alter any of the other variables in the experiments to compensate.

The presence of *people* on a project is just such a crucial element of project outcome.

Those who do not have the *people* element in their parsing pattern will simply not notice the effects of the people on their projects. When reading articles that recount the effect of using a particular new process (for example, Webb 1999), you may notice that the body of the narrative comments on people but that the conclusion omits commentary regarding people. Researchers who miss this key element in their operating vocabulary cannot use it to adjust the outcome of a project.

The same argument applies to every practitioner, methodologist, and researcher, including me. It is one reason I waited 13 years before writing this book. Much like discovering the difference between texture and taste in evaluating steaks, I kept discovering new parsing patterns for development projects. The results of using the different patterns were so different that I could not commit to any one of them.

These days, when I study a project, I am periodically reawakened to the fact that I don't know what it is that I don't know but should know—what I *should* be paying attention to but don't have a parsing element for.

This concept of being limited in our awareness of underlying parsing patterns does not reflect something abnormal. The world is not kind enough to give us in advance the yin and yang shapes to use in our daily experiences. We are not first given the parsing pattern and then asked what the result looks like. Rather, we are given a complex experience on which any number of parsing patterns work and in which secondary artifacts easily command our attention. Although this condition can cause difficulty, it is normal and is worth reconsidering from time to time.

DETECTING PARSING PATTERNS

My role as a research and field methodologist is to parse software development experiences that happen at full speed, detect boundaries fit for parsing, and give the pieces names that can be recalled for the next project. Detecting and naming these distinctions provides additional filters through which to examine the software development experience. This work does not create new techniques; it allows us to better detect what is already occurring in the projects and put the pieces back together in ways that will more closely match future experiences.

These days, I ask people to tell a story from a project (preferably something that worked, but any relevant episode will do). Then I see if I can reconstruct the story using the labels that I have in mind about project experience. With slowly increasing frequency, I can. When I can't, I store the story for later comparison. When two stories contain similarities, I look for words I can use to label the common parts.

We are still in the infancy of naming what is really happening on software development projects. The answer is not *process, modeling,* or *mathematics,* although those play parts. The answer has much more to do with *craft, community, pride,* and *learning,* as we will discuss.

The next step is for methodologists to partner with ethnographers, sociologists, and anthropologists to see if they have words to capture other parts of the experience. Through such a partnership on one project, I learned that system architects act as storytellers. They keep alive the promise and vision of the future system, which is particularly valuable during the confusing early periods of a project. Partnering with social specialists is something I strongly recommend to both researchers and contract software companies who are learning how to work more effectively.

THINKING INEXACT THOUGHTS

We don't notice what is in front of us, and we don't have adequate names for what we do notice. But it gets worse: When we go to communicate, we don't even know exactly what it is we mean to communicate.

In an ideal world, we would have in mind an exact idea of what we wanted to communicate, and our job would be merely to locate the words necessary to communicate that idea. Usually, however, what we want to express sits in a crack between all the words we possess. We use various words, shifting them around, trying to make them convey what we think we intend to say.

On some occasions, the idea we want to communicate is not even available to our conscious thought. The idea is just a sense that some such idea ought to be there. As we speak, we fish around inside ourselves, hoping that some set of sentences we utter will pull forth the thought we would like to have, to express to our conversation partners.

See how many words it takes you to express a thought, and then pay attention to the fact that what you expressed wasn't what you meant, and that quite possibly, what you had in mind wasn't even what you felt.

This has implications for both designing and communicating.

In the book *Sketches of Thought*, Vinod Goel (1995) investigates the idea that significant useful mental processing happens in a realm of imprecise thought, proto-thoughts of ideas whose boundaries have not yet been demarcated by the mind.

The study participants commented on the damage done to the developing ideas when the undemarcated thoughts are forced into a precise expression too early. Some processing works best while the proto-thoughts are still undemarcated.

Two of the participants complained about working with precise images: "You almost get committed to something before you know whether you like it or not" and "I have to decide beforehand what I want before I can draw it" (Goel, p. 200). One person said:

> "One gets the feeling that all the work is being done internally with a different type of symbol system and recorded after the fact, presumably

because the external symbol system cannot support such operations" (Goel, p. 200).

Pelle Ehn describes software design similarly. Recognizing that neither the users nor the designers could adequately identify, parse, and name their experiences, he asked them to *design by doing*. In the article reproduced in Appendix B he writes:

> "The language-games played in design-by-doing can be viewed both from the point of view of the users and of the designers. This kind of design becomes a language-game in which the users learn about possibilities and constraints of new computer tools that may become part of their ordinary language-games. The designers become the teachers that teach the users how to participate in this particular language-game of design. However, to set up these kinds of language-games, the designers have to learn from the users.
>
> "However, paradoxical as it sounds, users and designers do not have to understand each other fully in playing language-games of design-by-doing together. Participation in a language-game of design and the use of design artifacts can make constructive but different sense to users and designers."

That takes us pretty well to the boundary of ignorance: We don't notice what is in front of us, we don't have adequate names for what we do notice, and when we go to communicate we don't know

exactly what it is we mean to communicate. The only thing that might be worse

is if we couldn't actually communicate
our message.

THE IMPOSSIBILITY OF COMMUNICATION

That little grimace
you just made across the dinner table
speaks volumes to me,
though it says nothing to the others around us.

You twisted your lips like that yesterday

to show how you felt about that fellow
who had behaved so awfully, when
you were trying to be nice.

I quite agree.

Actually, he rather reminds me of the man
on your left.
I raise my eyebrows a hair
and glance lightly in his direction.

From the stiffening of your top lip as you
continue to chew, it is clear you think so too.

Oh, oh. We've been spotted.
No matter.
Our conversation, although discovered,
will have no meaning to anyone else.
And the poor man on your left will always suffer

from the label we gave him

in this short conversation.

—Alistair Cockburn, 1986

What *is* the information content of a raised eyebrow?

Don't look for the answer in Claude Shannon's seminal papers about information theory (Shannon 1963). He analyzed *constrained channels*, those in which the communication vocabulary is known in advance. In real-world communication, the channel is unconstrained. When or whether you raise your eyebrow is not prearranged. The "stiffening of your top lip" is the invention of a moment, referencing a *shared experience* with your conversation partner. In the poem above, the partner had that shared experience but the spotter did not. And so the spotter did not derive the same information content as the partner.

Biologists Maturana and Varela have investigated this in the context of biological systems. The following wording from *The Tree of Knowledge*, (Maturana 1998, p. 196) describes their results:

"Our discussion has led us to conclude that, biologically, there is no 'transmitted information' in communication. Communication takes place each time there is behavioral coordination in a realm of structural coupling. This conclusion is surprising only if we insist on not questioning the latest metaphor for communication . . . [in which] communication is something generated at a certain point. It is carried by a conduit (or tube) and is delivered to the receiver at the other end. Hence, there is a something that is communicated, and what is communicated is an integral part of that which travels in the tube. Thus, we usually speak of the "information" contained in a picture, an object, or more evidently, the printed word. . . . According to our analysis, this metaphor is basically false. . . . [E]ach person hears what he hears according to his own structural determination. . . . The phenomenon of communication does not depend on what is transmitted, but on what happens to the person who receives it. And this is a very different matter from 'transmitting information.'"

To put it into words that are simpler, although perhaps less accurate biologically, each living being exists inside a membrane that transfers impinging events into *internal* signals, which initiate internal activities. It is really only the internal signals that the being "notices," not the external signals. The surprising thing is that the internal signals can also be generated by activities and events *inside* the being!

A being that "notices" something cannot be sure whether that something originated from an internal or external signal. Thus we "see" images in dreams and hallucinations, when the eyes are closed. Maturana and Varela studied this effect in color vision, finding that we regularly see a color in a scene that does not explicitly contain that color. We generate the color's presence through internal mechanisms.

The "behavioral coordination in a realm of structural coupling" is the correlation between those things impinging on the membrane from the outside and the internal activities that follow. Obviously, we wouldn't last very long as beings if there weren't a fairly good correlation between the outside events and the internal activities generated. It is important to recognize, however, that the internal activities are equally determined by the internal state of the being, its "own structural determination." The information received is not what impinges upon the receiver, but what happens inside the receiver afterwards.

To put this into a concrete example, consider that someone runs into the room and shouts "Fire!" in Japanese. A Japanese-speaking listener receives a lot of information and immediately leaps up and runs to the exit. The Japanese person next to him, who happens to be asleep, receives no information at all. The external stimulus was never converted into an internal signal. A person who speaks no Japanese notices that someone came in and shouted something, but he received no particular information from the sounds uttered. What each person receives from the shout depends on his internal condition.

INTERNAL RESTRUCTURING

Information at the receiver's side is not a static, externally determinable quantity but rather a transient, dynamic personal quantity. The information *received* is a measure of the internal restructuring that follows the impingement of the signal. It is the quantity representing the size of the change in the receiver's predictive model of the world after receiving it.

Consider these few examples to see this in action:

"I am thinking of a set of numbers. The set includes 1, 3, 7, 11, 13, . . ."

At this point the listener has built up a predictive model that holds those numbers, the fact that they are in the set, and that 5 and 9 are conspicuously missing. They are conspicuously missing because the typical person constructed a second model, "the odd numbers without 5 and 9," alongside the first.

The speaker continues with:

". . . 15 is in the set . . ."

On hearing this, the model grows by one element, that "15 is in the set." No new patterns show up.

The speaker continues with:

". . . 5 and 9 are in the set . . ."

At this point, the model changes dramatically, because the sentence contained a lot of "information" for the listener, much more than the earlier arrival of the number 15. Instead of adding two more to the list of numbers in the set, the listener reduces the model to be "the odd numbers." Hearing that 5 and 9 are in the set added more than two small units information: It converted two medium-sized, competing models into a single, small model. The change in the size of the predictive model was relatively large.

The "information received," being a measure of the momentary change in the receiver, is a transient quantity. Hearing the same sentence twice does not bring the same information the second time. Typically, the receiver's internal predictive model does not change as much, because the restructuring is usually smaller.

Suppose the speaker repeats,

". . . 5 and 9 are in the set . . ."

The listener already knows that 5 and 9 are in the set. At this point, the speaker can keep naming odd numbers without disturbing the predictive model of the listener. Each new number adds increasing certainty about the model, but not much more.

If the speaker names an even number, then the listener scrambles to recall which odd numbers were named. He must throw away the "odd numbers" model and remember each number individually again. The moment of adding an even number provides a lot of information for the listener.

TOUCHING INTO SHARED EXPERIENCE

How do you ever know what message your listener receives? In conversation he returns messages, and you convince yourself that he really understood your intended message (at least closely enough).

Of course, sometimes you misunderstand his return message and falsely conclude that he understood your message. When you eventually find out, you exclaim, "But I thought my message was clear!"

The success of communication, then, lies in the sender and receiver having a shared experience to refer to.

GRIMACE AT THE STORE

Yesterday, when you and I were at the store, I grimaced when the sales clerk made a particular remark. Today, I make the same grimace. Your mind flashes back to the situation with the sales clerk. Comparing the situation at the current moment with that one, you detect commonality and transfer yesterday's emotional state to today's situation. You *get* my intended meaning, because we share a memory of the grimace.

When you have an experience sufficiently in common with another person, all you need to do is re-evoke that experience within him. When you touch a second experience in close succession, you link the two, creating new information. The fact of considering those two experiences as relevant to the moment is a new, shared experience for the two of you, one that you can later refer to. In this way, people jointly construct new concepts a little at a time, building new touch points from known experiences. Someone joining in at the end of the conversation lacks those intermediate touch points and must be "brought up to speed"; that is, given sufficient touch points to join in.

These touch points grow as a person progresses in experience from beginner to junior, expert, and eventually working partner.

Beginners attend a programming school, where they pick up an initial vocabulary on which to build. They learn standardized notations and simple idioms, which create touch points for the low-level elements of design. Those who are learning object-oriented design become familiar with *subclassing* and *polymorphism* at the early stages, *sequence charts* and *cardinality* soon after, and perhaps a few of the *Design Patterns* (Gamma 1995). An experienced person trying to communicate a design to someone with this background can only work from these low-level terms. The experienced designer typically experiences this as tedious and missing the overall intention behind the design.

A junior programmer joins a series of projects, building common vocabulary and ideas in stages. The experienced person describing a design to a person at this stage might review some source code, do some joint programming, role-play the operation with some index cards, draw UML diagrams of various kinds, and draw arbitrary scribbles on the whiteboard while talking. The experienced person helps build a different vocabulary in the junior person, and the two of them create new experience they can later refer to.

Two experienced programmers who have not been on projects together refer to common, advanced idioms of design. Their conversation might include fragments such as "... Just use *Composite* here, with a *Decorator* for the side view," "... Set them up as dot-h files, but incorporate ..." and so on. Through these large elements of description and additional squiggles on the whiteboard, one can convey an understanding of the design structure and perhaps reach the intention of the design.

Programmers who have worked together for years have many touch points of shared experience. Their descriptions of requirements and design can be very brief, built on references to previous projects. "... It's the same pseudo-DNA structure we used on the Fox project, but this time separating out the ..." The short-cut expressions allow them to communicate and move at a speed not possible with even advanced outsiders. They are able to convey much better the intentions they had while designing.

In professional life, people don't have time to rebuild the vocabulary from the ground up each time they need to communicate. They look for the highest level of common experience they share and build new experiences from there. In no case can they ever be sure the listener really understands what was intended.

MANAGING IMPERFECT COMMUNICATION

Communication is never perfect and complete. Such a thing is not even possible. Even assuming for the moment that you, yourself, know what you intend, the receivers of the communication must jump across a gap at some point and must jump it all on their own.

People with similar experience can jump a large gap, working even from mumblings and gestures.

The more different another person is from you, the smaller the communication gap that he can jump. You have to back up, explain basic concepts, and then work forward until he builds his own bridge of experience and understands what you are saying.

There is no end to this backing up. No matter how much you back up, there is always someone who will not understand.

The irony is apparent: In the computer industry, we write specification and design documents *as though* we can actually explain what we mean. We can't. We can never hope to completely specify the requirements or the design.

We have to assume that the reader has a certain level of experience. If we can assume more experience, then we can write less. If we have to assume less experience, then we have to write more.

THE RUSSIAN PROGRAMMERS

A group in an American firm that was contracting their programming to a Russian company contacted me. They wanted me to teach them how to write use cases for Russian programmers who knew neither English nor the domain very well.

I said, "You can't hope to teach them the domain inside the requirements document. First teach them the domain; then write a short requirements document that speaks to someone knowledgeable in the domain."

After trying for hours to get me to reveal the secret of communicating across this enormous gap, they finally admitted they had previously (and successfully) worked simply by putting the key people in the same room. They were just hoping that I had a way to communicate the requirements across the ocean perfectly using use cases.

In the end, they improved on my suggestion. They wrote a short requirements document for their local domain experts and then flew one of those experts to Russia to translate, explain, and generally ensure that the programmers were doing the right thing.

The domain expert could jump the large gap presented by the short use case document and then produce, *as needed, and only as needed*, communication to fill in and reduce the size of the gaps so that the Russian programmers could jump across.

The domain expert did not attempt to communicate perfectly. He managed the continuous incompleteness of the communications by interacting with the programmers in person and watching what they produced. Luke Hohmann (1997) refers to this as "reducing the equivocality" in the communication.

What the domain expert understood was that he did not have to reduce the equivocality to zero. He only had to reduce it to the point that the Russian programmers could take meaningful action.

Given that complete communication is never possible, the task on a project is not to try for complete communication but *to manage the incompleteness of our communications*.

The target is to reduce equivocality enough for appropriate action to be taken. That means guessing how much is needed, where to stop, when and how to make the gaps smaller, and how to help the receivers to jump larger gaps.

Software projects are short on time and money, and making the gap smaller costs both. You need to discover how large a gap you can get by with at each moment, how much equivocality you can tolerate, and stop there.

THREE LEVELS OF LISTENING

People who are learning and mastering new skills pass through three quite different stages of behavior: *following*, *detaching*, and *fluent*.

People in the *following* stage look for one procedure that works. Even if 10 procedures could work, they can't learn 10 at once. They need one to learn first, one that works. They copy it; they learn it. In this stage, practitioners measure success by (a) whether the procedure works and (b) how well they can carry out the procedure.

THE 1708 CARD READER

We watched a Humanities major encountering the Univac 1708 card readers for the first time in her first programming class (this was 1974).

Her short program didn't compile. Upset at this failure, she requested help from the student assistant. When the program failed to compile a second time, she became nearly hysterical, and shouted at the assistant in tears: "But you *promised* me it would work!"

Her reaction is typical of stage one learning. The reward for success in this first stage is the sense of, "at least this thing works," and "I can at least manage to accomplish that."

People moving to some new skill domain, whether software or some other, want explicit instructions. In terms of written software development methodologies, this means a thick, detailed manual. The thickness and the detail offer signs of safety for the learning.

In the *detaching*, or Level 2, stage, people locate the limitations of the single procedure and look for rules about when the procedure breaks down. They are actually in the first stage of a new learning; namely, learning the limits of the procedure. The person in the detaching stage learns to adapt the procedure to varying circumstances. He is now more interested in learning the 10 alternative procedures, in learning when each is most applicable and when each breaks down.

A large-scale technique breakdown of this sort occurred in our industry when large software contracting firms, finely tuned to developing software using Information Engineering (IE) architectures, had to begin delivering object-oriented software. After years of unsuccessfully trying to adapt IE methods, they had to develop completely new development methodologies, often regressing through quite unstructured development before discovering new structures to support the new projects. Most of these organizations now have two methodologies, one for IE and another for object-oriented (OO) development.

In the third, *fluent* stage, it becomes irrelevant to the practitioner whether he is following any particular technique or not. His knowledge has become integrated throughout a thousand thoughts and actions. Ask him if he is following a particular procedure, and he is likely to shrug his shoulders: It doesn't matter to him whether he is following a procedure, improvising around one, or making up a new one. He understands the desired end effect and simply makes his way to that end.

A team leader who has led a number of projects in different areas doesn't care about "methodology" anymore: "Just leave us alone and we'll deliver it," he says. He simply observes and senses that more discipline is needed here, more freedom there, more communication in some other place. This is the Level 3 practitioner.

THE THREE LEVELS AND METHODOLOGIES

The same three levels apply to listening, coaching, or reading about software development. It is important to respect all three levels, as the following story illustrates.

LEVEL MIX-UP WITH CRC CARDS

Three of us, unaware of these levels of learning, accidentally crossed to the wrong level on our first design mentoring assignment. We decided to lead small design sessions using Class-Responsibility-Collaborator (CRC) cards. (See Beck 1989.)

The three of us worked slightly differently, which upset the designers, who were newcomers to object-oriented design. They said, "You are all doing something different! Which one of you is right, and why don't the others do that, too?!"

We tried saying, "It doesn't matter. They all work." But that did not help the beginners, who were confused: Should they hold the cards up or leave them on the table? Should they write down all the instance variables, or some, or none? And so on.

We knew that the session could be made to work using any of those variants, but the beginners were still in Level 1 and needed one defined way of working that they could apply several times in a row.

A programming book aimed at the Level 1 audience would work to assure the reader that there really is a way of developing software that works, and that if the reader will just follow it, success is assured. Such a book might be called *The Science of Programming* (Gries 1981) or *A Discipline for Software Engineering* (Humphrey 1995).

A methodology text aimed at the Level 1 audience describes processes, techniques, and standards in detail. The very detailed templates in the Rational Unified Process (RUP) serve Level 1 practitioners. The big methodologies of Andersen Consulting, Ernst & Young, and the like fall into this category.

A programming book aimed at the Level 2 audience might be called *The Art of Computer Programming* (Knuth 1997, 1998). It would show the reader several techniques for working, with examples and notes about when each is more useful.

A book aimed at combined Level 2 and Level 3 audiences might be called *The Laissez-Faire of Programming* (think of that as an alternate title for this book) or *The Pragmatic Programmer* (Hunt 2000). It would name issues to bear in mind and identify techniques that the practitioner might learn, pick up, and put down as needed. The expert will find it a useful library of ideas, but the beginner finds it lacking specific rules.

The Level 3 listener knows that all the published software development techniques are personal and somewhat arbitrary. Discussions among Level 3 people sound distressingly Zen:

"Do whatever works."

"When you are really doing it, you are unaware that you are doing it."

"Use a technique so long as it is doing some good."

To someone at the fluent level of behavior, this is all true. To someone still detaching, it is confusing. To someone looking for a procedure to follow, it is useless.

My book *Writing Effective Use Cases* (Cockburn 2001c) is a technique book with different information for readers at the three levels.

For practitioners at the first level in use case writing, it details the minutiae of use case writing. It provides them with specific procedures to follow. For practitioners at the second level, it contains rules and tips for varying the basic rules. The book does not try to teach anything specific to the Level 3 reader, who will, in any case, find something new in it to try out one day. Instead, it assures the Level 3 reader that the rules are not binding, that a lot of different ways of working can be effective, and that the people at Levels 1 and 2 are being told this, too.

To the extent that book is successful, it permits the Level 1 reader to get specific advice, the Level 2 reader to learn the boundaries of the rules, and the Level 3 reader to move with freedom.

One member in the Crystal family of methodologies is Crystal Clear. Crystal Clear can be described to a Level 3 listener in the following words:

> "Put four to six people in a room with workstations and whiteboards and access to the users. Have them deliver running, tested software to the users every one or two months, and otherwise leave them alone."

I did, in fact, describe Crystal Clear in those words to a savvy project sponsor. He followed those instructions and reported five months later, "We did what you said, and it worked!"

I interviewed the team leader some months later and his report was about as short as my instructions:

> "Following your suggestion, the four of us took over this conference room, which has network connections. We kept it for all four months, drawing on the whiteboards over there, delivering software as we went. It worked great."

If you are an experienced software developer and can apply those instructions, then you have no need for an entire book called *Crystal Clear*. If either you or your sponsor is not at that stage, then you need the book-length version. This version describes key techniques in detail, exposes the principles involved, considers the zone of applicability for this minimalist methodology, and says how to move out of Crystal Clear when the project moves out of the zone of applicability.

One lesson to take away from all this is that if you are reading methodology texts at Level 1, don't become depressed that there are so many techniques and principles to master. Wishing the world were so simple as to only need a single software development technique is a wasted wish. Hire someone who is at Level 2 or 3.

If you read methodology texts at Level 2, note the alternative techniques and look for places to vary them.

If you are reading methodology texts at Level 3, recognize the continued need for methodology definition at Level 1. There will always be people entering the field who will need explicit direction at first, even if you don't.

Kent Beck, author of *Extreme Programming Explained* (Beck 2000), described the use of Extreme Programming (XP) using similar levels. Asked about XP and the five levels of the Software Engineering Institute's "Capability Maturity Model," he replied with XP's three levels of maturity:

1. Do everything as written.
2. After having done that, experiment with variations in the rules.
3. Eventually, don't care if you are doing XP or not.

THE THREE LEVELS AND THIS BOOK

As described in the preface, this book is aimed mostly at Level 2 and 3 readers. It has little to offer a Level 1 software practitioner looking for a simple procedure to follow. In fact, a key point of the book is that all methodologies have limitations—areas where they are more or less applicable. It is not possible to name one best and correct way to develop software. Ideally, the book helps you reach that understanding and leads you to constructive ideas about how to deal with this real-world situation. In that sense, the book is aimed at moving some Level 2 readers to Level 3.

Topics for the Level 2 readers include heuristics for selecting a project's base methodology and the ideas behind agile methodologies.

If you are a Level 3 reader, I hope you will find words to help express what you already know.

A few topics in this book are likely to be new even to experienced developers. Most people are Level 1 readers when it comes to the vocabulary for describing methodologies and just-in-time methodology tuning. These are therefore written in more detail.

SHU-HA-RI

The three levels of practice are known in other skill areas. In Aikido, they are called *shu*, *ha*, and *ri* (roughly translating as *learn*, *detach*, and *transcend*). To look up information about shu-ha-ri, you might start with a Web search or at www. aikidofaq.com/essays/tin/shuhari.html. The following extract is from that site's article, "Shu Ha Ri," by Ron Fox (1995). (In this extract, the references in square brackets refer to references Ron Fox provides inside his article.) I find it fascinating how his portrayal so accurately predicts our mistaken, early attempt to teach design using CRC cards.

"Shu, or Mamoru means to keep, protect, keep or maintain [1]. During the Shu phase, the student builds the technical foundation of the art. Shu also implies a loyalty or persistence in a single ryu or, in the modern interpretation, a single instructor [2]. In Shu, the student should be working to copy the techniques as taught without modification and without yet attempting to make any effort to understand the rationale of the techniques of the school/teacher [3]. In this way, a lasting technical foundation is built on which the deeper understanding of the art can be based.

"The point of Shu is that a sound technical foundation can be built most efficiently by following only a single route to that goal. Mixing in other schools, prior to an understanding of what you're really up to is an invitation to go down a wrong path. A path where the techniques developed will not have sound theoretical or practical value. In the traditional interpretation of the Shu stage, it is the instructor that decides when the student moves on from Shu to Ha, not the student. It's up to the student to follow the instructor's teaching as an empty vessel to be filled up [1].

"Ha, is the second stage of the process. Ha means to detach and means that the student breaks free from the traditions of the ryu to some extent [2]. In the Ha stage, the student must reflect on the meaning and purpose of everything that he has learned and thus come to a deeper understanding of the art than pure repetitive practice

can allow. At this stage, since each technique is thoroughly learned and absorbed into the muscle memory, the student is prepared to reason about the background behind these techniques [3]. In academics, the Ha stage can be likened to the stage where enough basic information is available to the student that research papers of a survey nature could be expected.

"Ri means to go beyond or transcend. In this stage, the student is no longer a student in the normal sense, but a practitioner. The practitioner must think originally and develop from background knowledge original thoughts about the art and test them against the reality of his or her background knowledge and conclusions as well as the demands of everyday life. In the Ri stage, the art truly becomes the practitioner's own and to some extent his or her own creation. This stage is similar in academia to the Ph.D. or beyond stage.

"[1] Kuroda, Ichitaro, 'Shu-Ha-Ri' in *Sempo Spring*, pp. 9–10, 1994.

"[2] McCarthy, Patrick, 'The World within Karate & Kinjo Hiroshi' in *Journal of Asian Martial Arts*, V. 3 No. 2, 1994.

"[3] Private conversations with Nakamura, L. Sensei Toronto. Spring, 1994."

With that basis in the three stages of listening and learning, we can continue resolving the mystery of how anything ever gets communicated at all, and what that portends for software development.

So, What Do I Do Tomorrow?

The mystery is that we can't get perfect communication. The answer to the mystery is that we don't need perfect communication. We just need to get close enough, often enough.

To become more comfortable with the ideas in this chapter, think about what sort of person would be able to understand your system's design from the available design documentation.

Notice the following kinds of communication events:

- People around you are blissfully unaware of missing each other's meaning in communication. Notice how often they manage to get by anyway.
- Someone gives you overly vague instructions, so that you can't catch the meaning.
- Someone gives you overly detailed instructions—so detailed that you can't listen.
- The people at your next meeting, speaking from different vocabularies, reach to touch into different experiences.
- People in a different field rely on very different shared experiences to convey information economically.

- Your waiter writes instructions for the cook in the back when you order a breakfast of "Two eggs over easy with hash browns, whole wheat toast, coffee." Ask to look at the order sheet. He probably wrote something like "#3 oe ww" (Menu item #3, over easy, whole wheat).

Notice how inefficient it would be if everyone had to break down their communications into units that could be understood by anyone walking by on the street.

Notice the level at which you are reading different topics in this book.

If you read this chapter at Level 1, work to get comfortable with the notion that the design documents don't contain all the design information. Get comfortable with the notion that experienced designers communicate in shorthand.

If you read this chapter at Level 2, experiment with conveying your system design using UML, design patterns, and references to previous designs. Watch the effects on your colleagues, and notice at what levels they are operating in the discussions.

If you read this at Level 3, see if you can communicate these ideas to someone else.

1

A Cooperative Game of Invention and Communication

A fruitful way to think about software development is to consider it as a cooperative game of invention and communication.

The first section asks the question, "What would the experience of developing software be like if it were not software we were developing?" The purpose of the section is to get some distance from the subject in order to explore other ways of talking about it.

The second section reviews the broad spectrum of activities called games and finds the place of software development within that spectrum. If you are already familiar with zero-sum, positional, cooperative, finite, and infinite games, you might skim rapidly through the first part of this section. The section continues with a comparison of software development with another team-cooperative game—rock climbing—and two common comparison partners, engineering and model building.

The third section examines the idea of software development as a cooperative game of invention and communication more closely. It considers the primary goal of the game—delivering working software—and the secondary goal—or residue of the game—setting up for the next game. The next game is altering or replacing the system, or creating a neighboring system.

The final section in the chapter relates the ideas to everyday life.

A Cooperative Game of Invention and Communication

SOFTWARE AND POETRY

What if software development were not software development? Then what would it be, and what would the experience be like? I suggest that it is like a community writing epic poetry together. I make this comparison not because I think you have experience in community poetry writing, but because I think you don't. Your imagination will supply you with the sorts of contradictions I am interested in evoking.

Imagine 50 people getting together to write a 20,000-line epic poem on cost and time. What would you expect to find? Lots of arguments, for one thing. People trying to be creative, trying to do their best, without enough talent, time, or resources.

Who are the players in this drama? First, the people who ordered the poem. What do they want? They want something they can use to amuse themselves or impress their friends, not too expensive, and *soon*.

Next we have the key poem designers.

As you might imagine, this began as a one-person project. But our mythical poet found herself promising *much* more than she could deliver in the given time frame. So she asked a few friends to help. They designated her the lead poet and poem designer. She blocked out the theme and the poem's sequencing.

Her friends started to help, but then they ran into problems with synchronizing and communicating their work. It also turned out that they couldn't get it all done in time. So they added a couple of clerical people, more friends, and in desperation, even neighbors. The friends and neighbors were not real poets, of course. So our lead designers blocked out sections of the poem that would not require too much talent.

What do you think happened?

There was good news: One person was good at descriptive passages, another was good at the gory bits, and another was good at passages about people. No one was good at emotion except the lead poet, who by now was pulling her hair out because she didn't have time to write *poetry*, she was so busy coordinating, checking, and delegating.

Actually, a couple of people couldn't leave well enough alone. Two of them wrote pages and pages and pages of material describing minor protagonists, and our lead poet could not get them to cut it down to size. Another few kept rewriting and revising their work, never satisfied with the result. She wanted them to move on to other passages, but they just wouldn't stop fiddling with their first sections.

As time progressed, the group got desperate and added more people. The trouble was that they were running out of money and couldn't really afford all these people. Communications were horrible, no one had the current copy of the poem, and no one knew the actual state of the poem.

Let's give this story a happy ending . . .

As luck would have it, they engaged a wonderfully efficient administrator who arranged for a plan of the overall poem, an inventory of each person's skills, a time frame and communication schedule for each part, standards for versioning and merging pieces of the poem, plus secretarial and other technical services.

They delivered the poem to satisfied clients, well over budget, of course. And the lead poet had to go on vacation to restore her senses. She swore she would never do this again (but we know better).

Groups surely have gotten together to write a long poem together. And I am sure that they ran into most of the issues that software developers run into: temperamental geniuses and average workers, hard requirements, and communication pressures. Humans working together, building something they don't quite understand. Done well, the result is breathtaking; done poorly, dross.

BALANCE IN SOFTWARE DESIGN

As I sat in on a design review of an object-oriented system, one of the reviewers suggested an alternate design approach.

The lead designer replied that the alternative would not be as *balanced*, would not *flow* as well as the original.

Thus, even in hard-core programming circles, we find designers discussing designs in terms of balance and flow.

Software developers have a greater burden than our hypothetical poets have: logic. The result must not only rhyme; it must behave properly—"accurately enough," if not correctly.

The point is that although programming is a solitary, inspiration-based, logical activity, it is also a group engineering activity. It is paradoxical, because it is not the case, and at the same time it is very much the case, that software development is:

- Mathematical, as C. A. R. Hoare has often said
- Engineering, as Bertrand Meyer has often said
- A craft, as many programmers say
- A mystical act of creation, as some programmers claim

Its creation is sensitive to tools; its quality is independent of tools. Some software qualifies as beautiful, some as junk. It is a meeting of opposites and of multiple sets of opposites.

It is an activity of cognition and expression done by communicating, thinking people who are working against economic boundaries, conditional to their cultures, sensitive to the particular individuals involved.

SOFTWARE AND GAMES

Games are not just for children, although children also play games. Games are invented and used by many people including novelists, mathematicians, and corporate strategists.

KINDS OF GAMES

If you are sitting around the living room on a winter's evening and someone says, "Let's play a game," what could you play?

You could play charades (play-acting to uncover a hidden phrase). You could play tic-tac-toe or checkers, poker or bridge. You could play hide-and-seek or table tennis. You could play "When I took a trip, . . ." a game in which each person adds a sentence onto a story that grows in the telling. You could, especially if you have younger children, end up having a wrestling match on the living room floor.

Games fall into many categories: zero-sum, non-zero-sum, positional, competitive, cooperative, finite, and infinite, to name a few (see Figure 1-1). As a way to help identify what kind of game software development could be, let's look at those choices.

Zero-sum games are those with two sides playing in opposition, so that if one side wins, the other loses. Checkers, tic-tac-toe, bridge, and tennis are examples. Software development is clearly not a zero-sum game.

Non-zero-sum games are those with multiple winners or multiple losers. Many of the games you would consider playing on that winter's evening are non-zero-sum

games: poker, parcheesi, and hide-and-seek. Software development is also a non-zero-sum game.

Positional games are those in which the entire state of the game can be discovered by looking at the markers on the board at that moment. Chess and tic-tac-toe are examples. Bridge isn't, because the played cards don't show which person played them.

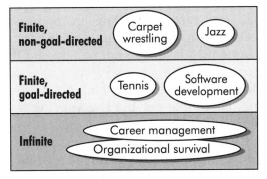

Figure 1-1 Different categories of games.

Some people try to play software development as a positional game, requiring that the documentation reflect the history *and* current state of the project. They intend that, should anyone leave the project, a replacement person will be able to join the team, read the documentation, and pick up where the other person left off. We will come to see that this is not an effective gaming strategy for software development.

(Positional games are actually far more interesting than the simple description above implies. John Conway, in his book *On Numbers and Games* (1976), was able to show how two-person, positional games form a superset of *all* numbers: real, imaginary, finite, and transfinite. He constructs the notion of *number* directly from two-person, positional games.)

All the above are *competitive* games, in which there is a clear notion of winning and losing.

In *cooperative games*, the people work either to win together or to continue the game as long as they consider it worth playing. The former are *goal-seeking* cooperative games, the latter *non-goal-seeking* cooperative games. Story telling, playing jazz, and carpet wrestling are non-goal-seeking cooperative games. In these latter games, the players do not seek to end the game by reaching a goal as fast as possible. They come to an end only when enough people get tired of playing and step out.

Charades, rock climbing, and software development are goal-seeking cooperative games (see Figure 1-1 again).

All of the above are *finite* games, games intended to end. *Infinite* games are those in which the players' primary intention is to keep the game going. Organizations, corporations, and countries play these. Their core purpose is to stay in existence.

A person's profession is also an infinite game. The person, wanting to continue the profession, makes a set of moves that permit her practice of that profession to continue.

Often, a person or company aims to play well on a particular project in order to get the best position on the next game. As with the card game appropriately named "So long, sucker," these sorts of teams and alliances change continually and without notice.

SOFTWARE AND ROCK CLIMBING

Of all the comparison partners for software development that I have seen, rock climbing has emerged as the best. It is useful to have such a comparison partner, to get some distance from the subject and open a vocabulary that we can reapply to software development. Rock climbing is not a metaphor for software development but a comparison partner, another member of the same class of games.

Let's see how some of the words and phrases associated with rock climbing relate to software development.

Cooperative and goal-seeking. A team of rock climbers work together to reach the top. They will evaluate the climb based on how well they climbed together and how much they enjoyed themselves, but the first measure of success is whether they reached the top. Reaching the endpoint is a primary goal, and the game is over when they reach the top.

(If you are a rock climber, you might well interrupt me here. For many rock climbers, the moment of reaching the end of the climb is a sad one, for it signals the end of the game. That is true of cooperative games in general. The game comes to an end when the endpoint is reached, but if the players have been enjoying themselves, they may not want to stop. Similarly, sometimes software developers do not want to finish their design, because then the fun part of their work will be over.)

Load bearing. The climbers must actually support their weight on their hands and feet. This is a particularly valuable point of comparison between the two: Software must run and produce reasonable responses. While multiple solutions are possible, not just any solution will do.

Team. Climbing is usually done in teams. There are solo climbers, but under normal circumstances, climbers form a team for the purpose of a climb.

Individuals with talent. Some people just naturally climb better than others do. Some people will never handle certain climbs.

Skill-sensitive. The rock climber must have certain proficiency. The novice can only approach simple climbs. With practice, the climber can attack more and more difficult climbs.

Training. Rock climbers are continually training on techniques to use.

Tools. Tools are a requirement for serious rock-climbing: chalk, chucks, harness, rope, carabiner, and so on. It is important to be able to reach for the right tool at the right moment. It is possible to climb very small distances with no tools. The longer the climb, however, the more critical the tool selection is.

Resource-limited. A climb usually needs to be completed by nightfall or before the weather changes. Climbers plan their climbs to fit their time and energy budget.

Plan. Whether bouldering, doing a single-rope climb, or doing a multiple-day climb, the climbers always make a plan. The longer the climb, the more extensive the plan must be, even though the team knows that the plan will be insufficient and even wrong in places.

Improvised. Unforeseen, unforeseeable, and purely chance obstacles are certain to show up on even the most meticulously planned climbing expeditions unless the climb is short and the people have already done it several times before. Therefore, the climbers must be prepared to change their plans—to improvise—at a moment's notice.

Fun. Climbers climb because it is fun. Climbers experience a sense of *flow* (Csikszentmihalyi 1991) while climbing, and this total occupation is part of what makes it fun. Similarly, programmers typically enjoy their work, and part of that enjoyment is getting into the flow of designing or programming. Flow in the case of rock climbing is both physical and mental. Flow in the case of programming is purely mental.

Challenging. Climbers climb because there is a challenge: Can they really make it to the top? Programmers often crave this challenge, too. If programmers do not find their assignment challenging, they may quit or start embellishing the system with design elements they find challenging (rather like some of the poets mentioned in the epic poetry project).

Dangerous. Probably the one aspect of rock climbing that does not transfer to software development is danger. If you take a bad fall, you can die. Rock climbers are fond of saying that climbing with proper care is less dangerous than driving a car. However, I have not heard programmers express the need to compare the danger of programming with the danger of driving a car.

Software development has been compared with many other things, including math, science, engineering, theater, bridge building, and law. Although one can gain some insight from looking at any of those activities, the rock-climbing comparison is the most useful for the purpose of understanding the factors involved in the activity.

A GAME OF INVENTION AND COMMUNICATION

We have seen that software development is a *group* game, which is *goal seeking, finite,* and *cooperative*. The team, which consists of the sponsor, the manager, usage specialists, domain specialists, designers, testers, and writers, works together with the goal of producing a working and useful system. In most cases, team members aim to produce the system as quickly as possible, but they may prefer to focus on ease of use, cost, defect freedom, or liability protection.

The game is finite because it is over when the goal is reached. Sometimes delivery of the system marks the termination point; sometimes the end comes a bit later. Funding for development usually changes around the time the system is delivered, and new funding defines a new game. The next game may be to improve the system, to replace the system, to build an entirely different system, or possibly to disband the group.

The game is cooperative because the people on the team help each other to reach the goal. The measure of their quality as a team is how well they cooperate and communicate during the game. This measure is used because it affects how well they reach the goal.

If it is a *goal-directed cooperative game*, what does the game consist of? What constitutes moves in the game?

The task facing the developers is this: They are working on a problem that they don't fully understand, one that lives in emotions, wishes, and thoughts and that changes as they proceed. They need to

- Understand the problem space
- Imagine some mechanism that solves the problem in a viable technology space
- Express that mental construct in an executable language, which lacks many features of expression, to a system that is unforgiving of mistakes

To work through this situation, they

- Use props and devices to pull thoughts out of themselves or to generate new ideas that might help them understand the problem or construct a solution
- Leave trails of markers for those who will come later, markers to monitor and test their progress and their understanding, and they use those markers again, themselves, when they revisit parts of their work

Software development is therefore a cooperative game *of invention and communication*. There is nothing in the game but people's ideas and the communication of those ideas to their colleagues and to the computer.

Looking back at the literature of our field, we see a few people who have articulated this before. Peter Naur did, in his 1985 article "Programming as Theory Building," and Pelle Ehn did, in "Scandinavian Design: On Participation and

Skill" (1992) and in his magnificent but out-of-print book, *Work-Oriented Design of Software Artifacts* (1988). Naur and Ehn did this so well that I include those two articles in near entirety in Appendix B. Robert Glass and colleagues wrote about it in "Software Tasks: Intellectual or Clerical?" (1992), and Fred Brooks saw it as such a wickedly hard assignment that he wrote the article "No Silver Bullet" (1995).

The potential consequences of this cooperative game of invention and communication are outlined in the remainder of this chapter. The remainder of the book examines those consequences.

SOFTWARE AND ENGINEERING

Considering software development as a game with moves is profitable, because doing so gives us a way to make meaningful and advantageous decisions on a project. In contrast, speaking of software development as *engineering* or *model building* does not help us make such advantageous decisions.

The trouble with using engineering as a reference is that we, as a community, don't know what that means. Without having a common understanding of what engineering is, it is hard to get people to work "more like engineering." In my travels, people mostly use the word *engineering* to create a sense of guilt for not having done enough of something, without being clear what that something is.

The dictionary is clear as to what "engineering" is: *"The application of science and mathematics by which the properties of matter and the sources of energy in nature are made useful to man"* (*Webster's New Collegiate Dictionary,* 1977).

That definition does not explain what *doing* engineering is about. In my experience, "doing engineering" involves creating a trade-off solution in the face of conflicting demands. Another person, though, wrote to me and said, "A basic concept of engineering is to address problems in a repeatable and consistent manner." Confusing the *act* of doing engineering work with the *outcome* of doing engineering work is a common mistake.

The *outcome* of doing engineering work is the factory, which is run while specific people watch carefully for variations in quantity and quality of the items being manufactured.

The *act* of doing engineering work is the ill-defined creative process the industrial engineer goes through to invent the manufacturing plant design. That process is not run with statistical controls, measuring quantity and quality of output. Like software development, it runs as a cooperative game of invention and communication, with individual people of different backgrounds huddling together to come up with a workable design.

When people say, "Make software development more like engineering," they often mean, "Make it more like running a plant, with statistical quality controls." But as we have seen, running the plant is not the act of doing engineering.

The other aspect of "doing engineering" is looking up previous solutions in code books.

Civil engineers who design bridges are not supposed to invent new structures. Given a river and a predicted traffic load, they are supposed to take soil samples and use the code books to look for the simplest structure that handles the required load over the given distance, building on the soil at hand. They base their work on centuries of tabulation of known solutions.

This only marginally fits the current state of software development. We are still in the stage where each team's design is supposed to be better than the neighbor's, and the technologies are changing so fast that few code books exist. As time goes by, more of these code books will be available. Today, however, there are still more variations between systems than there are commonalities.

Let's return to considering "engineering" to mean "thinking and making trade-offs." These are appropriate phrases. We would like our software developers to think, and to understand the trade-offs they select. However, these phrases do not provide guidance in running projects.

SOFTWARE AND MODEL BUILDING

Many people have advocated model building over the last decade, including Ivar Jacobson, who declared, "Software development *is* model building."

Characterizing software development as engineering may not provide much guidance for running projects, but characterizing it as *model building* leads directly to inappropriate project decisions.

If software development were model building, then a valid measure of the quality of the software or of the development process would be the quality of the models, their fidelity to the real world, and their completeness. However, as dozens of successful project teams around the world have told me:

> "The interesting part of what we want to express doesn't get captured in those models. The interesting part is what we say to each other while drawing on the board.

> "We don't have time to create fancy or complete models. Often, we don't have time to create models at all."

Where I found people diligently creating models, software was not getting delivered. Paying attention to the models interfered with developing the software.

Constructing models is not the purpose of the project. Constructing a model is only interesting as it helps win the game.

The purpose of the game is to deliver software. Any other activity is secondary. A model, as any communication, is *sufficient, as soon as* it permits the next person to move on with her work.

The work products of the team should be measured for *sufficiency with respect to communicating with the target group*. It does not matter if the models are incomplete, drawn with incorrect syntax, and actually not like the real world *if* they communicate sufficiently to the recipients.

As Jim Sawyer so colorfully wrote in an e-mail discussion about use cases (Cockburn 2001c):

"... as long as the templates don't feel so formal that you get lost in a recursive descent that worm-holes its way into design space. If that starts to occur, I say strip the little buggers naked and start telling stories and scrawling on napkins."

The *effect* of the communication is more important than the form of the communication.

Some successful project teams have built more and fancier models than some unsuccessful teams. From this, many people draw the conclusion that more modeling is better.

Some successful teams built fewer and sloppier models than some unsuccessful teams. From this, other people draw the conclusion that less modeling is better.

Neither is a valid conclusion. Modeling serves as part of the team communication. There can be both too much and too little modeling. Scrawling on napkins is sufficient at times; much more detail is needed at other times.

Understanding how much modeling to do, and when, is the subject of this book. Thinking of software development as a cooperative game that has primary and secondary goals helps you develop insight about how elaborate a model to build or whether to build a model at all.

A Second Look at the Cooperative Game

The Cooperative Game Principle

Software development is a (resource-limited) cooperative game of invention and communication. The primary goal of the game is to deliver useful, working software. The secondary goal, the residue of the game, is to set up for the next game. The next game may be to alter or replace the system or to create a neighboring system.

Programmers as Communications Specialists

Saying that "software development is a cooperative game of invention and communication" suddenly shines a very different light on the people in our field.

Programmers are typically stereotyped as noncommunicative individuals who like to sit in darkened rooms alone with their computer screens.

It is not a true stereotype, though. Programmers just like to communicate about things *they* like to communicate about, usually the programs they are involved in. Programmers enjoy trading notes about XML-RPC or the difficulties in mapping object-oriented designs to relational databases. They just don't like joining in the chitchat about things they consider irrelevant.

There has been a surprisingly high acceptance of programming in pairs, a technique in which two people sit together and co-write their program (Beck 2000). I say "surprising" because many programmers first predict that they won't be able to work that way and then find they actually prefer it, after trying it for a week or two (Cockburn, 2001b).

As far as the stereotype is true, it accents the "invention" portion of the cooperative game. Programming has, up until recently, been more focused as a game of invention than as a game of communication. The interest of programmers to discuss programming matters with each other gets in the way of them discussing business matters with sponsors, users, and business experts.

We can attribute part of the cause for this to our educational curricula. Imagine some people thumbing through the university's curriculum guide. They see two tracks: One calls for a lot of reading, writing, and speaking, and some programming. The other calls for less reading, writing, and speaking, and more of working alone, building artifacts. We can easily imagine the verbally oriented people selecting the first curriculum and the less verbally oriented people selecting the second.

Historically, success in our profession came from being able to sit alone for long hours without talking to anyone, staring at papers or screens. Those who didn't like that mode of work simply left the field. Newer, and particularly the "agile" methodologies, emphasize communication more. Suddenly the people who elected to join a profession that did not require much interpersonal communication are being asked to become good at it.

Only the universities can reverse the general characteristics, by creating software

development curricula that contain more communication-intensive courses.

At the University of Aalborg, in Denmark, a new Informatics major was defined that involves both software design and communication skill (Mathiassen 1999). The department head, Lars Mathiassen, reports that the difference in people's personalities is noticeable: The new curriculum attracts those who are willing to accept the communications load, and the old curriculum attracts those who have less interest in communication.

To the extent that software development really *is* a game of invention and communication, we will have to see a greater emphasis on communication in the university curricula.

GAMING FASTER

We should not expect orders of magnitude improvement in program production.

As much as programming languages may improve, programming will still be limited by our ability to think through the problem and the solution, working through the details of how the described solution deals with the myriad cases it will encounter. This is Naur's "programming as theory building" (Appendix B).

To understand why exponential productivity growth is not an appropriate expectation, we need only look at two other fields of thought expression: writing novels and writing laws. Imagine being worried that lawyers are not getting exponentially faster at creating contracts and laws!

In other words, we can expect the game of invention and the business of communicating those intentions to a computer to remain difficult.

MARKERS AND PROPS

Intermediate work products help with Naur's "theory building" and Ehn's "language games," as *reminders for our reflection*. They provide shared experiences to refer to or serve as support structures for new ideas.

The former need only be complete enough to *remind* a person of an earlier thought or decision. Different markers are appropriate for different people with different backgrounds.

The latter act as props to incite new thoughts.

LASER PRINTER MOCK-UPS

Ehn's team considered introducing laser printers to a group that had no experience with them, back in 1982. They constructed cardboard mock-ups, not to remind the participants of what they already knew, but to allow them to invent themselves into the future, by creating an inexpensive and temporary future reality to visualize.

These mock-ups are not second-class items, used only due to some accidental absence of technology. Rather, they are a fundamental technique used to help people construct thoughts about new situations. Any work product that helps the group invent a way forward in the game is appropriate. Whether they keep the mock-up around as a reminder of the discussion is up to them in the playing of their game.

DIMINISHING RETURNS

Because the typical software development project is limited in time, people, and money, spending extra of those resources to make an intermediate work product better than it needs to be for its purpose is wasteful. One colleague expressed it this way:

DIMINISHING RETURNS

It is clear to me as I start creating use cases, object models, and the like, that the work is doing some good. But at some point, it stops being useful and starts being both drudgery and a waste of effort. I can't detect when that point is crossed, and I have never heard it discussed. It is frustrating, because it turns a useful activity into a wasteful activity.

The purpose of each activity is to move the game forward. Work products of every sort are sufficiently good as soon as they permit the next move.

Knowing this permits a person to more easily detect the crossover from value adding to diminishing returns, to hit the point of being *sufficient-to-purpose*. That point has been nicknamed "satisficing" (Simon 1987, Bach URL).

SUFFICIENCY FOR THE PRIMARY GOAL

Intermediate work products are not important as models of reality, nor do they have intrinsic value. They have value only as they help the team make a move in the game. Thus, there is no idea to measure intermediate work products for completeness or perfection. An intermediate work product is to be measured for *sufficiency*: Is it sufficient to remind or inspire the involved group?

These three short stories illustrate how quickly sufficiency can be reached:

SUFFICIENCY IN A MEETING

On a project called "Winifred" (Cockburn, 1998), I was asked partway through the project to review, for the approximately 40 people on the project, the process we were following and to show samples of the work products. The meeting would be held in the cafeteria.

I copied onto overhead transparencies a sample of each work product: a use case, a sequence chart, a class diagram, a screen definition, a fragment of Smalltalk code, and so on.

As luck would have it, the overhead projector bulb blew out just before my little presentation. As I was wearing a white shirt that day, I asked everyone to move closer and held up the sample use case in front of my shirt.

"I can't read it!" someone called out, not too surprisingly, from the back.

"You don't need to read it," I said. (The group laughed.) "All you need to see is that a use case is paragraphs of text, approximately like this. There are lots of them online for you to look at. We write them as requirements, . . ." and I described who was

writing them, who was reading them, and how they were being used.

I held a sample class diagram in front of my shirt.

"I can't read it!" someone called out again.

"You don't need to read it." (The group laughed again.) "All you need to see is that it is a diagram with boxes and lines. It is written by . . ." and I discussed the role of the class diagram in the project.

I went through the work products this way. In each case, all that the group needed was a visual image of what one of these things looked liked, who wrote it, who read it, and how it served the project. Real examples were all online and could be examined by anyone on the project.

This was communication *sufficient* to the purpose that people could have a visual memory of what each product looked like, to anchor the sentences about how they were used.

We did have a drawing showing the process we were following, but as far as I know, nobody other than the project managers and I ever looked at it.

SUFFICIENCY OF WORK PRODUCTS

Project "Winifred" was a fixed-time, fixed-price project costing about $15 million, lasting 18 months, with 24 programmers among 45 people total. We ran it with the cooperative game principle in mind (the principle hadn't been defined back then, but we knew what we wanted), with as much close, informal communication as possible.

At the time, use cases weren't very well defined, and so the writers wrote just a few paragraphs of simple prose describing what was supposed to take place, and some of the business rules involved.

The analyst responsible for a use case usually went straight from each meeting with the end users to visit the designer-programmers, telling them the outcome of the meeting. The designer-programmers put their new knowledge directly into their programs, based on the verbal description.

This worked effectively, because the time delay from the analyst's hearing the information in the meeting to the programmer's knowing of its effect on the program was just a matter of hours.

There was an odd side effect, however. Halfway through the project, one of the programming leads commented that he didn't know what purpose the use cases were supposed to serve: They certainly weren't requirements, he said, because he had never read them.

The point of the story is that the casual use cases were "sufficient to the task" of holding the requirements in place. The communication channels and the shared understanding between the writers and readers was rich enough to carry the information.

CHRYSLER'S ULTRALIGHT SUFFICIENCY

Chrysler's Comprehensive Compensation project (C3 1998) ran even lighter than project Winifred. The 10 programmers sat together in a single, enormous room, and the team tracker and three customers (requirements experts) sat in the next room, with no door between them.

With excellent intra-team communications and requirements available continuously, the group wrote even less-than-casual use cases. They wrote a few sentences on an index card for each needed system behavior. They called these "user stories."

When it came time to start on a user story, the programmers involved asked the customer to explain what was needed and then designed that. Whenever they needed more information, they asked the nearby customer to explain. The requirements lived in the discussion between the participants and were archived in the acceptance and unit test suites.

The design documentation also lived in a mostly oral tradition within the group. The designers invented new designs using CRC card sessions (Wilkinson 1995). In a CRC-card design session, the designers write the names of potential classes on index cards and then move them around to illustrate the system performing its tasks. The cards serve both to incite new thoughts and to hold in place the discussion so far. CRC cards are easy to construct, to put aside, to bring back into play, and are thus perfectly suited for an evolving game of invention and communication.

After sketching out a possible design with the cards, the designers moved to the workstations and wrote a program matching the design, delivering a small bit of system function.

The design was never written down. It lived in the cards, in memories of the conversations surrounding the cards, in the unit tests written to capture the detailed requirements, in the code, and in the shared memories of the people who had worked together on a rotating basis during the design's development.

This was a group highly attuned to the cooperative game principle. Their intermediate work products, while radically minimalist, were quite evidently *sufficient* to the task of developing the software.

The team delivered new function every three weeks over a three-year period.

SUFFICIENCY IN THE RESIDUE

Thus far, the topic of discussion has been the *primary* goal of the game: delivering working software. However, the entire project is just one move within a larger game. The project has two goals: to deliver the software and to create an advantageous position for the next game, which is either altering or replacing the system or creating a neighboring system.

If the team fails to meet the primary goal, there may be no next game, and so that goal must be protected first. If the team reaches the primary goal but does a poor job of setting up for the next game, they jeopardize that game.

In most cases, therefore, the teams should create some markers to inform the next team about the system's requirements and design. In keeping with Naur's programming as theory building and the cooperative game principle, these markers should be constructed to get the next team of people *reasonably close* to the thinking of the team members who completed the previous system. Everything about language games, touching into shared experience, and sufficiency-to-purpose still applies.

The compelling question now becomes this: When does the team construct these additional work products?

One naive answer is to say, "As the work products are created." Another is to say, "At the very end." Neither is optimal. If the requirements or designs change frequently, then it costs a great deal to constantly regenerate them—often, the cost is high enough to jeopardize the project itself. On the other hand, if constructing markers for the future is left to the very end of the project, there is great danger that they will never get created at all. Here are two project stories that illustrate this point:

CONTINUOUS REDOCUMENTATION

Project "Reel" involved 150 people. The sponsors, very worried about the system's documentation becoming out of date and inaccurate, mandated that whenever any part of the requirements, design, or code changed, all documentation that the change affected had to be immediately brought up to date.

The result was as you might expect. The project crawled forward at an impossibly slow rate, because the team members spent most of their time updating documentation for each change made.

The project was soon canceled.

This project's sponsors did not pay proper attention to the economic side of system development, and they lost the game.

JUST NEVER DOCUMENTATION

The sponsors of the Chrysler Comprehensive Compensation project eventually halted funding for the project. As the people left the development team, they left no archived documentation of their requirements and design other than the two-sentence user stories, the tests, and the program source code.

Eventually, enough people left that the oral tradition and group memory were lost.

This team masterfully understood the cooperative game principle during system construction but missed the point of setting up the residue for the following game.

Deciding on the residue is a question that the project team cannot avoid. The team must ask and answer both of these questions:

- How do we complete this project in a timely way?
- When do we construct what sorts of markers for the next team?

Some people choose to spend more money, earlier, to create a safety buffer around the secondary goal. Others play a game of brinksmanship, aiming to reach the primary goal faster and creating as little residue as possible, as late as possible.

In constructing responses, the team must consider the complexity of both the problem and the solution, the type of people who will work on it next, and so on. Team members should balance the cost of overspending for future utility against the risk of under documenting for the future. Finding the balance between the two is something of an art and is the proper subject of this book.

A GAME WITHIN A GAME

Although any one project is a cooperative and finite game, the players are busy playing competitive and infinite games at the same time.

Each team member is playing an infinite game called *career*. These individuals may take actions that are damaging to the project-as-game but that they view as advantageous to their respective careers.

Similarly, the company is playing an infinite game: its growth. To the company, the entire project is a single move within that larger game. In certain competitive situations, a company's directors may deliberately hinder or sabotage a project in order to hurt a competitor or in some other way create a better future situation for itself.

Watching military subcontracting projects, it sometimes seems that the companies spend more time and money jockeying for position than developing the software. Thinking about any one project in isolation, this doesn't seem to be sensible behavior. If we consider the larger set of competitive, infinite games the companies are playing, though, then the players' behavior suddenly makes more sense. They use any one project as a playing board on which to build their position for the next segment of the game.

The cooperative game concept does not imply that competitive and infinite games don't exist. Rather, it provides words to describe what is happening across the games.

OPEN-SOURCE DEVELOPMENT

Finally, consider open-source projects. They are grounded in a different economic structure than commercial projects: They do not presume to be resource-limited.

An open-source project runs for as long as it runs, using whatever people happen to join in. It is not money-limited, because the people do not get paid for participating. It is not people-resource limited, because anyone who shows up can play. It is not time limited, because it is not run to a schedule. It just takes as long as it takes.

The moves that are appropriate in a game that is not resource-limited are quite naturally different from those in a resource-limited game. The reward structure is also different. Thus it is to be expected that an open-source project will use a different set of moves to get through the game. The creation of the software, though, is still cooperative and is still a game of invention and communication.

One may argue that open-source development is not really *goal seeking*. Linus Torvalds did not wake up one day and say, "Let's finish rewriting this UNIX operating system so we can all go out and get some real jobs." He did it first because it was fun (Torvalds 2001) and then to "make this thing somewhat better." In other words, it was more like kids carpet wrestling or musicians playing music than rock climbers striving to reach the top.

While that is true to some degree, it is still goal-directed in that a person working on a section of the system works to get it to "the next usable state." The people involved in that section of the system still work the cooperative game of invention and communication to reach that goal.

WHAT SHOULD THIS MEAN TO ME?

As you practice this new vocabulary on your current project, you should start to see new ways of finishing the job in a timely manner while protecting your interests for future projects. Here are some ideas for becoming more comfortable with the ideas in this chapter:

Read "Programming as Theory Building" in Appendix B. Then, watch

- The people on the design team build their theories
- The people doing last-minute debugging, or program maintenance, build their theories
- The difference in the information available to the latter compared with the former
- How their different theories result in different programs being produced

- How your understanding of your problem changes over time and how that changes your understanding of the solution you are building

Look around your project, viewing it as a resource-limited cooperative game of invention and communication. Ask:

- Who are the players in this game?
- Which are playing a finite, goal-directed team game?
- Which are playing their own infinite game instead?
- When are my teammates inventing together, and when they are laying down tracks to help others get to where they are? Track this carefully for five consecutive workdays, to see them move from one to the other.

View the project decisions as "moves" in a game. Imagine it as a different sort of game, crossing a swamp:

- Recall the project setup activities as a preliminary plan of assault on the swamp, one that will change as new information emerges about the characteristics of the swamp and the capabilities of the team members.
- Watch as each person contributes to detecting deep or safe spots and builds a map or walkway for other people to cross.

Reconsider the work products your team is producing:

- Who is going to read each?
- Is the work product more detailed than needed for that person, or is it not detailed enough?
- What is the smallest set of internal work products your team needs to reach the primary goal?
- What is the smallest set of final work products your team needs to produce to protect the next team?
- Notice the difference between the two.

Consider running the project as two separate subprojects:

- The first subproject produces the running software in as economic a fashion as possible.
- The second subproject, competing for key resources with the first, produces the final work products for the next team.

Think about developing a large, life-critical, mission-critical system:

- Will that project benefit more from increasing the invention and communication or from isolating the people?
- Notice which sorts of projects need more final work products as their residue and which need fewer work products.

Finally, notice the larger game within which the project resides. Notice

- The distractions on your project, such as giving demos to visitors, taking the system to trade shows, and hitting key deadlines
- How those "distractions" contribute to the larger game in play
- That moves in the larger game jeopardize your local game
- How you would balance moves in the project-delivery game against the moves in the larger game

The point of all this watching and reconsidering is to sharpen your sense of "team," "cooperative game," "moves in a game," "invention and communication," "theory building," and "sufficiency."

After watching software development for awhile, reexamine the engineering activities around you:

- Identify where they too are cooperative games of invention and communication and where they are more a matter of looking up previous solutions in code books.

When you have achieved some facility at viewing the life around you as a set of games in motion, practice

- Adding discipline on your project at key places
- Reducing discipline at key places
- Declaring, "Enough! This is sufficient!"

2

Individuals

That it is *people* who design software is terribly obvious . . . and ignored. Weinberg's discussion of people written in 1969 was followed by a stunning silence that lasted 15 years. The silence was finally broken by DeMarco and Lister's *Peopleware* (1999). Another silence followed that book. We shouldn't have to wait another 15 years before learning more about how people's characteristics affect software development.

This chapter discusses people's general "funkiness," their failure modes, their success modes, and their general mode of operation, in the following sections:

"Them's Funky People" discusses how different and unpredictable people are. A theme is that although general rules of operation may apply to this human device, any useful generalization is limited by the variations among people.

"Overcoming Failure Modes" discusses the weak points of the human device. If we are going to create systems of people working together, we should not rely on aspects of behavior that are points of failure for most people.

"Working Better in Some Ways Than Others" asks, "What is the natural mode of operation of the human device?" When we try to apply these ideas, we have to bear in mind the variations among people.

"Drawing on Success Modes" asks, "What permits us to succeed ever, given all the ways we have of failing?" The answers may surprise you for how vague they initially sound and how powerful they are in their end effect. The end of this section shows how success modes combine for a stronger effect.

The final section relates the ideas to everyday life.

Individuals

THEM'S FUNKY PEOPLE

There is some resistance in our industry to the idea that people factors dominate software development.

As I participated in initiatives for formal program specification, advanced programming environments, and new development processes, I kept discovering that successful teams were still delivering software without using our latest energy-saving ideas.

Initially, I viewed this as a nuisance: "Why can't those people just realize how much better off they would be if they used our ideas?!"

Eventually, it went from a nuisance to a curiosity.

Slowly, it became a discovery.

I reversed my assumptions and found that the opposite correlation held: Purely people factors predict project trajectories quite well, overriding choice of process or technology.

I found no interesting correlation in the projects that I studied among process, language, or tools and project success. I found successes and failures with all sorts of processes, languages, and tools.

A well-functioning team of adequate people will complete a project almost regardless of the process or technology they are asked to use (although the process and technology might help or hinder them along the way).

Dave A. Thomas, founder of Object Technology International, a company with a long record of successful projects, summarized his success formula to me one day: "Some people deliver software, some don't. I hire those that have delivered."

THE QUEST FOR A CHARACTERISTIC FUNCTION

If we are going to build systems out of people, we should understand people's operating characteristics.

With some trouble over the centuries, we have created mathematical models of rods, hinges, springs, resistors, capacitors, wires, transistors, and other devices. These mathematical models have served us well in constructing systems from those devices.

If the behavior of a device is complicated, engineers will often go out of their way to redesign the system so that the device needs to work only in a region of simpler behavior. Transistors, for example, produce output voltage nonlinearly to their input. This makes them wonderful amplifiers. As the circuit being designed grows in complexity, though, that nonlinearity gets in the way, and the mathematics soon become too hard to handle.

Transistors have a flat output when they are over-driven. This flat output is quite useless for amplifiers but is very handy for putting together the millions of components needed for a digital computer. The computer industry is built on the fact that transistors can be driven into two simple states. The industry would not work if designers could only work with them as nonlinear devices.

If transistors in the active region are complicated, people are more complicated still. They are not linear and not even decently nonlinear.

If humans were linear, we could double a person's output by doubling some input. As nature has it, though, neither doubling the rewards offered, the punishment threatened, nor even the time used has a reliable double effect on a person's thinking quality, thinking speed, programming output, or motivation.

A person who works 40 hours one week might double his output the next week by working 60 hours, because he isn't being distracted for those extra 20 hours. He is unlikely to double his output again by working 120 hours the next week. In fact, he is unlikely to produce even the same work in the next 60-hour week, because fatigue sets in.

We are nowhere near creating a model of humans that is both simple and accurate enough to be used in designing a system composed of humans.

ELEMENTS OF FUNKINESS

Humans are spontaneous, both for good and for bad. Each of the following might happen at any time on a project, sometimes with great consequences:

- Jenny happens to notice, at some arbitrary moment and for no discernible reason, something that needs attention and initiates an activity that helps the project recover.
- Ron, who always hated testing, suddenly gets the testing bug and starts regression testing his programs.
- Ron says something seemingly innocuous to Jenny, and Jenny explodes in anger.

- Ron suddenly quits the project over a seemingly minor event.

Humans are happily contradictory.

- Jenny is sloppy at one type of work and obsessively detail-oriented on another.
- Ron is communicative in one situation and close-mouthed in another.

Humans are stuffed full of personality. They vary by hour, by day, by age, by culture, by temperature, by who else is in the room, and so on. Personal style and chemistry are significant matters between people.

Depending on almost anything, a person can be cooperative with one person at one moment and belligerent the next moment or with the next person. A classroom full of children can be well behaved with one teacher and rowdy with the next teacher. The same applies among project managers.

People don't work through their problems in a nice and tidy fashion:

- Jenny fills in crossword puzzles starting with the first clue and going through to the back.
- Ron fills in clues haphazardly.
- Both get the crossword puzzles done.
- Some programmers derive their programs mathematically (Gries, 1981).
- Some people shuffle index cards to visualize interactions before coding (Beck 1989, Wilkinson 1995).
- Some people design their code by looking at the textual structure.

- As often as not, people go back and forth, up and down, and forward and backward while producing a solution (Guindon 1992).

Thus, legislating how a person is to solve problems invites trouble.

A person who is averse to detail-oriented work will have a hard time rechecking interface specifications for minor omissions. A concrete thinker is likely to have trouble inventing an object-oriented software framework. A noncommunicator will cause difficulty when assigned to manage a team.

An individual's personality affects his ability to perform particular job assignments:

- The cross-team manager on a large project was very concerned about being liked. He refused to make the hard decisions that the teams needed from him, and the project suffered accordingly.
- The best programmer was put in charge of a team of beginners. Not having the patience to tutor his people, he changed their code in the middle of the night! Although his designs were wonderful, his team neither enjoyed working with him nor learned much about programming.
- The person creating the program specs was a stereotypic salesman. His relations with the customers were great, but he could not bring himself to write his needs down. He needed a detail-oriented aide to do the writing.

In each of the above stories, it was not the process that was at fault. It was that the characteristics of the individual people did not fit the characteristics needed for the job role.

An individual's personal style affects the surrounding people.

Imagine the leaders of two well-functioning and stable teams:

- The first is list-oriented and uses a command-and-control leadership style. The group is used to this.
- The second has a casual manner, gives brief instructions, and wants decisions made through discussion. The group is used to this.

Now imagine that the two leaders trade places. Each team will suffer for a period, as they adapt to (or fail to adapt to) the new leadership style.

Collaboration styles vary by culture. Just as the personal styles of the key project individuals affect the collaboration patterns, so do the locally dominant cultural styles. I am indebted to Laurence Archer for contributing this example of crossing cultural style boundaries several times:

CROSSING CULTURES

My early experience was with a consulting company in England, where the manager had to set the project up single-handedly, developing the scope, objectives, strategy, plan, etc., and then get a team together and present the project to the team.

I tried to do this as a project manager in Italy. At the team briefing the message I got was, "That is your plan; you work to it. If you want us to work together, we plan together." Powerful message.

Then I went to Australia, where the prevailing corporate culture is that the managers make all the mistakes and everyone else just does as they are told.

I set up my first project the Italian way. I called the team together in a room with clean whiteboards, described the scope and objectives, and said, "Now let's work out together how we are going to do this."

The response was, "You are the manager. You work it out, and we'll just do whatever you say."

You can imagine the similar dissonance resulting from dropping a Japanese development methodology onto an Indian team (or the reverse), or from using a methodology for designing military aircraft in an e-commerce startup (or the reverse).

INESCAPABLE DIVERSITY

As a result of the differences between people, many technical approaches have been invented. For each fervent philosophy, its reverse is being used equally fervently somewhere else. No one approach has gained domination. Rather, each has found support with a sympathetic programmer and has grown in use as the programming population has increased. Just as the number of ways of creating software will probably continue to grow, the differing approaches will become stable as they find their support clusters.

This all seems obvious—right up to the moment of applying it on a particular project. People have a tendency to forget it, though, as they prescribe software development methodologies for a project and announce the "correct" way of working. Worse, they often expect everyone on the project to work using that one approach.

It is good to have variety on your team: abstract and concrete thinkers, orderly and random approaches, with some people who enjoy diving into the innards of a system and others who enjoy designing the user interface, documenting the system structure, or selling the final product. Having people with different characteristics on your team allows individuals to work in areas in which they are strong. The same diversity that presents communication difficulty and personality friction also allows for efficiency, so that mixed teams often outperform homogeneous teams (Sully 1998).

People being different does not mean that all general statements about humans are false. Some things that we can say are valid in a broad sense and vary primarily by degree and population. We will build upon such statements, even while accepting that people differ.

What we can't do, however, is expect people to be either predictable or the same as each other.

THE PLACE OF TECHNOLOGY

Technology increases effectiveness under any of these four circumstances:

- When it lets people express their thoughts more easily. High-level languages let people express ideas more succinctly. Some high-level languages let a person think in a technology space that is closer to the problem space, reducing interfering thoughts about implementation constraints.
- When it performs tasks that can't be done manually. Measuring and profiling tools gather data that otherwise can't be gathered. They are cited by programmers as essential tools to have.
- When it automates tedious or error-prone activities. Compilers, spreadsheets, and software configuration management tools are so basic that some people don't even refer to them as tools but simply assume their presence.
- When it facilitates communication across people. In the world of distributed software development, all kinds of communication tools help the team.

Note that with the exception of compilers, the tools let people make the decisions. The tools provide feedback and let the people consider the result.

In the case of compilers, people complained for decades that the compiler could not allocate registers and sequence instructions as well as people could. As it eventually became clear that the compiler could do that, people forgot about register allocation and moved their thoughts closer to the problem space, working on algorithms and program structure.

Technology does not increase effectiveness to the extent that it works against the grain of human cultural values and human cognition.

CONSULTANTS NOT TRADING NOTES

A consulting firm, wanting to leverage its consultants' technical experience, installed Lotus Notes and encouraged the consultants to trade technical notes and help each other.

They forgot that consultants retain their competitive value by owning secrets. To those consultants, knowledge was not just power; it was income.

The Notes database stayed mysteriously empty, despite constant exhortations from upper management for the people to share their secrets.

CONFLICTING GENERALIZATIONS

As you proceed through the next sections, please bear in mind that when talking about people, seemingly conflicting ideas come into play at the same time.

People do vary, *and* it is possible to make a few broad generalizations, *and* there will be exceptions to those generalizations.

This section discussed the idea of the exceptions. Now let's take a look at some of the generalizations.

OVERCOMING FAILURE MODES

Trygve Reenskaug cautioned me about discussing human failure modes. "If you give a dog a bad name," he reminded me of the old saying, "you might as well hang him." The hazard is that some people will use my naming of failure modes as excuses for poor work. Trygve reminded me that often what passes as a human failure has more to do with the working environment, as discussed in the last section and illustrated in this story he told me:

THE SMALL-GOODS SHOP

There was a small-goods and buttons shop nearby that was always in a terrible shape. The place was a mess, and the girls were either doing their nails or on the phone and didn't have much time for the customers.

That business closed, and another small-goods and buttons shop opened in its place. This place was wonderful! It was clean, tidy, and the girls were attentive to their customers. The only thing was . . . it was the same two girls!

C3 CULTURE SHIFTS

The Chrysler Comprehensive Compensation project experienced several shifts as in this story (C3 1998).

The team initially valued "thinking ahead," "subtle but extensible designs," and "my code is private."

The team, largely under the impetus of Kent Beck, rebuilt itself with the core values "make it simple and clear," "you don't really need that subtle item," "all code is public," and "any pair of people sitting together may change anything." With these shifts, the same people also adopted a different and highly disciplined set of practices.

Those caveats having been placed, I do notice people having certain kinds of "failure modes." I regularly see methodologies and projects fail for not taking these human characteristics into account. We can build systems of people that are less likely to fail by explicitly taking these characteristics into account.

The five failure modes to take into account are people

- Making mistakes
- Preferring to fail conservatively
- Inventing rather than researching
- Being creatures of habit
- Being inconsistent

MAKING MISTAKES

That people make mistakes is, in principle, no surprise to us. Indeed, that is exactly why *iterative* and *incremental* development were invented.

Iterative refers to a scheduling and staging strategy that allows rework of pieces of the system.

Iterative development lets the team learn about the requirements and design of the system. Grady Booch calls this sort of learning "gestalt, round-trip design" (1994), a term that emphasizes the human characteristic of learning by completing.

Iterative schedules are difficult to plan, because it is hard to guess in advance how many major learnings will take place. To get past this difficulty, some planners simply fix the schedule to contain three iterations: draft design, major design, and tested design.

Incremental refers to a scheduling and staging strategy in which pieces of the system are developed at different rates or times and integrated as they are developed.

Incremental development lets the team learn about its own development process as well as about the system being designed. After a section of the system is built, the team members examine their working conventions to find out what should be improved. They might change the team structure, the techniques, or the deliverables.

Incremental is the simpler of the two methods to learn, because cutting the project into subprojects is not as tricky as deciding when to stop improving the product. Incremental development is a critical success factor for modern projects (Cockburn 1998).

The very reason for incremental and iterative strategies is to allow for people's inevitable mistakes to be discovered relatively early and repaired in a tidy manner.

That people make mistakes should really not be any surprise to us. And yet, some managers seem genuinely surprised when the development team announces a plan to work according to an incremental or iterative process. I have heard of managers saying things like,

"What do you mean, you don't know how long it will take?"

or

"What do you mean, you plan to do it wrong the first time? I can go out and hire someone who will promise to do it right the first time."

In other words, the manager is saying that he expects the development team not to make any major mistakes or to learn anything new on the project.

One can find people who promise to get things right the first time, but one is unlikely to find people who actually get things right the first time. People make mistakes in estimation, requirements, design, typing, proofreading, installing, testing . . . and everything else they do. There is no escape. We must accept that mistakes will be made and use processes that adjust to the fact of mistakes.

Given how obvious it is that people make mistakes, the really surprising thing is that managers still refuse to use incremental and iterative strategies. I will argue that this is not as surprising as it appears, because it is anchored in two failure modes of humans: preferring to fail conservatively rather than risk succeeding differently, and having difficulty changing working habits.

PREFERRING TO FAIL CONSERVATIVELY

There is evidence that people generally are risk-averse when they have something in their hands that they might lose and risk-accepting if they are in the process of losing something and may have a chance to regain it (Piattelli-Palmarini 1996).

Piattelli-Palmarini describes a number of experiments involving risks and rewards. The interesting thing is that even when the outcomes are mathematically identical, the results are different depending on how the situation is presented.

ILLUSIONS OF CHOICE

Piattelli-Palmarini cites a dual experiment. In the first, people are given $300 and then have to choose between a guaranteed $100 more or a 50/50 chance at $200 more.

People prefer to take the guaranteed $100.

In the second, people are given $500 and then have to choose between having $100 taken away from them or a 50/50 chance of having $200 taken away from them.

People prefer to risk having $200 taken from them.

(Piattelli-Palmarini, p. 58)

Mathematically, all outcomes are equal. What is interesting is the difference in the outcomes depending on how the problem is stated.

Piattelli-Palmarini sums up the aspect relevant to project managers: *We are risk-averse when we might gain.*

Consider a manager faced with changing from waterfall to incremental or iterative scheduling. The waterfall strategy is accepted as a normal, conservative way of doing business, even though some people think it is faulty. The manager has used this strategy several times, with varying success. Now, one of his junior people comes to him with a radically different approach. He sees some significant dangers in the new approach. His reputation is riding on this next project. Does he use the normal, conservative strategy or try out the risky new strategy?

Odds are that he will use the normal, conservative strategy, a "guaranteed" standard outcome, rather than one that might work but might blow up in strange ways.

This characteristic, "preferring to fail conservatively rather than to risk succeeding differently," gets coupled with people's fear of rejection and the difficulty they have in building new work habits. The three together explain (to me) why managers continue to use the long-abused one-pass waterfall development process. Based on this line of thinking, I expect that people will continue to use the waterfall process even in the presence of mounting evidence against it and increasing evidence supporting incremental and iterative development. Use of the waterfall process is anchored in a failure mode.

In keeping with variations among people, some people have the opposite tendency. Often, though, the most adventuresome people are those who have little to lose personally if the project fails.

The good news is that there are opportunities for both sorts of people. The bad news is that these people probably find themselves on the same project.

INVENTING RATHER THAN RESEARCHING

This behavioral mode may be peculiar to American and European software developers. (I don't have enough experience with Indian and Asian developers to comment on their habits.) It is the tendency to avoid researching previous solutions to a problem and just invent a new solution on the spot.

This tendency is usually described as a sickness, the Not-Invented-Here (NIH) Syndrome. I prefer not to view it as a disease but rather as a natural outgrowth of cultural pressures. One might instead call it the Invent-Here-Now Imperative. It grows in the following way:

From earliest school days, students are instructed not to copy other people's work, not to help each other, and to be as original as possible in all but rote memory acts. They are given positive marks for originality and punished for using other people's solutions. (Recently, a *fourth* grade teacher told her students not to call each other to discuss homework problems—not even to ask for which problems to do!)

Through the university level, assignments are designed to produce grades for individual work, not for teamwork. This reaches a culmination in the Ph.D. dissertation, where originality is a core requirement.

Somewhere in these years of schooling, some people join the profession of "programmer," a person whose job is to program and who advances in the profession by writing harder and more uniquely original programs.

Under these circumstances, it is hardly surprising that the people internalize the Invent-Here-Now Imperative.

Upon showing up at work, though, these same people are told by the business owners that they should not write new programs but should scavenge solutions created throughout the industry over the history of the field. They should use as many existing solutions as possible, without violating intellectual property rights.

The rewards offered for this behavior are meager. People continue to receive low evaluations for reusing code instead of writing new code. Promotion comes to those who do the most and the best programming, not those who successfully hook together existing components. Technical authors still refer to people who do such work as low-level "component assemblers."

Frakes and Fox did a survey and found that education and attitude—just showing people that the culture values reuse over developing new solutions—showed the greatest correlation with increased reuse (Frakes 1995). Reward structures did not show a significant effect, nor did object-oriented technology, CASE tools, or a myriad of other factors.

Texas Instruments fought its "Not Invented Here" syndrome with an unusual award, the "Not Invented Here But I Did It Anyway" award (Dixon 2000). This NIHBIDIA award not only rewards people who make use of previous results, but it pokes fun at people caught up in the NIH syndrome at the same time. In this way, it creates a social effect of the type Frakes and Fox were referring to.

People who are professionals in some *different* field do practice effective reuse. These people, using the computer to accomplish some assignment of value in that other field, develop their sense of accomplishment from the program's effect in that other field, not from the cleverness of the programming. They are therefore motivated to put the software together to get on with their other work. They happily accept a less glamorous design if it can be put into use quickly.

BEING INCONSISTENT CREATURES OF HABIT

Asking a person to change his habits or to be consistent in action are the two most difficult requests I can think of. We are creatures of habit who resist learning new behaviors, and at the same time we tend toward inconsistency.

This may seem like a harsh judgement, and so I illustrate it with a conversation I heard among four people. Each was a senior manager or had a Ph.D., and so these were people you would most expect to be able to handle changing habits and being consistent.

THE CLEAN DESK TECHNIQUE

One of the four said, "I'm suffering from the flood of paper that comes into my office. I can't think of how to manage it."

A second offered, "It's easy. Keep your desk entirely clean. Put four baskets on one side and a set of folders in the top drawer. When a new piece of paper shows up, deal with it directly, and put it into its correct filing place . . ."

He didn't actually get that far before the other three jumped in together:

"Keep the desk clean!? I can't do that!"

The second speaker never got to finish explaining his technique. The demand was that the people act with care at 100 percent consistency. A few people can accomplish this. Most people, though, vary from hour to hour, having a good hour followed by a bad one. Some people even celebrate being inconsistent and careless.

Worse than asking them to be consistent, the second speaker asked them to both change their habits *and* be consistent in that change.

This story tells me, as a methodologist, that if we ever do discover an optimal design process, people will resist using it and then use it sporadically or carelessly.

If only people could just act consistently . . .

Of course, if they could do that, they could keep their desks clean, avoid cavities, lose weight, give up smoking, play a musical instrument, and possibly even produce software on a regular and timely basis.

We already know of a number of good practices:

- David Gries detailed how to derive correct programs in *The Science of Programming* (1981).
- Beck and Cunningham (1989) and Wilkinson (1995) described using CRC cards in object-oriented design.
- Beck (2000) and Jeffries (2001) described pair programming and test-first design in the context of Extreme Programming.
- Careful design checking and statistical testing were detailed in the Cleanroom methodology (Becker 1996).
- Humphrey (1997), in his Personal Software Process, provided detailed instructions about how programmers can become more effective through checking where errors are introduced.

Consistent application of any of the above ideas would improve most of the projects I have visited. As Karl Wiegers quipped, "We are not short on *practices*; we are short on *practice*."

COUNTERING WITH DISCIPLINE AND TOLERANCE

Methodologists deal with people's common weaknesses with *discipline* or *tolerance*:

- Create mechanisms in the methodology that hold strict behavioral standards in place.
- Design the methodology to be tolerant of individual variations.

Most choose discipline.

Because consistency in action is a human weakness, high-discipline methodologies are fragile. Even when they contain good practices, people are unlikely to keep performing those practices over time. Performing a disciplined activity daily is just as hard in software development as keeping the desk clear in the clean-desk technique just mentioned.

To remain in practice, a high-discipline methodology must contain specific elements that keep the discipline in place.

Let's look briefly at three high-discipline methodologies: Cleanroom, Personal Software Process, and Extreme Programming.

In Cleanroom, production code is not allowed to be compiled before being checked in. Typing errors and syntax errors are considered part of the statistical process being controlled (new language features and system calls are learned on nonproduction code). The team doing the compiling can then detect the rate at which errors are introduced during program entry.

This is a high-discipline rule and requires explicit management support and checks.

In the Personal Software Process, the practitioner is to write down how long each activity took and to tabulate at what point errors were introduced. From these notes, the person can determine which activities are most error-prone and concentrate more carefully next time. The difficulty is, of course, that the logs take effort to maintain, requiring consistency of action over time. Not producing them properly invalidates PSP.

PSP contains no specific mechanisms to hold the high-discipline practices in place. It is, therefore, not terribly surprising to find the following experience report coming from even a highly disciplined development group. The following words about PSP were written by a military group that had been trained in PSP and had achieved the Software Engineering Institute's Capability Maturity Model Level 5 rating (Webb 1999):

PSP REPORT

"During the summer of 1996, TIS introduced the PSP to a small group of software engineers.

Although the training was generally well received, use of the PSP in TIS started to decline as soon as the classes were completed. Soon, none of the engineers who had been instructed in PSP techniques was using them on the job.

When asked why, the reason was almost unanimous: 'PSP is extremely rigorous, and if no one is asking for my data, it's easier to do it the old way.'"

Extreme Programming (XP) is the third methodology to call for high-discipline practices. It calls for programming in pairs (with pair rotation), extensive and automated unit tests completed prior to code check-in each day, adherence to the group's coding standards, and aggressive refactoring of the code base.

Based on the discussion above, I expected to find adherence to the XP practices to be short-lived in most groups. My interview results were somewhat surprising, though.

People report programming in pairs to be enjoyable. They therefore program in pairs quite happily, after they adapt to each other's quirks. While programming in pairs, they find it easier to talk each other into writing the test cases and adhere to the coding standards.

The main part of XP that is high-discipline and resistant to the pressure of programming in pairs is the code refactoring work. I still find that most people on the team do not refactor often, generally leaving that to the senior project person.

However, unlike PSP, Extreme Programming contains a specific mechanism to help with the discipline. It calls for one person to act as "coach" and keep the team members sensitive to the way in which they are using the practices.

It is interesting to note that all three of these methodologies were invented by people who were, themselves, consistent in the habits they required. So it is not as though high-discipline methods can't be used. They just are "fragile."

The alternative to requiring discipline is being tolerant of individual variation.

Adaptive Software Development (Highsmith 2000) and the Crystal methodology family described in this book are the only two methodologies I know that are explicitly about being "variation tolerant." Each

methodology calls for the team members to form consensus on the minimum compliance needed in the work products and practices. Each suggests the use of standards but does not require that standards be enforced.

For "tolerant" methodologies to work, the people on the project must care about citizenship issues and generally take pride in their work. In such projects, the people develop a personal interest in seeing that their work is acceptable. Getting this to happen is no more guaranteed than getting people to follow standards, but I do see it accomplished regularly. It was also reported by Dixon (2000, p. 32).

Which is better: high-discipline or high-tolerance methodologies?

- Strict adherence to strict (and effective) practices should be harder to attain but may be more productive in the end.
- Tolerant practices should be easier to get adopted but may be less productive.

Part of the difficulty in choosing between them is that there currently is no consensus as to which practices are effective or ineffective under various circumstances. As a result, project leaders might enforce strict adherence to practices they consider effective and be surprised at the negative result they encounter.

The "Continuous Redocumentation" story in the last chapter gave one example of false adherence to discipline. The sponsors required that every change to any part of the system be immediately reflected in all documentation. They probably thought this would be an effective practice. In their context, though, it proved too costly, and the project was canceled.

In other words, although strict adherence to effective practices leads to an effective team, strict adherence to ineffective practices leads to an ineffective team.

If only we knew which was which.

WORKING BETTER IN SOME WAYS THAN OTHERS

Reminding ourselves that people vary, that certain broad generalizations hold, and that there are exceptions to each generalization, let's look at some of people's natural ways of working.

People generally work better by starting with something concrete and tangible, such as examples, by altering rather than creating from scratch, by watching, and by getting feedback.

One of my favorite sentences comes from Wenger and Lave (1993) about the power of the concrete:

> "The world carries its own structure, so that specificity always implies generality (and in this sense, generality is not to be assimilated to abstractness). That is why stories can be so powerful in conveying ideas, often more so than an articulation of the idea itself."

CONCRETE

Cognitive research provides support for the idea that our minds operate directly from concrete examples (an idea that is remarkably in harmony with the properties of neural networks).

Johnson-Laird and Byrne (1991) suggest that people perform logical deduction by imagining concrete situations and concrete counterexamples rather than from manipulating predicate calculus in their heads. For example, in a problem about billiard balls, "it is possible to frame rules that capture [the] inference, but it seems likely that people will make it by imagining the layout of the balls."

They suggest that in performing deduction, we:

1. Construct an internal model of the state of affairs that the premises describe
2. Formulate a brief description of the models constructed—one that ideally asserts something not explicitly stated in the premises
3. Search for alternative models of the premises in which the putative conclusion is false

Notice that even the third step, the validation step, involves constructing concrete examples.

Robert Glass (1995, p. 178) relates a remarkably similar version of the software design process. Citing other researchers, he relates that people do the following when composing plans:

1. Build a mental model of a proposed solution to the problem.
2. Mentally execute the model to see if it does indeed solve the problem, providing sample input to the model to see if it produces correct output.
3. When sufficient sample inputs have passed the test, assume the model to be a suitable design model and begin representation of the design.

If people really do make use of concrete situations in their thinking, we should find such artifacts among programmers' work products. User composites and interaction diagrams are two such artifacts.

In the user composites technique, the development team creates a composite sketch of one or more fictitious users of the system. Ideally, they invent several: one user who is lazy, one who is fanatically detail-oriented, one who is an expert in all the shortcuts, another who is slow to learn, and so on. They make these composite sketches as concrete and real as possible, even giving the imaginary people names. By putting very concrete images of future users in front of the design team, the team can more easily imagine how each would react differently to the system and can create system capabilities suited to those different sorts of people.

Interaction diagrams (of which there are two forms, collaboration diagrams and sequence charts) tell the story of objects interacting over time. They are created by drawing object instances on the page and drawing arrows showing the messages between them. In collaboration diagrams, the objects are placed anywhere on the page, and the arrows are drawn between them and numbered to show the time sequencing of the messages. In sequence charts, the objects are all placed as column heads at the top of the page. The interactions are shown going down the page as arrows from one column to the next.

Of the two, sequence charts are a recommended part of many OO design techniques. Collaboration diagrams, which are mathematically isomorphic to sequence charts, are so rarely mentioned in methodology texts that it was only after several years of teaching and coaching that I noticed that beginners often showed me their discussion results in collaboration diagrams, not sequence charts or class diagrams.

I suspect the reason that collaboration diagrams are not mentioned in methodologies is that they are temporary artifacts. They are useful in creating designs and in communicating about specific situations, but they are not preserved in the heavily distilled design documentation the project team feels obliged to produce.

As we become better at preserving records of transient discussions, I expect to see such diagrams used more in design and documentation.

TANGIBLE

Beyond concrete is providing something tangible, something that people can touch.

Pelle Ehn used paper prototypes in the mid-1980s, helping a typesetter's union to discover how computer systems might help them. He used cardboard boxes and bits of paper to represent the computer screen and its contents, to understand how the as-yet-unimagined system might work. The people worked through their daily operations to discover ways in which a computer might be useful. They felt comfortable manipulating these tangible, movable, and unfinished-looking props. Paper-based user-interface prototypes have grown to be a favorite of professional user-interface designers (Hohmann, forthcoming).

During the early, discovery phases of designing a user interface, such "low-fidelity" prototypes are considered even more effective than the screens simulated with care on a live computer screen. They are not only tangible but almost invite a person to change them.

ROUGH ARCHITECTURE DRAWINGS

An architect designing a hospital told me that he never shows the customers a computer-drawn plan of the building. The customers view it as too far along to change, no matter what he says.

He therefore always draws the plan in pencil, so they feel comfortable drawing over it.

An extension of the low-fidelity mock-up technique is one called *informance* (Burns 1994). An informance is an interactive performance, showing the not-yet-built system in use in its predicted future setting, using a mock-up so concrete that people can interact with it. Informance allows trial users to live the life of the future user in a realistic future environment.

One reported informance showed a hair stylist using a proposed system while cutting hair. In another, the group built a walk-through apartment in which actors playing patients used computers to talk with each other and build community while staying in bed.

By making the informance setting concrete, everyone involved in development can see the strong and weak points of the proposed idea.

A popular design technique that takes advantage of tangibility is the Class-Responsibility-Collaborator (CRC) card technique mentioned earlier. In this technique, an index card is put on a table to represent a specific instance of an object nominated for use in a design. The designer picks the card up and moves it around, at the same time discussing its behavior with respect to the other cards on the table.

CRC cards are concrete and tangible examples that let designers work multimodally through concrete situations. People consistently report that moving the cards online reduces their effectiveness.

There is something about picking up a couple of cards and saying, "This object sends . . . this other object . . . the request to do XYZ . . . No, that's not right, let's try another one . . ." that triggers an emotional, physical response about the quality of the design.

SOMETHING TO ALTER

Copying and altering previous work is a standard mode of operation used almost daily by people in all fields.

Faced with starting a new letter, invoice, proposal, document, program, or project plan, a person finds a previously done sample, copies it to a new work area, and changes all the particulars until the work product becomes what he needs. A cook will copy a recipe and vary just one part. A project manager takes over the previous project's plan and changes the line items to reflect the current project. A requirements document or database schema gets similarly copied and altered. Children (and adults) learn hypercard programming by copying someone else's program and guessing at the simple things to change.

THE *TALKINGPARROT* PROGRAM

My first Smalltalk program was a direct-manipulation editor for sequence charts.

Not yet knowing Smalltalk, I copied the *TalkingParrot* example from the Smalltalk tutorial and then changed every line in the program until I got my editor. Nothing was left of the original *TalkingParrot* except its use of the sophisticated MVC Model-View-Controller architecture (which I had never heard of, at the time).

A year later, my colleagues were having trouble changing their program to accept input from the network instead of from the keyboard, and I wasn't. It turned out that the MVC architecture I had inadvertently picked up from *TalkingParrot* was what was making my life so easy.

This copy-alter technique has been applied even to completed applications.

Airline companies traded frequent-flyer applications in the late 1990s. A frequent flyer application, by itself, provides little competitive advantage to an airline company. So one company would recover development costs by selling its frequent flyer application to its competitor. The buyer received a graphical model that generated application code that would need tuning, and the actual, generated and tuned code from the previous company. The buyer recognized that the application would not be quite correct but that it would take less effort to alter it than to build it from scratch.

Glass (1995, p.182) tells that a first design model

> "may very well be a reused model rather than one created by the designer in response to this particular problem. Visser (1987) discovered that, for problems encountered before, designers employ an 'example program' as their starting point, and then observed, 'Designers rarely start from scratch.'"

You can and should start taking advantage of people's strengths in copying and altering work samples. Create a small, online library of real samples for work products produced on your (or some previous) project. Other people can then simply copy one of the samples as the base for their own work. In copying it, they will pick up both the structure and style from the sample, while changing the details to fit their purpose.

The implication is, of course, that you would like the work samples you collect to be relatively "good," having structure and style you don't mind having copied. They don't have to be perfect, of course, just "good enough."

One book already does this. *Developing Object-Oriented Software: An Experience-Based Approach* (IBM OOTC 1997) is a collection of work product samples used by IBM's OOTC on various projects during the mid-1990s. The OOTC avoided fighting over methodology by providing examples of various work products and letting each project team choose the examples they felt compelled to use.

You may notice that many of the foregoing stories use surprising low-tech items, with much use of paper and cardboard. O'Dell (1998) wrote about the World Bank's successful knowledge management and transfer experiences with an appropriate lesson:

> "For best results, take one spoon of low-tech and one spoon of high-tech. Mix and drink."

WATCHING AND LISTENING

Humans have a knack for learning by watching as well as by doing.

Wenger and Lave (1993) discuss success and failure in apprenticeship-based professions. They highlight the value of line-of-sight and line-of-hearing learning in these professions. After I read the book, I made the following unhappy discovery:

LINE-OF-SIGHT DESIGN LEARNING

As I walked into our programmer's room, I saw all the programmers staring at their own screens! There was no line-of-sight learning anywhere in the room.

I had the chance to change the situation somewhat a few weeks later. When someone asked a design question, I made sure we discussed it at the whiteboard or said our ideas out loud.

It took another month or two, but eventually I could hear the designers talking about their designs using the words and ideas we had been building up in the room over the previous month.

This room setup is the basis for the "Expert in Earshot" strategy (Cockburn 2000a), which is further developed in "Convection Currents of Information" on page 77.

Programming in pairs is a programming technique that provides line-of-sight-and-hearing learning. Larry Constantine (1995) found this technique so effective that he nicknamed Brian Kernighan's use of pair programming "dynamic duo" teams. Pair programming has been repopularized largely through Extreme Programming (Beck 2000). Groups who practice pair programming report faster learning of both programming techniques and problem domain, as well as faster code production and lower defect rates (Cockburn 2001b).

SUPPORTING CONCENTRATION *AND* COMMUNICATION

Software development as a both thinking-intensive and communication-intensive activity presents an interesting dichotomy.

Programmers need sufficient quiet time to get into a quiet and productive mode known as *flow* (Csikszentmihalyi 1991). After spending 20 minutes getting into a state of flow, it takes only a minute or two of other conversation to disrupt it.

Every project team should find a way to provide quiet times sufficient to get into flow and should protect those times. DeMarco and Lister (1999) suggest designating two hours as quiet time every day, turning off all phones and banning all meetings during this time. I watched one organization adopt this convention. It was so appreciated, from the CEO on down, that among three dozen suggestions for improvements to the company's working habits this was uniformly acclaimed the most critical.

XP recommends a "caves and common" room layout (Auer 2002). The center of the room is used for group work: tables with two to six workstations and space for two people at each workstation (see Figure 3-13).

The outside of the room is set up with individual areas where people put their bags, make phone calls, answer e-mail messages, and so on. With this layout, the people have close access to other people while they are designing and private space for their personal needs.

I have found no consensus on the question of private offices versus shared workspace. People regularly tell me that they have produced their best work when they shared an office with someone else on the project or worked in war-room seating. Some say that they enjoyed the quiet of their private offices but produced better work when they didn't have a private office. Others, however, are so strongly attached to their private offices that they would quit rather than move into a shared workspace. That may be too high a price to pay for communication.

PERSONALITY-MATCHED WORK ASSIGNMENTS

For people to perform as well as they can, it helps if their job assignments are aligned with the strong points of their personalities, not their weak points. Methodologies name the roles that must be present on a project but don't mention the personality characteristics required for each role.

Here are three examples of a person whose personality characteristics did not match those required for the role:

THE SOCIALLY MINDED MANAGER

Once, on a large multiteam project, the cross-team manager was socially minded to the extent that he did not want to offend anyone.

As a result, he would not make those hard personal and priority decisions that are exactly what the cross-team manager is hired to make.

THE NONVERBAL TEAM LEAD

The person hired as lead programmer and mentor was a stereotypical noncommunicating programmer.

Rather than coach the novice programmers on improving their programming skills, he simply changed their code when they weren't around!

THE CONCRETE-THINKING OO DESIGNER

One person on our OO project desperately wanted to learn object-oriented programming. He seemed unable to get his thinking to an abstract enough level to generate good OO designs, though.

After much coaching for six months, his programs still looked like the user interface or the relational database.

What could be done with these people instead? On the first project, the person was too high on the project ladder to be replaced, and so the project continued to suffer. On the second project, the person was eventually replaced with someone who had good communication skills, who taught the novice programmers basic OO design skills.

On the third project, we were luckier. The person was spectacularly good at defining requirements, where his careful thinking and attention to detail paid off. In exchange for his working on the requirements, he continued doing OO design and programming on sections of the system where the quality of the design was not a critical issue. Everyone benefited: He had fun doing the programming, and the project was safer due to the high quality of his requirements work.

TALENT

The best programmers on the team may be so much better than the rest that just a few of the best programmers can put out more than all the rest combined.

eBUCKS.COM GOES LIVE

Vincent Coetzee, CTO at eBucks.com, told of how their group got the company's new eBucks system out in just three months.

The best two programmers programmed most of it.

I nodded as I heard this. "The old solution. Get the best two programmers to sit together and program it up rather than coordinate 20 people through a fancy methodology."

But that left an open question. I knew that he had many other duties and would have to attend so many meetings that he couldn't possibly concentrate enough to program. I asked him about that.

He answered, "I attended meetings until 5 p.m. or so and then wrote code from 6 p.m. until 2 a.m. each day."

Oh. Another far-too-obvious solution. Have the two best people work back-breaking hours for several months.

Painful, but effective.

This combination of talent and practiced skill I call *personal prowess*. Although a manager can increase the skill of the team members by encouraging them to learn and sending them to courses, he can't change the talent level of the team. A talented designer will still outperform an average designer with good skills.

John Wooden, the famously successful college basketball coach, considers talent such a key issue that he labeled his first coaching secret, "Secret #1: The team with the best players almost always wins" (Hill 2001, p. 63).

REWARDS THAT PRESERVE JOY

Inventing reward structures is tricky. I recently got tripped up on this myself, in what I thought was a simple work-reward situation:

PICKING DANDELIONS

Dandelions were beginning to clutter our backyard. Having three children aged 10 and under, I concocted a brilliant solution: I offered them one cent per yellow flower and ten cents for any dandelion in the seeding stage. For five to ten dollars a year, I thought, we'd get rid of dandelions in a few years.

The kids brought in bags of dandelions, and I paid out the cash.

On the third year, I commented to my now 12-year-old, Cameron, that it looked like we had more dandelions than the previous year.

He said, "Sure. Last year I ran around, dancing and waving all the white dandelions around. When Sean asked why I wasn't just putting them into the bag, I said, 'I'm planting money for next year!' "

If I had that much trouble with that simple situation, how much harder is it to find an appropriate reward for creating software? Should you reward

- Lines of code sent to the test department?
- Low defect rates delivered to the test department?

- Function points delivered each month?
- Number of lines reused from a corporate library?

In a Dilbert cartoon, the manager offers rewards related to the number of program bugs discovered. A programmer immediately announces: "I'm writing myself a minivan this afternoon!" (How like the dandelions!)

Even if you can name an appropriate reward structure, what does the organization actually reward? Is it aligned with what is most important for the company?

LINES-OF-CODE-BASED PAY

A large company I dare not name ran an initiative to encourage reuse. Programmers' performance, however, was evaluated based on the number of lines of code sent to the test department each month.

One person I knew incorporated components from the company's reuse library, as encouraged. She was, however, only given credit for the lines she wrote herself, not those she reused. As a result, she received a low evaluation for her programming performance.

Programmers detect the mismatch and sometimes find subtle ways in which to retaliate.

GOLDPLATING

A team leader in a small start-up company complained to me that one of the programmers was adding unnecessary complexity to his design—"goldplating" it—to make it more "interesting" for himself.

When we looked at the matter together, we saw that this person was earning a small, fixed salary in a high-risk position in a start-up company. His risk exposure for working there was high, his reward low.

He had evidently made his own self-reward scheme, inventing "cool" code that either would make his daily life interesting or would enhance his employability for the next job.

This sort of mismatch leads to programmers behaving in ways that hurt the company, just as Cameron's "investment" view of dandelion picking hurt my plans for the back yard.

One person wrote to me that he feels stock options are a form of reward that aligns the good of the company with the programmer's behavior. He wrote that he is now working in maintenance, not because it is more fun but because it is the best way to protect his stock ownership in the company.

Reward schemes are an even more slippery subject than I have implied so far, though. Alfie Kohn (1999) writes that rewards actually reduce the intrinsic joy and output quality of an otherwise fun activity:

"Young children who are rewarded for drawing are less likely to draw on their own than are children who draw just for the fun of it. Teenagers offered rewards for playing word games enjoy the games less and do not do as well as those who play with no rewards. Employees who are praised for meeting a manager's expectations suffer a drop in motivation. . . . In one study, girls in the fifth and sixth grades tutored younger children

much less effectively if they were promised free movie tickets for teaching well. The study, by James Gabarino, now president of Chicago's Erikson Institute for Advanced Studies in Child Development, showed that tutors working for the reward took longer to communicate ideas, got frustrated more easily, and did a poorer job in the end than those who were not rewarded."

If rewarding intrinsically motivated behavior destroys intrinsic motivation, what rewards might retain a person's intrinsic motivation?

- Pride-in-work
- Pride-in-accomplishment
- Pride-in-contribution

Pride-in-Work

Pride-in-work is exemplified by an ad for Scotch whiskey that I saw some years ago (sorry, it was long enough ago that I have to paraphrase this example). The ad ran something like this: "If you want a set of hand-carved golf clubs from Ian McGregor, you'll have to wait two years. There are three people ahead of you. (Good things take time)."

The ad made it clear that Ian McGregor took pride in his work, and as a result, he did an outstanding job (as did the Scotch distillery, by extension). The clientele could tell the difference and were willing to wait.

I only recently became aware of the possible role that pride-in-work might play on a project, but it wasn't long before I heard a programmer say this:

> "Well, the system's OK . . . I mean it functions, but I can't really take any pride in my work. I'd like to go home feeling good about my program, but I don't. It's just a big mess that barely works."

He continued by saying that he wasn't really happy with his job, even though things were "working."

Pride-in-Accomplishment

Winning is a great reward. We create a "small win," a powerful motivator, whenever we complete something (Weick 2001).

In software, we create an early win by delivering running, tested, useful code quickly. Using the principle of small wins as a motivating reward, a team delivers as early as possible the smallest thing that will count as a win for the team. That early delivery demonstrates to both the sponsor and the team that the team can work together and deliver. It boosts the morale of both.

To keep with Weick's principle of small wins, the team will then deliver more running, tested, useful function at regular intervals. This is the "Early and Regular Delivery" strategy underlying incremental delivery, described in *Surviving Object-Oriented Software* (Cockburn 1998).

One question that arises with Early and Regular Delivery is what to deliver first. On the one hand, it seems a good idea to leave the hardest thing until the end so that the team knows everything possible about the system before attacking the hardest problem. This is the "hardest-last" strategy. It has a surprisingly bad track record, because many projects simply can't be done by the people assigned. Continually deferring the hardest part to the end, the project schedule does not become more reliable over time but stays unstable until the last piece of design magic is found . . . or the sponsors run out of money.

The opposite strategy is to get the hardest part out of the way, using a "worst-things-first" strategy. This is better, but it has a weakness in that if the team cannot solve the hardest problem right away, no one knows what is wrong: Is the problem too hard? Is the team wrong? Is the process wrong? Are the tools wrong?

The repaired strategy is "simplest first, worst second." By constructing a "walking skeleton," a barely connected version of the system that can handle just one small type of action, the team learns how to work together and gains an early win.

With one victory under its collective belt, the team is in a stronger position to attack the worst problem. If the team can succeed with this, it once again gains doubly: The hardest part of the project is over (stabilizing the project plan), and the team accomplishes a major win.

If the team is not yet strong enough to attack the worst problem, team members attack the hardest problem they are sure they can solve. This gives them more practice on their assignment, a bigger win for their morale, and greater confidence in their ability to attack the hardest problem. They continue in this way until they solve the hardest problem, and the project starts to become easier.

Pride-in-Contribution

The third possible intrinsic reward is pride-in-contribution. People's desire to contribute is so strong that I regularly see programmers damage their health and private lives in their effort to contribute to the team.

Here is a story of a key developer who changed his attitude toward the project when it was made clear to him what his contribution to the project and the community meant.

REALIGNING COMMITMENT

The programmer was a senior-level contract programmer who was working on the most complicated and critical portion of the system. He was already being paid well.

The executive involved was a socially astute person.

At some point, the executive had a conversation with the programmer. The executive made it clear how important this particular programmer was to the success of the entire corporation, and he did it in a way that illustrated to the programmer that building a really clever, beautiful, and perfect solution that was hard for the other people to use would be to the detriment of the entire community and that the programmer could make a very positive contribution to everyone involved by making a simple and workable solution, even if it was less aesthetic or less mathematically sound.

Almost immediately, the programmer shifted his behavior. Rather than sneer at the company and the technology, he became interested in delivering value, contributing to the group. He was already a core contributor but now delivered a workable solution and stayed on long enough to see the solution deployed.

The interesting thing to me is that the executive did not draw on the programmer's feeling of pride-in-work with respect to the perfection of the design. Instead, he drew on pride-in-contribution to the community

COMBINING REWARDS

Laubacher and Malone at MIT's Sloan School of Management highlight the combination of rewards needed for high-tech workers (Laubacher 2000). They start with this caution:

> "We'll get and keep the best" is not a viable strategy for most companies. Such an approach may be possible for leaders like Sun Microsystems and Cisco, that can offer a compelling package of salary, stock options and challenging work. But not every firm has these resources."

They amend that with the following:

> "Because so many of its engineers have become millionaires through company stock options, Cisco Systems likens its workforce to volunteers and manages them accordingly. This is an extreme example, but in many highly skilled fields, talent is seeking something more than the biggest package of stock options. Interesting, rewarding work or a chance to join in a compelling mission now become valuable tools for attracting and keeping talented people."

Open-source projects seem to offer all three of the intrinsic reward mechanisms. The people involved comment on their pleasure in contributing, on the pride they feel about their work, and on their own and others' accomplishments. Those who contribute to open-source software are a notably committed group of people who generate very high-quality code. In their case, software creation clearly is a cooperative "game," done more for fun than for profit.

Even with all of the above discussion in place, it is still not true that a single reward mechanism will work for all people. The space shuttle projects, for example, benefit from people who take pride in finding every mistake and who therefore take their time and review every work artifact carefully. It may be difficult to find appropriate rewards on a project like this if the people involved are looking for high-risk projects that will let them go fast and get rich quickly.

This difference among people is good, because so many different kinds of systems need to be built.

FEEDBACK

People benefit from clear and frequent feedback. In general, the quicker the feedback, the better the effect.

SEYMOUR CRAY FIDDLES

Seymour Cray, inventor of the world's fastest computers for several decades, gave some talks about his early design techniques.

Fresh out of the university, he was the proud owner of an extra-large radial slide rule. He immediately used it on his first assignment, diligently calculating the parameters for several days.

Walking the halls one day, he met an experienced designer who showed him that it was simpler just to apply a few rules of thumb and build a prototype. He could then test it to see where it was off, make a few adjustments to the design, and bring it to spec.

Seymour Cray illustrated that a little bit of feedback can replace a lot of analytical work.

Of all the published methodologies, Extreme Programming (XP) perhaps puts the most emphasis on feedback, both during design and in the overall project.

XP calls for programmers to work in pairs during design and programming. The second person catches many programming errors during program entry.

The programmers keep unit tests in an automated test suite. Whenever they change a section of code, they run the test suite to discover right away whether they have broken something that had been working.

They produce running, tested code every few weeks. The on-site customers evaluate the new parts of the system and give feedback on the usefulness of the system while the work is still fresh in everyone's minds.

They review their own working habits every few weeks, reflecting on how well they worked in the previous iteration.

Actually, every development team should review its working habits every few weeks, whether or not it uses pair programming or XP. The project "post-mortem" that some teams hold at the end of a project happens too late to help the project. Holding regular reflection sessions *during* the project is much more effective. The team has a chance to incorporate feedback along the way and to work in the time needed to benefit the project.

Periodic mid-project reflection sessions are the single practice common across all of the Crystal methodologies described in Chapter 6. Every two to six weeks, depending on the project's cycle duration, the team gathers to discuss what went well, what didn't, and what to try out during the next period.

With regular feedback reflection periods in place, the team can construct other methods, such as Highsmith's product review sessions (2000), to gain feedback about the project.

DRAWING ON SUCCESS MODES

The surprising thing about human success modes is how nebulous and improbable they seem. They include

- Being good at looking around
- Being able to learn
- Being malleable
- Taking pride in work
- Taking pride in contributing
- Being good citizens
- Taking initiative

Are these the mechanisms that consistently pull projects through to safety?

In my interview notes, I find that one answer showed up repeatedly when I asked what caused a project to succeed in the end:

> "A few good people stepped in at key moments and did whatever was needed to get the job done."

For the first eight years of my interviews, I assumed that the speakers meant that they had messed up, and only personal heroics had saved the project.

Slowly, though, as I kept hearing it, I realized that I could not explain *why* people did that or the overall role of this sort of action on the project. It was by investigating this sentence that I started to see the powerful effects of the human success factors just mentioned, effects that are relevant no matter whether a tight or loose process is being used.

Let's look at these success factors.

GOOD AT LOOKING AROUND

That people are *good at looking around* is reflected in the ways they organize the paper in their lives: books, reports, addresses, and so on. A common, human way of sorting is to use the "shell sort" algorithm: We build piles ordered according to the sorting criterion (for example, alphabetically, or by date) but leave things unsorted within any pile. We then break each pile into smaller piles and repeat until each pile is small enough to sort by eye and by hand. Except ... we often don't do that final sort. When the pile is small enough to sort by eye and by hand, we often just leave it like that and find any item of interest just by scanning the contents of the pile.

The standard address book is a perfect example of this. An address book is sorted into sections by starting letter, but the entries within a section are not sorted. They are just written in any order, and we scan the section to find the entry of interest.

A more extreme example is the way many people sort papers in their offices. They have stacks of papers in general piles and locate reports by looking through the relevant stacks.

The important thing to notice is that this lack of final sorting is not bothersome. Most people do not even notice it but work on the assumption that they can locate things fast enough through scanning and by memory associations.

Trygve Reenskaug gave the following example of *being good at looking around* on a project:

OFFSHORE OIL PLATFORM DESIGN

Trygve tried to get a designer of offshore oil platforms interested in a computer-aided design system. Trygve suggested that the system could add value to the project by tracking all the design update activity touching any part of the platform.

The engineer replied, "Just have it store the phone numbers of the people working on each part. I'll call them and find out."

A second example of people using their ability to look around is the way code maintenance is done.

Keeping traceability and design documents up to date is very expensive and unreliable (particularly given the weakness of humans with regard to consistency). In most projects, it is not long before the documentation doesn't match the code.

If keeping the two in sync were essential, project teams would not be able to continue through the maintenance phase. However, code maintainers expect this mismatch, and so they use the faulty documentation simply as a means of getting "close" to the area that will need changing.

As soon as they are close, their eyes and intelligence take care of the rest. They plan on *just looking around* until they find the section of code to change.

Inside the theory of the cooperative game, we can use this human ability and plan on making the documentation "good enough to get close," close enough to use the native human ability to look around and find the right place to make a change.

A third place where we count on people being *good at looking around* is the role of technical lead.

The title "Technical Lead" contains the assumption that this person has done something similar enough before, that he has a sense of when the project is all right and when it is off track. The Technical Lead is not given any instructions about to how to do this. He is simply supposed to "look around and notice" when something is not right and somehow invent a way to get back into the safety zone.

"Looking around and noticing when something is not right" is something that everyone on the project does. I have found people in every possible job description who have detected something amiss with some aspect of the project—very often not their own—and have reported it to the person who should deal with it. Or, they have just dealt with it themselves, specifically stepping outside their own job descriptions to take care of it.

PEOPLE LEARN

Novices don't stay novices forever. People who are novices on one project become experienced by the end of the same project and often are senior designers a few projects later.

This ability to learn along the way helps many projects. Within a single project's time frame, the people learn new technology, new problem domain, new process, and how to work with new colleagues.

Often, a team struggles through the first two increments, becoming stronger and stronger until successful results at the end are almost a given. In long-running projects and in situations where there is a steady flow of small initiatives, senior people leave and junior people—who have become senior—take their places.

We take advantage of people's ability to learn *within* a project by splitting it into subprojects (incremental development again). This provides not only the small wins and feedback discussed earlier but also the opportunity for people to learn how the process works. "Oh!" they might say, *"That's* why we had to write the input validation fields in the data structures table." They use their ability to look around to detect what needs improvement, and then they invent new ways of working to try out in the next increment.

MALLEABLE

People are remarkably able to act differently given new motives and new information. This is the mechanism in the two stories at the start of the "Overcoming Failure Modes section": the small-goods shop and the C3 project.

In the story of the small-goods shop, we don't have enough information to know why the girls changed their work habits.

In the story of the Chrysler Comprehensive Compensation (C3) project, Kent Beck needed to shift the team's cultural values away from creating clever code to creating simple solutions, a notoriously difficult task.

One technique he used was the peer-pressure ritual. In one such ritual, the group formed a procession, placed a propeller beanie on the head of someone with an overly clever solution, and then spun the propeller on the beanie, commenting on the "cleverness" of the solution. The negative attention from peers caused people to move away from clever solutions; appreciation for simple designs drew them to simple solutions.

True to people being different, not everyone on the team was "malleable" enough to adopt XP. One person did not enjoy the new working style with its requirements for conformity and close cooperation and eventually left the project.

CONTRIBUTING AND TAKING INITIATIVE

In the previous section I discussed pride-in-contribution and pride-in-work as strong intrinsic motivators. Now I suggest that they are also core contributors to project success.

People who have pride in their work do a better job than those who do not, and they are also more likely to step outside of their own job descriptions to repair or report some other problem that they notice. Even though their only reward may be that they have done a good deed, I continually encounter people for whom this is sufficient.

Notice that we are back to the spontaneous behavior I mentioned at the start of the chapter. At that time, I described spontaneity as a difficulty in building a predictive model of humans working in a system. Now I include it as one of the human success modes.

Start with some pride-in-work and a sense of citizenship. Add being good at looking around and acting spontaneously. With these, we see people taking initiative to get the job done every day, an ongoing activity that keeps the project operating at peak form.

This is not an indication of process failure. Even the best process won't be able to account for every surprise that occurs on the project. Therefore, it becomes important that people notice, mention, and resolve problems that they see. The good thing to notice is that as the team gets better at pride-in-work, communication, citizenship, and initiative, the process can become less formal, based more on noticing what needs doing.

COMBINING SUCCESS MODES

Is it possible to construct a development methodology just around pride-in-work, citizenship, community, people being good at looking around, and taking initiative?

It is. The following excerpt (Hock 1999, pp. 205–207) is a description of how the first VISA clearing program was developed in 60 days. Note Dee Hock's use of the phrase "self-organization," synonymous with people taking initiative in a community.

DEE HOCK'S VISA STORY

"We decided to become our own prime contractor, farming out selected tasks to a variety of software developers and then coordinating and implementing results. Conventional wisdom held it to be one of the worst possible ways to build computerized communications systems.

"We rented cheap space in a suburban building and dispensed with leasehold improvements in favor of medical curtains on rolling frames for the limited spacial separation required. . . .

"Swiftly, self-organization emerged. An entire wall became a pinboard with every remaining day calendared across the top. Someone grabbed an unwashed coffee cup and suspended it on a long piece of string pinned to the current date. Every element of work to be done was listed on a scrap of paper with the required completion date and name of the person who had accepted the work. Anyone could revise the elements, adding tasks or revising dates, provided that they coordinated with others affected. Everyone, at any time, could see the picture emerge and evolve. They could see how the whole depended on their work and how their work was connected to every other part of the effort. Groups constantly assembled in front of the board as need and inclination arose, discussing and deciding in continuous flow and then dissolving as needs were met. As each task was completed, its scrap of paper would be removed. Each day, the cup and string moved inexorably ahead.

"Every day, every scrap of paper that fell behind the grimy string would find an eager group of volunteers to undertake the work required to remove it. To be able to get one's own work done and help another became a sought-after privilege. Nor did anyone feel beggared by accepting help. Such Herculean effort meant that at any time, anyone's task could fall behind and emerge on the wrong side of the string.

"Leaders spontaneously emerged and reemerged, none in control, but all in order. Ingenuity exploded. Individuality and diversity flourished. People astonished themselves at what they could accomplish and were amazed at the suppressed talents that emerged in others.

"Position became meaningless. Power over others became meaningless. Time became meaningless. Excitement about doing the impossible increased, and a community based on purpose, principle, and people arose. Individuality, self-worth, ingenuity, and creativity flourished; and as they did, so did the sense of belonging to something larger than self, something beyond immediate gain and monetary gratification.

"No one ever forgot the joy of bringing to work the wholeness of mind, body, and spirit; discovering in the process that such wholeness is impossible without inseparable connection with the others in the larger purpose of community effort. Money was a small part of what happened. The effort was fueled by a spontaneous expansion of the nonmonetary exchange of value. . . .

"No one ever replaced the dirty string and no one washed the cup. . . . The BASE-I system came up on time, under budget, and exceeded all operating objectives."

According to traditional software engineering methods, this project should have been a shambles. According to the cooperative game theory, it is clear why it works.

Is it a repeatable process? The answer depends on how well the group manages to keep those key factors alive.

HEROES AS ORDINARY PEOPLE

One point I wish to make is that in well-run projects, people in any job description can notice when something is out of kilter and act to correct it or notify someone who can.

Although heroes who work overtime may be needed to save poorly run projects, there is a much more interesting phenomenon to observe: ordinary people doing their work with a sense of pride and community and in doing that work noticing something wrong, passing information to someone who can fix the problem, or stepping out of their job descriptions to handle it themselves. This is an indicator of a community in action, not an indicator of a poor development process. Note the strength of this community effect in the VISA story above.

Pride-in-work, citizenship, and communication even have an effect in strongly "engineering" cultures. Here is an example, from computer hardware design:

FINDING ERRORS IN PC BOARDS

When designing computer hardware, one person has the job of examining with a magnifying glass the photographic negatives used to produce the printed circuit boards. The person is to any find hairline cracks that may be in the negatives and to paint over them with black ink.

One day, the woman who was doing this work noticed a strange looping pattern in the line she was following. Deciding that it couldn't be correct, she notified the department head.

He first dismissed the idea that she could have found anything substantive but at her insistence took the time to investigate further.

As it turned out, a circuit drawing error had resulted in two signals being tied together. The error showed up in the original circuit design. It had somehow slipped past all the design, drawing, and board layout reviews.

I wish to draw two morals from this story: The first is that everyone on a project is in a position to detect a mistake, regardless of the type of system being designed.

The second is a lead-in to a key topic in the next chapter: After a person detects a mistake, the cost of getting that information to the right person starts to drive the cost of the project.

I close this section with this summary from NASA's "Deorbit flight software lessons learned" (NASA 1998, my italics added for emphasis).

> "Perhaps most important for the long term, during the course of the project, a capable core team for rapid development of GN&C systems evolved. This included finding *talented team members*; training in and gaining experience with the tools, processes and methodology, and integrating into a cohesive team.
>
> "After working together in the RDL for a year, team members have acquired expertise in methods, tools and domain. *A helpful and cooperative atmosphere has encouraged* and enabled cross training. A willingness on the part of team members to *address any and all* project issues has proven invaluable on many occasions . . . this team can be a long-term asset to the division and to the agency."

WHAT SHOULD I DO TOMORROW?

Tomorrow, start noticing the strengths, weaknesses, and oddities of the people around you. Notice

- How some fit their jobs well and some don't
- How some people are good at being consistent and others aren't
- The presence of both list-makers and those who dislike lists
- Some people taking unnecessary risks, and more people being conservative
- What your boss says the next time you offer a suggestion for improvement

About the time you start to wonder how on earth anything gets done in your company with such a mixture of fit and misfit, notice

- The teamwork in place
- The citizenship displayed by people
- The initiatives being taken spontaneously (what process could you possibly put in place that would eliminate the need for such initiative-taking?)

Improve your environment:

- Collect a few work samples: an example of some good code, a well-written class comment, use case, project plan, meeting minutes, design memo, or user interface.
- Enlist a few others to do this, and put the small collection of work samples online for everyone to copy from.
- Reduce interruptions. Create a small period each day, just two hours long, in which you don't take interruptions. See if a larger group in your office will do the same.
- Reduce the need for mechanisms that rely on the weaknesses of people.
- Increase the use of mechanisms that draw on the strengths of people and let them use their talents.

3

Communicating, Cooperating Teams

This chapter considers the effect of the physical environment, communication modalities used for jumping the inevitable communication gaps, the role of amicability and conflict, and subcultures on the team. These issues highlight the fact that projects need people to notice important events and to be both willing and able to communicate to others what they notice.

"Convection Currents of Information" compares the movement of information to the dispersion of heat and gas. The comparison yields several useful associations: the energy cost of information transfer, osmotic communication, information radiators, and information drafts.

"Jumping Communication Gaps" examines people's efficiency in conveying ideas using warmer and cooler communication channels. It introduces the idea of adding "stickiness" to information and looks at how those two topics relate to transferring information across time.

"Teams as Communities" discusses amicability and conflict, the role of small team victories in team building, and the sorts of subcultures that evolve on a project. We will see that the differing cultural values are both useful to the organization and difficult for the team to deal with.

"Teams as Ecosystems" considers a software development team as an ecosystem in which physical structures, roles, and individuals with unique personalities all exert forces on each other. That each project produces its own, unique ecosystem makes the job of methodology design even more difficult.

Communicating, Cooperating Teams

CONVECTION CURRENTS OF INFORMATION

Saying that software development is a cooperative game of communication implies that a project's rate of progress is linked to how long it takes information to get from one person's mind to another's. If Kim knows something that Pat needs, the project's progress depends on

- How long it takes Pat to discover that Kim knows something useful
- How much energy it costs Pat and Kim together to get the knowledge transferred to Pat

Let's see how much this costs a project.

DELAYS AND LOST-OPPORTUNITY COSTS

A programmer these days costs a company about $2.10 per minute, and so adding one minute to getting a question answered adds $2.10 to the cost of the project. Standing up and walking to another table can add that minute.

Suppose that people who program in pairs ask and get answers to 100 questions per week. Adding that minute's delay costs the project $210 per programmer per week. On a 12-person team, this is about $2,500 per week for the team, which adds up to $50,000 for a 20-week project.

The project gets delayed almost a full week and costs an extra $50,000 *for each minute of delay* in getting questions answered, not assuming any other damage

to the project for the questions taking longer to answer!

The delay is more on the order of five minutes if a person has to walk down the hall. If Kim is not there, it is likely that when Pat returns to his office, he has lost the train of thought he was working on and has to spend more time and energy recovering it.

Even worse, the next time Pat has a question, he may decide against walking upstairs, because Kim might not be there. For not asking the question, he makes an assumption. Some percentage of his assumptions will be wrong, and each wrong assumption results in Pat introducing an error into the program. Finding and fixing that error costs the project anything from multiple minutes to multiple days.

Thus, Pat's not asking his question and getting it answered represents a large *lost-opportunity cost*. Over the course of the project, the lost-opportunity cost is far greater than the cost of walking upstairs.

I hope you palpably feel the project's development costs rising in the following six situations:

1. Kim and Pat pair-program on the same workstation (Figure 3-1). Pat wonders a question out loud, and Kim answers. Or, Kim mentions the answer in passing as part of their ongoing conversation, and Pat recognizes it as useful information. This takes little work by each person and takes the least time to accomplish.

Figure 3-1 Two people pair programming.

(Photo courtesy of Evant Solutions Corporation)

2. Kim and Pat sit at separate workstations, but right next to each other (side-by-side programming). Using peripheral vision or the usual chitchat that develops when sitting close together, Kim notices that Pat is looking for something on the Web and asks what the question is. Or, Pat simply asks. Kim answers, possibly without looking away from the screen. Not much work; not much time involved.

3. Kim and Pat work on opposite sides of a room, facing away from each other (Figure 3-2). Kim is not likely to notice that Pat is looking for something, but Pat can easily see whether Kim is available to answer a question. At that point, Pat asks and Kim answers.

4. Kim and Pat sit in adjacent offices, separated by a wall. Kim can't see when Pat is looking for something, and Pat can't see if Kim is available. Pat must get up, peek around the door frame to see if Kim is in, and then ask Kim the question.

Figure 3-2 Two people sitting at opposites sides of the room.

(Photo courtesy of Thoughtworks, Inc.)

5. Kim and Pat sit on different floors or in adjacent buildings. Pat walks upstairs only to find that Kim is out! Now Pat has lost time, energy, the train of thought he was holding while he was working downstairs, and the motivation to walk upstairs the next time he has a question. The lost-opportunity cost starts to mount.

6. Kim and Pat sit in different cities, possibly with several time zones between them. In this setting, not only will they not ask each other questions as often, they also will have to use less efficient, less rich communication channels to discuss the question and its answer. They expend more energy, over a longer period of time, to achieve the same communication result.

The main question is, if you were funding this project, which working configuration would you like Kim and Pat to use?

What we see is that even minor differences have an impact on the rate of information flow.

Figure 3-3 Pair programming and working across a partition. Between which pair of people will information discovery happen fastest?

(Photo courtesy of Thoughtworks, Inc.)

Notice, in Figure 3-3, the two different situations occurring at the same time. The two people on the left are pair programming. It may be nice for them to have a small separation from the person on the right. However, if it happened to be the two people across the partition who needed to work together, the partition would soon become a problem. Indeed, I visited two people who were working across a partition, and it wasn't long before they removed the partition. As one of them explained, "I couldn't see his eyes."

ERG-SECONDS

Comparing the flow of information with that of heat and gas is not as far-fetched as it may at first seem. With every speech act, Kim radiates both information and energy into the environment around her. That information or energy gets picked up by people within sight or hearing. Pat also radiates, with every speech act.

In his case he radiates his need for information. Sooner or later, either Kim detects Pat's information need, or Pat detects that Kim has the information. Whichever way the discovery goes, they then engage in conversation (or Pat reads Kim's document, if Kim's information is in written form).

In gas-dispersion problems, one analyzes the distance that molecules travel in a certain amount of time. The unit of measure for molecules is *moles* and that for distance is *meters*; therefore, gas dispersion is measured in *mole-meters/second* (how many moles of the gas travel how far, in how much time).

We can analyze the movement of ideas—*memes*, to borrow an appropriate term from *The Selfish Gene* (Dawkins 1990)—using similar terms. We are interested in how many useful memes flow through the project team each minute.

A meter is not the correct unit, though, because ideas travel through phone lines, e-mail notes, and documents, rather than through space.

What we care about is the amount of energy it takes to move a meme from one mind to another. The appropriate units are *erg-seconds*. An *erg* is a unit of work (such as walking up the stairs), and a *second* is a unit of time (such as time spent on the telephone); therefore, the term *erg-seconds* captures the cost in both labor and time to get a question answered.

(Bo Leuf comments that its inverse is also useful: *argh-minutes*, a measure of the pain of expending energy and *not* managing to convey the idea.)

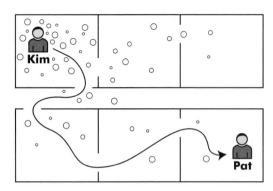

Figure 3-4 Energy and information moving through a barrier complex.

Using this metaphor, let's look at office layouts to see the energy cost associated with detecting that someone else has some needed information.

Suppose that Kim and Pat sit in offices some distance from each other (Figure 3-4). The walls between them keep Pat from seeing or hearing Kim. Kim radiates information as she walks around on her daily travels. The people in her room detect the greatest amount of information, and the people in earshot of her movement detect the next greatest amount. Information reaches Pat either as Kim walks into his office, or indirectly, through other people.

If their offices are next to each other, Kim is more likely to pop into Pat's office, or vice versa (Figure 3-5, top). Just as gas molecules or convected heat move more easily between neighboring rooms, so also does project information.

If Kim and Pat share an office (Figure 3-5, middle), then just as Pat will smell Kim's perfume sooner than anyone outside the office will, so will he notice if Kim radiates information that is useful to him.

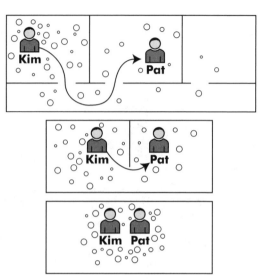

Figure 3-5 Gas canisters (or people) in three different configurations.

The greatest rate of information movement occurs if they are sitting side by side. In the case of information, the information transmission is greater if they are working on the same task, pair programming, than if they are merely sitting side by side, working on different tasks (this has more to do with their focus of attention than the radiation).

Describing information transmission costs in *erg-seconds* captures the effect of distance and communication modality on project costs.

Assume face-to-face communications, sitting in your own office, versus walking 50 meters to a colleague's office. Walking down the hall takes work (ergs) and time (seconds). Energy and cost increase, and the information transfer rate decreases. Move people closer, to the office next door. As the distance decreases, work required to visit the colleague decreases and so do energy and project cost while the information transfer rate increases.

Similarly, describing an idea on the phone takes more time than describing it in person. In this case, the time factor increases, and so does cost to the project.

The *erg-seconds* formula accounts for these changes well.

Of course, the formula does not account for wasted energy, such as jumping up and down while talking on the phone or walking around the building the long way in getting to a colleague's office. It also does not guarantee that two people who work in the same room will ever actually understand each other. (See "The Impossibility of Communication" on page 8.) What it does say is that project costs increase in proportion to the time it takes for people to understand each other.

OSMOTIC COMMUNICATION

While writing, reading, typing, or talking, we pick up traces of the ongoing sounds around us, using some background listening mode even though we are not consciously paying attention.

If someone says something interesting, we may perk up and join the conversation. Otherwise, the sound goes through some background processing, either just above or just below our conscious level.

In some cases, we register enough about the conversation to be able to develop what we need directly from memory. Otherwise, we may recall a phrase that was used or perhaps only *that* a particular person was discussing a particular topic. In any case, we register enough to ask about it.

This taking in of information without directly paying attention to it is like the process of osmosis, in which one substance seeps from one system, through a separator, into another.

Osmotic communication further lowers the cost of idea transfer.

If Pat and Kim work in the same room, with Pat programming and Kim having a discussion, Pat may get just enough information to know that Kim has talked about the idea. If multiple people are working in the same room, then Pat knows that someone in the room has the answer.

We have seen three separate effects that office layout has on communication costs within a project:

- The lost-opportunity cost of not asking questions
- The overall cost of detecting and transferring information (erg-seconds)
- The reduction in cost when people discover information in background sounds (osmotic communication)

The three magnify the effects of distance in office seating. People who sit close by each other benefit in all three effects; people who sit in separate locations suffer in all three.

According to this theory, sponsors should think twice before sponsoring a geographically distributed project.

One might think that we now have an easy answer to the riddle of how to seat people: "Obviously, put them into open and shared workspaces." Unfortunately, people are not so uniform or simple that this will work in all cases.

Three more issues affect the answer in any one particular setting:

- The sort of information being shared
- People's personal preferences
- Drafts

The team members exchange both business and technical information.

Suppose that Chris is the business expert in the group. If Chris, Pat, and Kim sit together, Chris can answer business questions as soon as Pat or Kim encounters them. Chris might even see what Pat and Kim are doing and guide them in a different direction. The three of them can put their heads together at any instant to jointly invent something better than any one of them could do.

This sort of *radical colocation* (as it has recently been called) only works for very small teams. Among 12 programmers and four business experts, who should sit close to whom? How does one arrange seating with two-person rooms?

The most common seating arrangement I encounter consists of programmers sitting on one side of the building and business experts on the other.

This seating arrangement produces two problems. The obvious one is the cost of business communication, including the lost opportunity cost of missed early interventions.

The second is that each group forms its own community and usually complains about the other group. The chitchat in the osmotic communication is filled with these complaints, interfering with the ability of people in each group to work with each other in an amicable way.

As is natural with osmotic communication, this emotionally loaded background noise soaks into each group's subconscious. In this case, it does not educate them but rather attacks their attitude. Going into a meeting with "those idiotic other people," they don't give full consideration to what the other people say and don't offer full information when speaking. The group's amicability suffers, with all the attendant costs just discussed.

My current preference is to find seating arrangements where one or more business experts sit close to two or more programmers. Where this is not possible, I look for other business and social mechanisms that will get the business expert in regular, meaningful collaboration with the programmers on a frequent (preferably daily) basis.

Cross-specialty teams that work together have been recommended by many authors. These teams have been given names such as *Holistic Diversity* (Cockburn 1998), CASE teams (Hammer 1994), and Feature teams (McCarthy 1995). When this can be done, the project as a whole moves faster, based on the increase in both information flow and amicability across specialties.

Another issue is the matter of people's personal preferences.

As I started asking people about working in shared rooms versus in private offices, several issues emerged.

Some people really value their quiet, private offices. They value them enough that they would feel offended if they had to give them up, some even to the point that they would quit the company. If that is the case, then any gain in communication is partially lost if the person stays, but feels offended, and is completely lost if the person leaves the company.

Thus, the clear theoretical argument for seating people close to the people they need to interact with is affected by personal preferences. Several people have told me, "I prefer having my own office, but considering all the projects I've been on, I would have to say that I was never so productive as when I shared an office with my project mate." I have moved out of private offices so often that I eventually noticed it as a pattern. As I noticed other experts doing it, it became a project-management strategy, which I call "Expert in Earshot" (Cockburn 2001a).

The third issue affecting the question of where to seat people concerns drafts.

Drafts

Drafty Cubicles

One day, while I was describing this peculiar notion of convection currents of information flow, one of the listeners suddenly exclaimed, "But you have to watch out for drafts!"

He went on to explain that he had been working in a place where he and the other programmers had low-walled cubicles next to each other and so benefited from overhearing each other.

On the other side of their bank of cubicles sat the call-center people, who answered questions on the phone all day. They also benefited from overhearing each other. But, and here was the bad part, the conversation of the call-center people would (in his words) "wash over the walls to the programmers' area." There was a "draft" of unwanted information coming from that area.

Drafts are the *unwanted information* in our newly extended metaphor.

Later, two programmers were talking about how their walls were too thin. They enjoyed their shared room but were bothered by their neighbors, who argued loudly with each other. Their room was *drafty,* in an information sense.

We now have a nice pair of forces to balance: We want to set up seating clusters that increase information flow among people sitting within hearing distance and balance that against draftiness—their overhearing information that is not helpful to them. You can develop a sense of this for yourself, as you walk around.

Osmosis across Distances

Is there anything that teams can do to improve communication if they do not sit together, for whatever reason?

Charles Herring, in Australia, describes applying technology to simulate "presence and awareness," a term used by a researcher in computer-supported collaborative work (Herring 2001). Following is a paraphrased summary of their experience:

E-Presence and E-Awareness

The people sat in different parts of the same building. They had microphones and Web cameras on their workstations and arranged small windows on their monitors, showing the picture from the other people's cameras.

They wanted to give each person a sensation that they were sitting in a group ("presence") and an awareness of what the other people were all doing.

Pat could just glance at Kim's image to decide if Kim was in a state to be disturbed with a question. In that glance, he could detect if Kim was typing with great concentration, working in a relaxed mode, talking to someone else, or gone.

Pat could then ask Kim a question, using the microphone or chat boxes they kept on their screens. They could even drop code fragments from their programming workspaces into the chat boxes.

They reported a low distraction rate. Charles added that while programming, he could easily respond to queries and even answer programming problems without losing his main train of thought on his own work.

Pavel Curtis and others at Xerox PARC were able to simulate "whispering" (when a user would like to speak to just one person in a room) through video and audio. They also had their online chat rooms produce background sounds as people entered or left (Curtis 1995).

Because memes (ideas) don't have to travel through air but travel through the senses, primarily audio and visual, we should be able to mimic the effects of convection currents of information using high-bandwidth technology. Still missing from that technology, of course, are the tactile and kinesthetic cues that can be so important to interpersonal communication.

INFORMATION RADIATORS

An information radiator displays information in a place where passersby can see it. With information radiators, the passersby don't need to ask questions; the information simply hits them as they pass.

Two characteristics are key to a good information radiator. The first is that the information changes over time. This makes it worth a person's while to look at the display. This characteristic explains why a status display makes for a useful information radiator and a display of the company's development process does not.

The other characteristic is that it takes very little energy to view the display. Size matters when it comes to information radiators—the bigger the better.

Hallways qualify very nicely as good places for information radiators. Web pages don't. Accessing the Web page costs most people more effort than they are willing to expend, and so the information stays hidden. The following story contributed by Martin Fowler, at Thoughtworks, reports an exception: This team found that a particular report worked best on a Web page.

AUTOMATED BUILD REPORT

A program auto-builds the team's system every 15 minutes. After each build, it sends e-mail messages to each person whose test cases failed and posts the build statistics to a Web page.

The information about the system is updated every 15 minutes on the Web page. Martin reports that a growing number of programmers keep that Web page up on their screen at all times and periodically just hit the Refresh button to check the recent system build history.

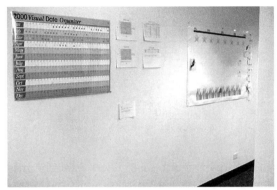

Figure 3-6 Hall with information radiators.

(Courtesy of Thoughtworks, Inc.)

The first information radiators I noticed were at Thoughtworks, while talking with Martin Fowler about Thoughtworks' application of XP to an unusually large (40-person) project (Figure 3-6 and Figure 3-7).

PROGRESS RADIATORS

Martin was describing that the testing group had been worried about the state of the system.

To assuage the testers' concerns, the programmers placed this poster in the hallway (Figure 3-6) to show their progress.

The chart shows the state of the user stories being worked on in the iteration, with one Post-It note per story. The programmers moved the notes on the graph to show both the completeness and the implementation quality of the user stories they were working on. They moved a note to the right as a story grew to completion and raised it higher on the poster as its quality improved. A note might stop moving to the right for a time while it moved up.

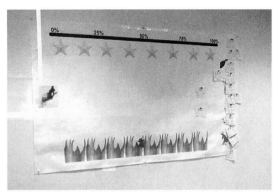

Figure 3-7 Status display showing completion level and quality of user stories being implemented.

(Courtesy of Thoughtworks, Inc.)

The testers could see the state of the system without pestering the programmers. In this case, they saw that the work was further along than they thought and soon became less worried about the state of the project.

The best thing was that they could see the progress of the work daily, without asking the programmers a question.

Just as a heating duct blows air into a hallway or a heater radiates heat into a room, these posters radiate information into the hallway, onto people walking by. They are marvelous for passing along information quietly, with little effort, and without disturbing the people whose status is being reported.

A second use of information radiators, suited for any project using increments of a month or less, is to show the work breakdown and assignments for the next increment (Figure 3-8). The following example also comes from Thoughtworks.

Figure 3-8 Large information radiator wall showing the iteration plan, one flipchart per user story.

(Courtesy of Thoughtworks, Inc.)

DISPLAYING WORK BREAKDOWN

The team created a flipchart for each user story. They put Post-It notes on the flipchart for the tasks they would need to do for that story.

They would move notes *below* a flipchart to show tasks being taken out of scope of the current iteration in order to meet the delivery schedule.

Evant's XP team also used whiteboards and flipcharts as information radiators. Figure 3-9 shows the tasks for iteration "Mary Ann" (each iteration was nicknamed for someone on the *Gilligan's Island* TV series).

Figure 3-9 Detail of an XP task signup and status for one iteration (nicknamed "Mary Ann").

(Courtesy of Evant Solutions Corporation)

A third use of flipcharts as information radiators is to show the results of the project's periodic *reflection workshop* (Figure 3-10). During these one- to two-hour workshops, the team discusses what is going well for them and what they should do differently for the next period. They write those on a flipchart and post it in a prominent place so that people are reminded about these thoughts as they work.

The wording in the posters matters. One XP team had posted "Things we did wrong last increment." Another had posted, "Things to work on this increment." Imagine the difference in the projects: The first one radiated guilt into the project room and was, not surprisingly, not referred to very much by the project team. The second one radiates promise. The people on the second team referred to their poster quite frequently when talking about their project.

Periodic reflection workshops such as these are used in Crystal Clear and XP projects.

A fourth use of information radiators is to show everyone the user stories delivered or in progress, the number of acceptance tests written and met, and so on. (Figure 3-11).

The systems operations team at eBucks.com constructed a fifth use of information radiators, this time to keep the programmers from pestering them.

DISPLAYING SYSTEM STATUS

The programmers kept asking, "Is system A up? Is system B up? Is the link to the back end up?"

The maintenance team wrote the status of each system and link on the whiteboard outside their area. Each day, they updated the status. It looked rather like a ski area posting the status of lifts and runs (so skiers don't keep asking the ski resort staff).

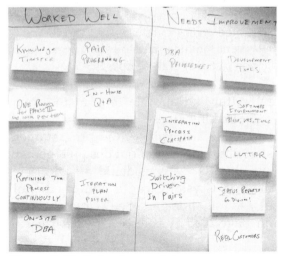

Figure 3-10 Reflection workshop output.

(Courtesy of Joshua Kerievsky, Industrial Logic, Inc.)

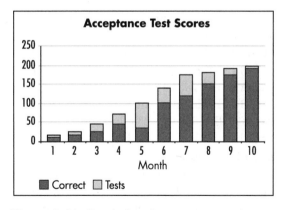

Figure 3-11 Graph showing growing completion.

(Courtesy of Ron Jeffries)

The group at eBucks.com came up with a sixth use of information radiators. This time it was the programmers who created the status displays:

DISPLAYING WORK PROGRESS

The programmers were being asked about the status of their work every hour or two, which caused them no end of frustration.

They wrote on the whiteboard outside their office their intentions for the current week. As they completed their tasks, carefully sized to be of the half-day to two-day variety, they marked the tasks complete.

After these boards had been tried by the programmers, several other groups started using them to broadcast their own priorities and progress.

APPLYING THE THEORY OF HOT AIR

People have long applied the above-described "hot air theory of software development."

Gerald Weinberg discussed the damaging effect of removing a soda machine from a computer help-desk area (Weinberg 1998). Thomas Allen, of MIT's Sloan School of Management, discussed the effect of building design on R&D organizations (Allen 1984). IBM and Hewlett-Packard have incorporated such research in their R&D buildings since the late 1970s.

As a result of these and others' work, it seems natural that research and development groups have whiteboards in the hallways or near coffee machines. What we have forgotten, though, is the significance of actually being within sight and earshot of each other.

Here are several examples. The first is from a Crystal Orange project. The second is from a project unsuccessfully trying to apply Crystal Clear. Next comes a discussion of the "caves and common" room design recommended by XP. The final example is a success story from Lockheed's Skunk Works group.

REPAIRING DESIGN DISCUSSIONS

On project "Winifred" (Cockburn 1998), the lead programmer announced at regular intervals that design was unnecessary and that code simply grew under his fingertips.

As a predictable result, the young programmers working in the room with him also felt it unnecessary to design. The code looked that way, too.

He eventually left and I took his place. To reverse the situation, I arranged for us to design by having conversations at the whiteboard. After some period of doing this, I started getting questions like, "Could you look at the responsibilities (or communication patterns) of these objects?"

By setting an audible tone in the room and making these design discussions legitimate and valued, the programmers started to converse about design together.

Colocation is considered a critical element in Crystal Clear, a light methodology for small teams. (See "Crystal Clear" on page 202.) A rule of Crystal Clear is that the entire team must sit in the same or adjacent rooms, in order to take advantage of convection currents of information and osmotic communications.

CRYSTAL UN-CLEAR

"Pat" asked me to visit his Crystal Clear project. When I arrived, he wasn't at his desk. The secretary said he was with his teammate.

I offered to go to that office, but she said, "You can't. There is a combination lock in the hallway over to that section."

"!! . . . ?"

Each time a team member wanted to ask a question, he had to stand, walk across the hall, punch in the lock combination, and walk to the teammate's office. Clearly, this team was not getting the benefit of osmotic communication or the low cost of information transfer. Fortunately, changing the team seating was a simple matter to arrange.

Caves and Common

The "caves and common" room arrangement recommended in XP makes use of all three information-exchange mechanisms. It is shown in action in Figure 3-12 and diagrammed in Figure 3-13.

"Caves and common" is very effective, but as Tom DeMarco correctly warns, it can easily be abused to become just a programming sweatshop. Therefore, not only the room layout is described in this section but also the social presuppositions that accompany its use: a single project team, good team dynamics, and provision for both private and project space.

The phrase *caves and common* refers to the creation of two zones in the room. The "common" area is organized to maximize osmotic communication and information transfer. For this to make sense, the people in the room must be working on the same project. It is perfect for XP's single team of up to 12 people programming in pairs (Figure 3-12).

Figure 3-12 The RoleModel Software team at work.

(Photo courtesy RoleModel Software)

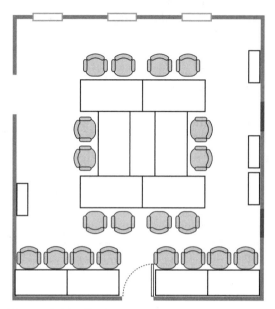

Figure 3-13 The "caves and common" room layout used at RoleModel Software.

(Picture courtesy of RoleModel Software)

The "caves" portion of the room is organized to give people a private place to do e-mail, make phone calls, and take care of their need for separation. In RoleModel Software's office, private workstations are set up along one wall (Figure 3-12). At Evant, a table came out from the walls on two sides of the room.

People who have worked in "caves and common" facilities say that there needs to be ample wall space for whiteboards and posted flipcharts, and two more types of rooms for the team to use: a food-preparation room and areas for small discussions to take place.

You can see from the picture that while the "caves and common" room is very efficient for transmitting information, it is also very efficient for transmitting coughs

and colds. People who work in this sort of room encourage their colleagues to stay home if they don't feel well and to return after they have recovered.

You can also see that it is drafty (in an information sense): The people sitting in this configuration should really *need* to overhear each other.

Finally, you can see that it is very effective as long as the morale of the group is good. If the social chitchat degenerates into negative chatter, the highly osmotic communication again magnifies its effect.

Skunk Works

It is useful to compare the above discussions against a group performing classical "engineering," one of the most effective aero-engineering groups: Lockheed's "skunk works" team. This team achieved fame for its rapid development of a series of radical new airplane designs in the second half of the 20th century, under the guidance of Jim Kelly and his successor, Ben Rich. Ben Rich wrote about their experiences in the book *Skunk Works* (1994).

Rich highlights that, among the rules of the group, Kelly insisted on people taking accountability for decisions from design through testing, and on their sitting close together. The following quotation is from that book:

SKUNK WORKS ROOMS

"Kelly kept those of us working on his airplane jammed together in one corner of our [building] ... My three-man thermodynamics and propulsion group now shared space with the performance and stability-control people. Through a connecting door was the eight-man structures group. ...

Henry and I could have reached through the doorway and shaken hands.

"... I was separated by a connecting doorway from the office of four structures guys, who configured the strength, loads, and weight of the airplane from preliminary design sketches.... [T]he aerodynamics group in my office began talking through the open door to the structures bunch about calculations on the center of pressures on the fuselage, when suddenly I got the idea of unhinging the door between us, laying the door between a couple of desks, tacking onto it a long sheet of paper, and having all of us join in designing the optimum final design.... It took us a day and a half...."

"All that mattered to him was our proximity to the production floor: A stone's throw was too far away; he wanted us only steps away from the shop workers, to make quick structural or parts changes or answer any of their questions."

Every project team should be on a quest to reduce the total energy cost of detecting and transferring needed ideas. That means noticing and improving the convection currents of information flow, getting the benefits of osmotic communication, watching for sources of drafts, and using information radiators. The end goal is to lower the *erg-seconds* required for team members to exchange information, whatever constraints their organization places on their seating, and with or without technology.

JUMPING COMMUNICATION GAPS

To make communications as effective as possible, it is essential to improve the likelihood that the receiver can jump the communication gaps that are always present. The sender needs to touch into the highest level of shared experience with the receiver. The two people should provide constant feedback to each other in this process so that they can detect the extent to which they miss their intention.

MODALITIES IN COMMUNICATION

Imagine a simple discussion at the whiteboard. How many communication mechanisms are at play? Consider these 11:

Physical proximity. Standing about one meter from each other, the people detect minute visual cues, tiny movements of eye muscles to overall muscle tension.

The speaker may move closer to indicate aggressiveness or enthusiasm. The listener may move closer to indicate interest, agreement, or the desire to speak; or, the listener may move away to indicate fear, disagreement, or the need to think privately for a moment. The speaker and listener manipulate their relative distance to express various emotions and stages of agreement, disagreement, aggressiveness, trust, and distrust.

The signals vary across cultures and personalities, but the signals are both present and used.

Three-dimensionality. The people notice visual parallax, or 3D information.

The parallax shift of the visual image is lost when the same people talk over a video link, even if they are similarly close to the camera and screen.

Smell. Smell is one of those senses that is unimportant to some people, very important to others, and important but subconscious to many.

One person reported that she can often sense sublimated fear and distress, probably through sense of smell. It certainly is the case that those cues are available at the whiteboard and are lost in remote communications.

Kinesthetics. Many people use kinesthetics (sensation of movement) to help them think and remember. The speaker might use it to help construct a new explanation or to help improve the building of a question.

Touch. One person touches another on the shoulder to mean, "Don't feel threatened by this discussion" or perhaps, "This is really important" or "I have something to say."

Touching is part of the overall manipulation of proximity and personal space. In some cases there are objects to touch whose feel is important to the conversation.

Sound. In the simple use of language, a speaker emphasizes points with colorful adjectives, exaggerations, metaphors, and the like.

Besides that simple use of language, the speaker uses pitch, volume, and pacing to differentiate and emphasize ideas in a sentence.

Visuals. People communicate through gestures as well as words, often making a point by gesturing, raising an eyebrow, or pointing while speaking.

The people may wave their hands to make shapes in the air or to accentuate the speaking. They may raise an eyebrow to indicate questioning or emphasis.

Again, they use pacing to differentiate and emphasize ideas, for example, moving rapidly over obvious parts of a drawing and slowing down or pausing for effect at less obvious or more important parts.

A person also draws on the whiteboard to present (particularly spatially oriented) information for the other to consider. The drawings may be standardized notations, such as class or timing diagrams. They may be loose sketches. They may even be squiggles having no particular meaning, whose sole purpose is to anchor in a public, static location the thought being discussed for later reference.

Cross-modality timing. One of the most important characteristics of two people at the whiteboard is the timed correlation of all of the above.

The speaker moves facial muscles and gestures while talking, draws while talking and moving, pauses in speech for effect while drawing, and carefully announces key phrases in time, while drawing lines between shapes.

Cross-modality emphasis helps anchor ideas in the listener's mind, enhancing the memory associations around the idea.

Drawing otherwise meaningless squiggles on the board while talking gives meaning to the squiggles—meaning that the speaker and listener can later refer to.

Low latency. Because the two are standing next to each other, watching and listening to each other, the round-trip time for a signal and a response is very small. This allows real-time question and answer, and interruptions:

- *Real-time question-and-answer.* The receiver asks questions to reveal ambiguity and missed communication in the speaker's explanation. The timing of the questions sets up a pattern of communication between the people.
- *Interruptions.* With the very fast round-trip times available in face-to-face communication, the listener can interrupt the speaker, asking for clarification on the spot. During the course of conversation, the speaker may be able to tune the presentation to fit the receiver's background. The listener can give the speaker feedback *in the middle of the expression of an idea*, perhaps through a raised eyebrow or other nonverbal modality. The speaker can then adjust the expression on the fly.

Trust and learning. Through modalities and rapid feedback, two people are likely to develop a sense of comfort and trust in communication with each other.

This is comfort and trust of the form, "Oh, when he speaks in that tone of voice he is not actually angry, but just excited." The two find ways to not hurt each other in communication and to know that they will not be hurt in the communication.

They build small emotional normalizing rituals of movement and expression to indicate things like, "I'm starting to feel attacked here" and "You don't need to, because this is not an attack on you."

Those rituals serve the people well over the course of the project, particularly when they can't see each other during the communication. At that juncture, touching into the shared experience of these rituals becomes crucial.

You see an example of the need for these normalizing rituals in the amount of airplane travel going on:

FLYING PLACES TO BE THERE

A senior executive of a video-communications firm returned to San Jose from London. It was her second trip in 10 days, each being for a single meeting.

The astonishment for us was that she obviously had access to state-of-the-art video-conferencing facilities and yet felt that she could not conduct her business over the video link. Her meetings still required the lowest latency, richest, multimodal communication possible: "in person."

We decided that it is easy to start negotiations over the phone or Internet but difficult to bring them to conclusion that way.

Use of a shared, persistent information radiator. The whiteboard holds the drawn information in place, while words dissolve in the air. The people can all see the board, draw on the board, and refer to the board just minutes later in the conversation.

THE IMPACT OF REMOVING MODALITIES

What happens when you remove some of those mechanisms and go to other communication settings?

Remove only physical proximity. With people at opposite ends of a video link, the visual and temporal characteristics should be very much the same as being in person.

Somehow, though, they aren't, as witnessed by the video-communications executive who still flew to London for single meetings.

My teammates, in Lillehammer, and I, in Oslo, often found that we only made design progress when we took the train trip together. Even walking to the train station together was a more effective design environment for us than talking over our video link.

Remove the visuals (use a telephone). Removing visuals also removes cross-modality timing. You lose the drawings, the gestures, the facial expressions, sight of the muscle tone, proximity cues, and the ability to link speech with action.

Remove voice (use e-mail). With this, you lose vocal inflection, the ability to pause for effect, to check for interruptions, to speed up or slow down to make a point, to raise your tone or volume to indicate surprise, boredom, or the obviousness of the transmitted idea.

Remove the ability to ask questions (but possibly reinstate one of the above modalities). Without the questions, the sender must guess what the receiver knows, doesn't know, would like to ask, and what an appropriate answer to the guessed question might be—all without feedback.

Now, the sender really doesn't know what the receiver needs to hear, where the communication gaps are too wide, or where the shared experience lies. (This, of course, applies to me, communicating with you. How many words—which words—do I need to spend on this idea?)

Finally, remove almost everything. Remove visuals, sound, timing, kinesthetics, cross-modality timing, question-and-answer, and you get . . . paper.

How surprising it is in retrospect that most projects require documentation in the least effective communication format possible! The person who is trying to communicate a design idea must guess at what will work for the reader, does not get to use timing, vocal, or gestural inflections, and gets no feedback along the way.

With this view in mind, it is not surprising that the busiest and best project team leaders say:

"Put all the people into one room."

"Don't give me more than four people, that's all I can get into one room and talking together."

"Give me printing whiteboards, and keep all the rest of your drawing tools."

"Make sure there are whiteboards and coffee corners all over the building."

The above are standard recommendations among successful project leaders, who count on using the highest communication mode: people, communicating face to face.

The discussion of communication modalities matches the findings of researchers, such as McCarthy and Monk (1994).

MAKING USE OF MODALITIES

The graph in Figure 3-14 serves to capture the above discussion visually. In the graph you see two sets of situations: those in which question and answer are available and those in which they are not.

The horizontal axis indicates the "temperature" of the communication channel. Warmer indicates that more emotional and informational richness gets conveyed. E-mail is cooler than audio or videotape, and two people communicating face to face is the hottest channel.

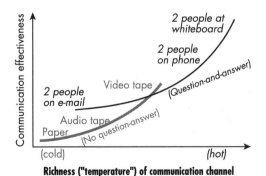

Figure 3-14 Effectiveness of different modes of communication.

What we see in the graph is communication effectiveness rising with the richness (temperature) of the communications channel. Two people at the whiteboard are using the richest form.

The graph provides an idea about how to improve the effectiveness of archival documentation:

VIDEOTAPED ARCHIVAL DOCUMENTATION

Have the designer give a short, 5- to 15-minute description of the design to one or two colleagues who are not familiar with the work. These one or two will act as ombudsmen for the viewers of the videotape. While the designer leads the discussion, the colleagues interrupt and ask questions as they need to.

Videotape the discussion.

At the end, capture and print the examples and drawings used in the discussion, to act as mnemonic anchors of the discussion.

You might consider posting the talk online, where others can access it using hyperlinked media.

Lizette Velasquez, of Lucent Technologies, reported that not only had she already used that technique with success, but she added that I had forgotten something important:

It is also important to mark and index places where "something interesting happened."

While much of the discussion proceeds at a relatively slow pace, occasionally a question triggers a flurry of significant discussion, and the viewers will want to refer to those sections.

Several people report that they have videotaped talks on their project, but we are missing experiments telling us about this technique in actual use: how to set up the room, how long the discussion can be, what sort of person should be used for the ombudsman. Most of all, I am still waiting for someone to perform this experiment and then, six months later, reflect on whether this was a good idea and what would make it better.

If you are willing to try out this experiment, please let me know these details: what you did, what happened, and what you thought about it months later.

As a thought experiment about the utility of the graph and the experiment, consider the book *Design Patterns* (Gamma 1995). This book is excellent but difficult. I still have trouble understanding the patterns that I have not yet used. I suppose that others have similar difficulties. Imagine that instead of trying to extract the meaning of the patterns from the book, you could see one of the authors explaining the pattern in a video clip. The authors would, of course, *rely* on tonal inflections, gestures, and timing to get the idea across. I'm sure that most people would understand those difficult patterns much more easily.

The lesson is that we should try to move team communications up the curve as far as possible, for the situation at hand. We should rely on informal, face-to-face conversation, not merely tolerate it. Face-to-face communication should become a core part of your development process.

There is a second lesson to pay attention to. Sometimes a cooler communication channel works better, because it contains less emotional content.

COOLER COMMUNICATIONS NEEDED

A project leader told me that her team deals better with her when they speak over the phone, because she is too aggressive with her emotions in person.

A married couple told me that they communicated in a more "even" and less emotional level over the phone than in person, just because the face-to-face setting flooded them with visual and emotional cues.

Hovenden (2000) describes a meeting in which a senior designer ruined a meeting's original plan by standing up and taking over the whiteboard for the rest of the meeting. In this case, the *lack of anonymity* created a social ranking that interfered with the intended meeting.

Bordia and Prashant (1997) describe that brainstorming improves when social ranking information is hidden from the participants.

McCarthy and Monk (1994) remind us that e-mail has the advantage of allowing people to reread their own messages before sending them, thereby giving them a chance to clarify the message.

Thus, warmer communications channels are more effective in transferring ideas, but cooler communications channels still have important uses.

STICKINESS AND JUMPING GAPS ACROSS SPACE

You can see, at this point, how the team of Russian programmers got low cost per idea transferred ("The Russian Programmers" on page 13). Sitting in a room together, they got convection currents of information, osmotic communication, face-to-face communication, and real-time question and answer.

So why did they need to write use cases at all?

The answer is: To give the information some *stickiness*. Information that is recorded on paper has a sort of stickiness—or permanence—that the information in a conversation doesn't, a stickiness you sometimes want.

The person who went to Russia with the use cases wanted to make sure that he did not forget what he was supposed to cover in his conversations. He wanted to make sure that after he explained the use cases to the Russian programmers, they could subsequently read the use cases, understand them, and recall the information without having to ask him again.

The use-case writer, knowing that the use cases were only game markers to remind them of what they already knew or had discussed, could balance the time he spent writing the use cases against the time that would be spent discussing other material. He could decide how much detail should go into the writing.

Large, sticky, revisable shared information radiators are often used by people to achieve greater understanding and to align their common goals. Figure 3-15 and Figure 3-16 show a useful mix of whiteboards (static information radiators) and people (dynamic information radiators).

Both whiteboards and paper are particularly good static information radiators and can be written on by all parties, making them *shared, sticky information radiators*.

Until recently, archivability and portability were still problems with whiteboards. If a discussion results in really valuable information being placed on the whiteboard, no one dares erase it and the group can't archive it. This slows the archiving of valuable information and shuts down the board for the next use. As

Figure 3-15 Two people working at a shared, sticky information radiator.

(Courtesy of Evant Solutions Corporation)

Figure 3-16 Dynamic and static information radiators at work.

(Courtesy of Evant Solutions Corporation)

Ron Jeffries put it, "If you never erase the whiteboards, you might as well write on the walls."

A colleague, Mohammad Salim, responded to this situation by covering *all* the walls and hallways with rolls of butcher paper so that people could literally draw on the walls wherever they were. He said, "If you have to take time to walk to a workstation or find a blank whiteboard, you just lost your idea." He continued, saying that when a section of paper gets full, to just roll it up and date it. That way all discussions are archived and can be pulled out for later examination. In his description of finding rolls of paper for later examination, he made use of the fact that humans are good at looking around, as discussed in the last chapter. He also worked hard to reduce the cost of invention and communication while preserving archivability for later discussions.

A number of people report that they are using digital cameras in conjunction with software that cleans up the image ("Whiteboard Photo" at www.pixid.com is one that they refer to). Printing whiteboards continue to be very practical. Often, people start a discussion thinking the outcome will not be significant but see at the end that the whiteboard holds valuable information. With a printing whiteboard, they can simply push the Print button if they wish.

Different information radiators are suited for different sizes of discussion groups, of course. A piece of paper works for two or three people; a whiteboard works for perhaps a dozen.

Recalling these differences will serve us well when we consider methodologies for different projects, in the next chapters.

STICKING THOUGHTS ONTO THE WALL

On one project, the business analysts were frustrated because their work was growing more and more interdependent. At that time they had no way of holding their thoughts in clear view, and still, while planning their joint work.

We held a discussion about cooperative games, game markers, and stickiness. The people saw that creating a large, persistent and revisable display of their mental territory would help them do their work. One of them immediately posted a picture of the domain on the corridor wall as a starting point.

They worked on it over the weeks, experimenting with representations of their concerns that would allow them to view their mutual interdependence.

There is an interesting and relevant aside to mention about this group, having to do with expectations and citizenship. For reasons I won't go into, this team of business analysts thought they were supposed to work in the XP style and that XP prohibited them from writing things down.

Notice four things about their situation:

1. They misunderstood XP. It does not forbid people to write things down.
2. Their citizenship was so strong that rather than be poor citizens and write down their thoughts on the domain model, they chose to be good citizens and not write down their business model at all!

3. Actually, they knew that the project wouldn't succeed if they really wrote nothing down. So they each clandestinely wrote pseudo use cases and other notes, which they passed to the programmers. They still did not create a domain model for themselves.

4. By writing down those notes, they subverted their own (mistaken) interpretation of the official process. I find this situation particularly interesting, because they were at war with themselves about whether to be good citizens and follow the process (at the expense of the project) or to be good citizens and protect the project (by violating the process).

What was significant in the end was that they posted an information radiator on the corridor wall, on which they scribbled individually and as a group, to give their thoughts and decisions some stickiness.

Jumping Gaps across Time

Finally, let us look at communicating across time and the twist that lies in store here.

You might expect, after the preceding discussion, that to preserve information across time you would definitely drop reliance on face-to-face communication in favor of paper, audiotape, and videotape.

However, on long-running projects, it turns out to be critically important that the chief architect stay around! This person's contribution is to keep memories of key ideas alive on changing development teams. Once again, *people* are used as the archival medium!

Individual people transfer information effectively across both time and space. As an IBM Fellow put it, while talking about technology transfer, "The way to get effective technology transfer is not to transfer the technology itself but to transfer the *heads* that hold the technology!"

TEAMS AS COMMUNITIES

We have looked at what it takes for someone to *notice* something of value on a project and what it takes for someone to *communicate* something of value. It is time to consider whether a person *cares* to notice and communicate anything.

On an effective team, the people pull approximately in the same direction. They actually all pull in slightly different directions, according to their personal goals, personal knowledge, stubbornness, and so on (Figure 3-17). They work together at times and against each other at times. The directions are more closely aligned on a more effective team than they are on a less effective team.

You can create a large overall effect on the project by eliciting small changes in each person's behavior. This is "micro-touch" intervention: getting people to make changes they don't mind making, in ways that get amplified by the number of people on the project. As each person pulls in a direction closer to the desired and *common* direction, the changes felt by any one individual are small but the composite effect is large (Figure 3-18).

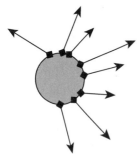

Figure 3-17 An average team working to pull toward a goal on the right.

The small changes come from people being given

- Additional information about the direction in which they should pull
- Additional information about the effects of their actions so that they notice which actions pull in a different direction
- A better reason to pull in the desired direction

The result is that people start contributing to each other's work as opposed to ignoring or accidentally working against each other.

With small changes like these, people see greater project output for similar amounts of energy and without having to learn major techniques or philosophies. As they notice this, they develop greater pride in their work and more trust in each other. Usually, morale improves, and the project team becomes a better community in which to live.

The Project Priority Chart

The project priority chart is one simple mechanism that every project team should use to help align team members' effort.

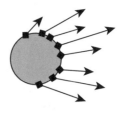

Figure 3-18 A slightly better aligned team.

This chart is also described in *Adaptive Software Development* (Highsmith 2000) and *Crystal Clear* (Cockburn, forthcoming).

At the start of the project, the executive sponsors and the developers discuss and write down the single aspect of the development that everyone should attend to. It may be time-to-market, defect reduction, response time, ease of learning to use, speed of expert usage, memory used, extensibility, or ease of maintenance. They may write a second one, such as time to market and ease of casual use.

They then select, from among all the other desirable characteristics the team should strive for, those three or four that the team should be willing to sacrifice in order to achieve the main two.

From this exercise, each person sees what sorts of trade-offs are permitted on the project and how to prioritize their actions. With a modicum of goodwill between team members, simply writing the choices down in a joint meeting and referring to it periodically gets goal alignment close enough.

The project priority contract addresses a common problem: The executive sponsor wants the software out soon (to hit a market window), but the programmers want to "design it *right*" (delaying their output to improve the design aesthetics). Or the reverse may be true: The programmers are used to working fast and sloppy to hit market windows, and the sponsors want them to take more time and make fewer mistakes. In these cases, the entire organization suffers for a simple, correctable miscommunication of the desired priorities (assuming that the reward structures in place align with the priorities being requested).

Sometimes the priorities need to change in the middle of a project. For example, a competitor may come out with a new product. At that instant, it may become important to reverse priorities, shifting from development speed to defect freedom or vice versa. Should this happen, the sponsors should get the team members together again and announce the shift in priorities.

AMICABILITY AND CONFLICT

Amicability is the willingness of people to hear the thoughts of another person with goodwill and to speak without malice.

Amicability is the weaker cousin to trust. Trust is wonderful and should be nurtured, but amicability is easier to achieve within a group and still confers advantages. I always watch the amicability level in an organization to learn to what extent information is being revealed versus concealed in conversations.

When people conceal information from their colleagues, they lower the rate of information discovery, which raises the lost-opportunity cost as well as the overall cost per idea developed.

Amicability permits successful conflict to occur when the project goes through a stressful period. The people, knowing that the others are not intending to be hurtful, can look past the current disagreement toward resolving the issues.

One might think that removing all conflict from a project team would be the best, but that turns out not to be the case. People need to be able to disagree, in order to identify design problems! I was surprised to find one organization that suffered from too little conflict:

NOT ENOUGH CONFLICT

In a church organization I visited, each staff member was employed for as long as she wished. The group cherished virtues of humility, peacefulness, and amicability. The unsuspected negative effect that accumulated was the absence of both disagreement and initiative!

Each person would think twice (or more) before criticizing someone else's idea, for fear of being seen as seeding discord or of disrupting the group. People would also think twice (or more) before taking initiative, lest they be considered glory hungry or power hungry.

The net result was that projects moved very slowly.

Before you start offering suggestions for this group, recall the values of the group. They will only improve their development practice when they can find ways to disagree without jeopardizing their values of humility and amicability.

Schrage (1999) describes the intentional use of small doses of conflict to get people to meet and learn to talk with each other. This is like introducing a weakened form of a virus so that the body can build ways of handling the stronger virus:

DELIBERATE CONFLICT

"[A]ccording to some reports, engineers on the 777 design-build teams deliberately introduced conflicts with other systems into their proposed designs.

". . . Although Boeing officially acknowledges only that interferences naturally evolved, according to at least one mechanical engineer, some of those interferences were intentional. Why? So that engineers in one part of Boeing could use the interference to find the people in other parts of the company with whom they needed to discuss future design issues. . . . [T]he software's ability to notify appropriate parties about interferences became, at least in some instances, a tool to forge interactions between various groups within Boeing.

". . . The resulting conversations and negotiations resolved design conflicts before more serious problems could emerge."

CITIZENSHIP WITHIN WORKING HOURS

Good citizenship is a matter of acting in ways that benefit others. Citizenship is illustrated by people

- Getting to meetings on time
- Answering questions from other people
- Bothering to mention things that they notice
- Following group coding conventions
- Using code libraries

Citizenship permits programmers who disagree about coding styles to nonetheless create a common coding standard for themselves. As many lead programmers have said, "It's not what I would like, but I recognize that many ways work and selecting any one of them is better than not selecting any at all."

Helping other people in the company is a characteristic of citizenship. Dixon (2000) reports on the strong effect of taking time to help other people. She cites, among many examples, a woman at Tandem Computers who was asked about taking away from her work time to answer questions posted on the corporate discussion boards. The woman responded, "Answering questions like this is part of being a good company citizen."

I often find that workers show citizenship and sacrifice from the moment they start work, and management takes too much advantage of it. People join a new company and work overtime, thinking that after they contribute this extra work the company will respond in kind and give them more recognition and time off. What they don't realize is that their bosses and colleagues assume that however they work in the first month is how they will work and act forever. As a result, people regularly get poor evaluations for dropping their working hours from 65 down to a *mere* 50!

I am afraid that managers will use the pretext of good citizenship to coerce people into working yet more overtime. Read *Death March* (Yourdon 1997) for examples of this.

Citizenship should be encouraged *within* normal working hours, not as a means of lengthening normal working hours. There are plenty of ways in which to apply citizenship within working hours.

HOSTILE XP VERSUS FRIENDLY XP

To round out this discussion, let's look at the consequences of working with and without attention to community. I choose to discuss Extreme Programming (XP), because although communication and community are core values within XP, I have seen it practiced with and without that community: "friendly" XP and "hostile" XP, as it were. The difference is profound.

The three following situations are some in which customers and programmers might magnify their differences and create a hostile XP environment:

- The customers are not quite sure what they want. The programmers insist, "Tell us what to build," so the customers say something. The programmers build exactly that and then say, "Tell us what to build next."

In this situation, neither group is really sure what the correct thing is to build next. The programmers escape the pressure of the situation by shifting the burden over to the customers (which they are allowed to do). The customers experience the situation as unsettling: There is little time to reflect, examine, experiment, and sort out options.

As a result, the customer's instructions over the course of succeeding iterations conflict with each other: "Build this. . . . No, now build this. . . . No, try building that now." Both parties become depressed about the lack of clear progress.

- The programmers do whatever the customers say, even if they are sure that the idea is silly.

As with the story "Not Enough Conflict," a project suffers when the developers don't mention problems they notice. The project loses the creative interplay of sharp programmers offering their insights to refine the requests of the customers.

- The customers tell the programmers that a particular feature will be coming up and ask if the programmers will please design the system to handle that gracefully. The programmers cite a series of the XP mantras: "Keep it simple," "You aren't gonna need it," "We'll do the simplest thing that will possibly work," and they ignore any suggestion of what to build into the software.

The consequence is that the designers run through a sequence of designs everyone knows are incorrect, until the critical requirements finally appear. By then, time has been spent redesigning the system several times. In the cases I have encountered, the programmers were happy about the exercise and the sponsors were unhappy.

In each of these cases, the programmers withheld information. Withholding their own thoughts and experience from the discussion, they abdicated responsibility toward the overall project. By doing so, they damaged the project by concealing from view superior development strategies.

In friendly XP, practiced with community, the three situations play out differently. In each case, the programmers actively share their views, experiences, cost estimates, and solutions.

- In the first situation, not knowing what to build next, the programmers help the customers gain experience in voicing what they want. They can do this by producing small working prototypes tailored to discovering the desired characteristics.
- In the case of the silly idea, the programmers volunteer their information through amicable dialogue: "I'm not sure you really want this thing you asked for. It will be so-and-so difficult to implement and has the following roll-on effects." The customer might still request the feature, but quite often, the person had no idea about those effects and is happy to have them mentioned. Usually, customers appreciate the insights, whether or not they change the request.
- In the story-sequencing situation, the programmers help the customers by finding those story cards that affect the decisions in question. They can then jointly consider in which order the cards should be tackled. The new order might not simply ask for more functionality along a business-value trajectory but might converge more quickly on the actual system the customers want.

Any development methodology, even one that advocates amicability and community, can be practiced without it to the detriment of the project.

BUILDING "TEAM" BY WINNING

Team spirit was once built through singing company songs and attending company functions. (Any of you still have your IBM songbook?) When singing on the job went out of style, nothing immediate took its place.

Some companies start projects with one or several days of offsite team building. This is good, even if it is good mostly because the people recognize the effort the company is putting forth to show that teamwork is important. Although not every team-building exercise actually builds a team, a number of successful teams have pointed to their team-building days at the start of the project as having helped them work together more effectively. As a result, their company leaders consider the money well spent and plan on continuing the tradition.

Programmers give mixed reviews to outside-of-work team-building exercises. Several said, roughly, "I'm not interested in whether we can barbeque together or climb walls together. I'm interested in whether we can produce software together."

What *does* build teams? Luke Hohmann offered this observation in an e-mail note:

"The best way to build a team is by having them be successful in producing results. Small ones, big ones. It doesn't matter. This belief has empirical support; see, for instance,

Brown (1990). Fuzzy team building is (IMO) almost always a waste of time and money."

Support for this is also found in Weick's description of the importance of "small wins" (Weick 2001) as well as in interviews of successful project managers.

One successful project manager told of a key moment when the project morale and "team"-ness improved. We found the following elements in the story:

- The people, who sat in different locations, met each other face to face.
- Together, they accomplished some significant result that they could not have achieved without working together.
- At some point, they placed themselves in some social jeopardy (venturing new thoughts, or admitting ignorance) and received support from the group when they might have been attacked.

The second of those characteristics is "producing results," as Luke Hohmann mentions. The first and the third build amicability, the positive absence of fear and distrust.

TEAM CULTURES AND SUBCULTURES

The project team itself creates a mini-culture. That mini-culture sits within the culture formed within the larger organization and also within the dominant national culture around it.

Often, the programming project ends up with its own culture, different from the national or corporate cultures in which it is embedded. People on the project find this useful, because they have a greater need to trade information about what is working and what is about to break.

Sometimes, the wider organization tolerates this different culture, and sometimes it fights back. One person who had experienced the resistance wrote, "Watch out for the organizational antibodies!"

Cultures and their values can be characterized in many ways. In one characterization (Constantine 1995), sociologists name four culture types by their communication, power, and decision-making habits (Figure 3-19). These four culture types are described in the following paragraphs:

Hierarchical cultures have the traditional top-down chain of command. Typically, older, larger corporations have a hierarchical culture. Many people internalize this as the dominant or natural or default corporate culture as they grow up, and they have to be trained away from it.

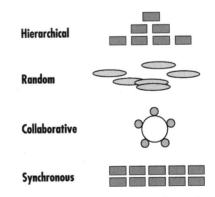

Figure 3-19 Four organizational paradigms.

Random is the opposite of hierarchical. It indicates a group in which there is little or no central control. Many start-up companies work this way. Some people consider *random* a fun way to work and regret the loss of the small, informal group when the company grows. Others find it stressful, because there are no clear points of control.

Collaborative groups work by consensus. I had the opportunity to encounter a collaborative group in action at Lucent Technology:

CONSENSUS CULTURE AT WORK

Someone in the organization decided that use cases would be a good way to capture requirements and asked me to teach a course to the people on a project.

I met the team leads (who are actually called *coaches*, because in a collaborative culture they don't lead, of course, they *coach*).

About a month later, I was called to teach it again, for more of the group.

Several months after that, I was asked to lecture one last time, for the entire department. Even though the coach had decided that use cases were good, the group was not going to use them until they had all had a chance to see and understand them.

The behavior of the coach in the final meeting was interesting: He programmed on his laptop while I taught. He was physically present in the room, but only just barely. Far from being insulting, I found his actions fully appropriate in light of the value systems in play around his situation. As a senior developer, he demonstrated that he was still contributing directly to the team's work. As a coach, he demonstrated support for the material being presented, which he was hearing for the third time. Thus, his behavior was a natural expression of his place in two professional societies: developer and coach.

Synchronous, or "silent," groups are the opposite of collaborative. They coordinate action without verbal communication, with people performing their roles without attempting to affect the other roles'work styles.

Constantine gives two examples of synchronous teamwork. The first comes from a scene in the movie *Witness*, in which members of the Amish community raise a new barn in a single day, scarcely uttering a word. The second comes from an accident that happened inside a hospital, when a heavy table fell on a person's leg. Without speaking to each other, the people in the room took coordinated action: Two lifted the table, one held the person's hand, one went to call for an X-ray, and one went to get a gurney.

In both cases, the people involved knew the rules of the situation and the goals and the roles involved. They could simply step into a needed role. Constantine points out that in a synchronous environment, "team members are aligned with the direction established by a shared vision and common values."

It may turn out, in an odd twist, that programmers operate within a silent or synchronous culture. If this is true, it will be interesting to see how the cooperative game gets reshaped to fit that cultural pattern. Certainly, the current wave of development methodologies, including XP and Crystal, require much more conversation than previous ones. Either the programmers will shift their culture, or the methodologies will have to adapt.

In many organizations, programmers are expected to work massive overtime. It was a great shock to me to move from one such organization to the Central Bank of Norway, where personal life was strongly valued and overtime discouraged:

OVERTIME LIGHTS AT NORGES BANK

At the Central Bank of Norway, the official workday ended at 3:30 p.m.

On a typical day, that is the time I suddenly waken from whatever else I am doing and ask myself what I *really* want to get done that day. As a result, I found myself wandering the halls at 3:45, trying to "really get some work completed before the end of the day" and unable to send faxes, get signatures on paper, or get questions answered. The staff really *did* go home at 3:30!

Then, at 5:00, the lights automatically turned off! I learned how to turn on the "overtime lights" but got a second shock when the light turned off again 7:00 p.m. ("*You really, really ought to go home now.*")

Cultures also differ by their attitude toward frankness and politeness in speech. The Japanese are renowned for working to preserve face, while Americans are considered frank. Frankness is taken to extremes in some places, such as MIT, Stanford, and Israel. An Israeli friend was coaching me in direct speaking: When I saw him after he had to miss a review meeting I said, "We missed you at the meeting." He replied, "In Israel we would say, 'Why weren't you there?'"

In other cultures, such as the church organization described earlier, even disagreeing mildly or taking initiative are considered slightly negative behaviors, signs of a person having excessive ego.

As a result of differences around frankness in speech, people coming from different cultures sometimes have difficulty working together. The overly frank person strikes the other as rash and abrasive, while the overly polite person strikes the other as not forthcoming, not contributing.

Professional Subcultures

Each profession also builds its own culture, with its own cultural values and norms. Project managers have theirs as do experienced object-oriented developers, relational database designers, COBOL programmers, salespeople, users, and so on. Even novices in each group have their own values and norms, distinct from the experts. Here are a few:

- Project managers need an orderly attitude to sort out and predict delivery dates and costs and the complex dependencies within the project.
- OO programmers need quiet time, abstract thinking ability, and the ability to deal with the uncertainty of simultaneously evolving programming interfaces.
- Requirements analysts rely on thorough thinking, going through the requirements and the interfaces one line at a time, looking for mistakes.
- Marketing people benefit from strong imaginations and people skills and dealing with the constant surprises that the market (and the programmers) throw at them.

Let's consider programmers' "noncommunicative and antisocial" behavior for a moment. Actually, as a number of them said when they wrote to me, they do like to talk ... about technical things. They just don't like talking about things they consider uninteresting (baseball games and birthday parties, perhaps). What they really detest is being interrupted during their work. It turns out that there is a good reason for this.

Software consists of tying together complex threads of thought. The programmer spends a great deal of time lifting and holding together a set of ideas. She starts typing, holding in her mind this tangled construct, tracing the mental links as she types.

If she gets called to a meeting at this point, her thought structure falls to the ground and she must rebuild it after the meeting. It can take 20 minutes to build this structure and an hour to make progress. Therefore, any phone call, discussion, or meeting that distracts her for longer than a few minutes causes her to lose up to an hour of work and an immense amount of energy. It is little wonder that programmers hate meetings. Antisocial behavior, meeting-avoidance in particular, is a protective part of their profession.

Thus, the values of each group contribute to their proper functioning, and the differences are necessary for the proper functioning of the total organization, even though they clash.

It would be nice to say that all of the values and norms are constructive. Not all are, though.

An example introduced earlier is the Invent-Here-Now Imperative. It is developed as a cultural value and norm all the way through college. In most organizations, however, inventing new solutions where old ones already exist is counter-productive to the aims of the organization. The ideal norm would be to scavenge existing solutions wherever possible and to invent only where it leads the organization past its competitors.

Adapting to Subcultures
Most people's initial reaction is to force one group's values on the other groups.

- Researchers in formal development techniques want more math to be taught in school.
- Managers who are uncomfortable with iterative development want their programmers to get the design right the first time.
- The programmers, frustrated with not being able to communicate with their managers, want the managers to learn object-oriented programming prior to managing a project.

There are two problems with the make-*them*-change approach:

- The less serious problem is that it is really, really hard to get people to change their habits and approaches.
- The more serious problem is that we don't yet understand the subcultures. To force them to change their values is a bit like prescribing medicine without understanding the defense mechanisms of the body.

In the face of this situation, there are things that the industry can do, things that a few individuals can do, and things that everyone can do.

As an industry, we can

- Encourage more ethnographic studies of software development groups, as Hovenden (2000) has done
- Identify and understand the norms in play, showing the contribution of each to the organization
- Experiment with cultural changes

Every consulting company can benefit from employing a social anthropologist or ethnographer. That person will help the consulting team understand the social forces in play on their projects, which will enhance the team's effectiveness.

People who are fluent in several specialties, such as programming and database design, programming and project management, or teaching and designing, can act as translators. These people help by converting statements phrased in one normative value set into sentences meaningful within a different value set. A number of people who perform this function have written to me to describe the difficulty and necessity of this role.

Finally, everyone can practice patience and goodwill in listening. Pretend that the other person's sentences, however crazy they may sound to you, make sense in the other culture's value system. Listen that way first, and *then* decide if you still need to disagree.

TEAMS AS ECOSYSTEMS

A software project sets up a small ecosystem made up of personalities from diverse cultures. We have seen some elements of the ecosystem, including

- Walls acting as barriers and open spaces acting as conduits
- People in their professional specialties acting as interacting subspecies
- Individuals with strong personalities changing the way in which the ecosystem works

Everything affects everything: the chairs, the seating, the shape of the building, whether people share a native language, even the air conditioning.

LIZARDS AND PENGUINS

At one company, moving from our old building to a new one nearly caused fights.

In the old building, we each had a private office, and each office had its own thermostat. In the new building, we would still have private offices, but there was only going to be one thermostat for every two offices. Each adjacent office pair had to use the same temperature setting.

Suddenly, the workforce polarized into those who liked warm offices (the "lizards") and those who liked cold offices (the "penguins"). People were jockeying for positions so they could share the thermostat with someone of similar temperature preferences.

In some work situations, it is hard for people to change companies. In other situations, people change jobs every few months. The two situations create different attitudes and behaviors in the workforce.

Every job role and every person affects every other. Key individuals play a more significant role in shaping the ecosystem than others. They focus or, more frequently, block conversations. When they leave, the entire network of relationships changes.

Each project's ecosystem is unique. In principle, it should be impossible to say anything concrete and substantive about all teams' ecosystems.

It is.

Only the people on the team can deduce and decide what will work in that particular environment and tune the environment to support them.

If the people on the team understand some key characteristics of humans and of methodologies, they can look around, introspect about what they observe, and construct a best first guess as to what conventions and policies might work well for them, suiting their own strengths and weaknesses.

The people on the teams will naturally reexamine and adjust their conventions over time, periodically or whenever a major event changes their ecosystem (as when a particularly influential individual joins or leaves the organization).

The set of conventions and policies I refer to as the team's *methodology*. As we will see in the next chapter, a methodology is a personal thing—"a social construction," to quote Ralph Hodgson of IBM.

Considering the methodology as the team's own social construction is useful. It highlights the idea that no methodology will work "straight out of the box." The team members will have to adapt both themselves and the methodology to work together to create their own, local, effective ecosystem.

Ecosystems and methodologies have this interesting characteristic in common: If the team members construct many complicated rules for themselves, they tie themselves to a narrow ecological niche.

However, narrow ecological niches are notoriously fragile, and the market has a nasty habit of changing the terrain around a company. The many rules that ensure effective behavior in one ecological setting are ill suited for use in another.

In biology, we use the phrase "become extinct." In business, the phrase is "go out of business."

If, on the other hand, the team creates and periodically updates a few well-placed guidelines, it can draw on the intelligence, pride-in-contribution, communication, and spontaneity of its members. The people will adapt those guidelines to the situation at hand, achieving robust behavior in the face of technological, social, and market surprises. Dee Hock, designer of the highly decentralized VISA system in the 1960s and 1970s, said this:

"Simple, clear purpose and principles give rise to complex, intelligent behavior.

"Complex rules and regulations give rise to simple, stupid behavior."

What Should I Do Tomorrow?

Walk around your place of work. Notice

- The convection currents of information
- The drafts
- The information radiators
- The separate communities of practice
- The background conversation complimenting or denigrating other groups in the organization

See

- How you can improve the flow of information and reduce the erg-seconds required to detect and transmit critical information
- If you can colocate your team
- What it takes to partition the project so that teams are located around their communication needs

Try

- Removing partitions between people
- Pair programming

- Arranging for daily visits between programmers and business experts
- Micro-touch intervention (people making small changes that they don't mind making but that result in their pulling more in the same direction)
- Listening to the words of someone in a different professional specialty according to *her* cultural norms, not your own
- Translating between two subcultures in their own cultural terms

Observe the interaction between your methodology's rules and your project's ecosystem. Note the fits and the misfits and the influence of a few key individuals.

Consider what conventions or policies might improve the way in which your group gets things done. They may be conventions about seating, tools, working hours, process, lighting, meetings: anything.

Do this, and you are halfway to tailoring your methodology to fit your organization.

4

Methodologies

The purpose of this chapter is to discuss and boil down the topic of methodologies until the rules of the methodology design game, and how to play that game, are clear.

"Methodology Concepts" covers the basic vocabulary and concepts needed to design and compare methodologies. These include the obvious concepts such as roles, techniques, and standards and also less-obvious concepts such as weight, ceremony, precision, stability, and tolerance. In terms of audience "levels," as described in "Three Levels of Listening" on page 14 of the introduction, this is largely Level 1 material. It is needed for the more advanced discussions that follow.

"Methodology Design Principles" discusses seven principles that can be used to guide the design of a methodology. The principles highlight the cost of moving to a heavier methodology as well as when to accept that cost. They also show how to use work-product stability in deciding how much concurrent development to employ.

"XP under Glass" applies the principles to analyze an existing, agile methodology. It also discusses how to use the principles to adjust XP for slightly different situations.

"Why Methodology at All?" revisits that key question in the light of the preceding discussion and presents the different uses for methodologies.

Methodologies

AN ECOSYSTEM THAT SHIPS SOFTWARE

"Methodology is a social construction," Ralph Hodgson told me in 1993. Two years went by before I started to understand.

Your "methodology" is everything you regularly do to get your software out. It includes who you hire, what you hire them for, how they work together, what they produce, and how they share. It is the combined job descriptions, procedures, and conventions of everyone on your team. It is the product of your particular ecosystem and is therefore a unique construction of your organization.

All organizations have a methodology: It is simply how they do business. Even the proverbial trio in a garage has a way of working—a way of trading information, of separating work, of putting it back together—all founded on assumed values and cultural norms. The way of working includes what people choose to spend their time on, how they choose to communicate, and how decision-making power is distributed.

Only a few companies bother to try to write it all down (usually just the large consulting houses and the military). A few have gone so far as to create an expert system that prints out the full methodology needed for a project based on project staffing, complexity, deadlines, and the like. None I have seen captures cultural assumptions or provides for variations among values or cultures.

Boil and condense the subject of methodology long enough and you get this one-sentence summary: "A methodology is the conventions that your group agrees to."

"The conventions your group agrees to" is a social construction. It is also a construction that you can and should revisit from time to time.

METHODOLOGY CONCEPTS

I use the word *methodology* as found in the Merriam-Webster dictionaries: "A series of related methods or techniques." A *method* is a "systematic procedure," similar to a technique.

(Readers of the Oxford English Dictionary may note that some OED editions only carry the definition of methodology as "study of methods," and others carry both. This helps explain the controversy over the word *methodology*.)

The distinction between *methodology* and *method* is useful. Reading the phrases "a method for finding classes from use cases" or "different methods are suited for different problems," we understand that the author is discussing techniques and procedures, not establishing team rules and conventions. That frees the use of the word *methodology* for the larger issues of coordinating people's activities on a team.

Coordination is important. The same average people who produce average designs when working alone often produce good designs in collaboration.

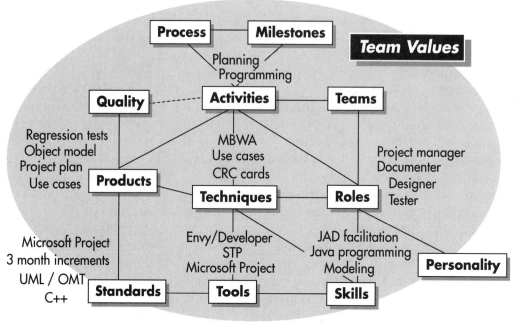

Figure 4-1 Elements of a methodology.

Conversely, all the smartest people together still won't produce group success without coordination, cooperation, and communication. Most of us have witnessed or heard of such groups. Team success hinges on cooperation, communication, and coordination.

STRUCTURAL TERMS

The first methodology structure I saw contained about seven elements. The one I now draw contains 13 (see Figure 4-1). The elements apply to any team endeavor, whether it is software development, rock climbing, or poetry writing. What you write for each box will vary, but the names of the elements won't.

Roles. Who you employ, what you employ them for, what skills they are supposed to have. Equally important, it turns out, are the personality traits expected of the person. A project manager should be good with people, a user interface designer should have natural visual talents and some empathy for user behavior, an object-oriented program designer should have good abstraction faculties, and a mentor should be good at explaining things.

It is bad for the project when the individuals in the jobs don't have the traits needed for the job (for example, a project manager who can't make decisions or a mentor who does not like to communicate).

Skills. The skills needed for the roles. The "personal prowess" of a person in a role is a product of his training and talent.

Programmers attend classes to learn object-oriented, Java programming and unit-testing skills.

User interface designers learn how to conduct usability examinations and do paper-based prototyping.

Managers learn interviewing, motivating, hiring, and critical-path task-management skills.

The best people draw heavily upon their natural talent, but in most cases adequate skills can be acquired through training and practice.

Teams. The roles that work together under various circumstances.

There may be only one team on a small project. On a large project, there are likely to be multiple, overlapping teams, some aimed at harnessing specific technologies and some aimed at steering the project or the system's architecture.

Techniques. The specific procedures people use to accomplish tasks. Some apply to a single person (writing a use case, managing by walking around, designing a class or test case), while others are aimed at groups of people (project retrospectives, group planning sessions). In general, I use the word *technique* if there is a prescriptive presentation of how to accomplish a task, using an understood body of knowledge.

Activities. How the people spend their days. Planning, programming, testing, and meeting are sample activities.

Some methodologies are work-product intensive, meaning that they focus on the work products that need to be produced. Others are activity-intensive, meaning that they focus on what the people should be doing during the day. Thus, where the Rational Unified Process is tool- and work-product intensive, Extreme Programming is activity intensive. It achieves its effectiveness, in part, by describing *what* the people should be doing with their day (pair programming, test-first development, refactoring, etc.).

Process. How activities fit together over time, often with pre- and post-conditions for the activities (for example, a design review is held two days after the material is sent out to participants and produces a list of recommendations for improvement). Process-intensive methodologies focus on the flow of work among the team members.

Process charts rarely convey the presence of loopback paths, where rework gets done. Thus, process charts are usually best viewed as workflow diagrams, describing *who* receives what from *whom.*

Work products. What someone constructs. A work product may be disposable, as with CRC design cards, or it may be relatively permanent, as the usage manual or source code.

I find it useful to reserve *deliverable* to mean "a work product that gets passed across an organizational boundary." This allows us to apply the term *deliverable* at different scales: The deliverables that pass between two subteams are work products in terms of the larger project. The work products that pass between a project team and the team working on the next system are *deliverables* of the project and need to be handled more carefully.

Work products are described in generic terms such as "source code" and "domain object model." Rules about the notation to be used for each work product are described in the work product standards. Examples of source-code standards include Java, Visual Basic, and executable visual models. Examples of class diagram standards could be UML or OML.

Milestones. Events marking progress or completion. Some milestones are simply assertions that a task has been performed, and some involve the publication of documents or code.

A milestone has two key characteristics: It occurs in an instant of time, and it is either fully met or not met (it is not partially met). A document is either published or not published, the code is delivered or not delivered, the meeting was held or not held.

Standards. The conventions the team adopts for particular tools, work products, and decision policies.

A coding standard might declare this: "Every function has the following header comment . . ."

A language standard might be this: "We'll be using fully portable Java."

A drawing standard for class diagrams might be this: "Only show public methods of persistent functions."

A tool standard might be this: "We'll use Microsoft Project, Together/J, JUnit, . . ."

A project-management standard might be this: "Use milestones of two days to two weeks and incremental deliveries every two to three months."

Quality. Quality may refer to the activities or the work products.

In XP, the quality of the team's program is evaluated by examining the source code work product: "All checked-in code must pass unit tests at 100 percent at all times."

The XP team members also evaluate the quality of their activities: Do they hold a stand-up meeting every day? How often do the programmers shift programming partners? How available are the customers for questions? In some cases, quality is given a numerical value; in other cases, a fuzzy value ("I wasn't happy with the team morale on the last iteration.").

Team values. The rest of the methodology elements are governed by the team's value system. An aggressive team working on quick-to-market values will work very differently than a group that values families and goes home at a regular time every night.

As Jim Highsmith likes to point out, a group whose mission is to explore and locate new oil fields will operate on different values and produce different rules than a group whose mission is to squeeze every barrel out of a known oil field at the least possible cost.

Types of Methodologies

Maier and Rechtin (2000) categorize methodologies themselves as being normative, rational, participative, or heuristic.

Normative methodologies are based on solutions or sequences of steps known to work for the discipline. Electrical and other building codes in house wiring are examples. In software development, one would include state diagram verification in this category.

Rational methodologies (no connection with the company) are based on method and technique. They would be used for system analysis and engineering disciplines.

Participative methodologies are stakeholder based and capture aspects of customer involvement.

Heuristic methodologies are based on lessons learned. Maier and Rechtin cite their use in the aerospace business (space and aircraft design).

As a body of knowledge grows, sections of the methodology move from heuristic to normative and become codified as standard solutions for standard problems. In computer programming, searching algorithms have reached that point. The decision about whether to put people in common or private offices has not.

Most of software development is still in the stage where heuristic methodologies are appropriate.

Milestones

Milestones are markers for where interesting things happen in the project. At each milestone, one or more people in some named roles must get together to affect the course of a work product.

Three kinds of milestones are used on projects, each with its particular characteristics. They are

- Reviews
- Publications
- Declarations

In a *review*, several people examine a work product. With respect to reviews, we care about the following questions: Who is doing the reviewing? What are they reviewing? Who created that item? What is the outcome of the review? Few reviews cause a project to halt; most end with a list of suggestions that are *supposed* to be incorporated.

A *publication* occurs whenever a work product is distributed or posted for open viewing. Sending out meeting minutes, checking source code into a configuration-management system, and deploying software to users' workstations are different forms of publication. With respect to publications, we care about the following: What is being published? Who publishes it? Who receives it? What causes it to be published?

The *declaration* milestone is a verbal notice from one person to another, or to multiple people, that a milestone was reached. There is no objective measure for a declaration; it is simply an announcement or a promise. Declarations are interesting because they construct a web of promises inside the team's social structure. This form of milestone came as a surprise to me, when I first detected it.

DISCOVERING DECLARATIONS

The first *declaration* milestone I detected was made during a discussion with the manager of the technical writers on a 100-person project. I asked how she knew when to assign a person to start writing the online help text (its birth event).

She said it was when a team lead told her that a section of the application was "ready" for her.

I asked her what "ready" meant, whether it meant that the screen design was complete.

She said it only meant that the screen design was *relatively stable*. The team lead was, in essence, making the following promise:

"We estimate that the changes that we are still going to make are *relatively small* compared to the work the tech writer will be doing, and the rework the writer will do will be *relatively small* compared to the overall work. So this would be a good time to get the writing started."

That assertion is full of social promises. It is a promise, given by a trained person, that in his judgement the trade-offs are balanced and that this is a good time to start.

A declaration ("It's ready!") is often the form of milestone that moves code from development to test, alpha delivery, beta delivery, and even deployment.

Declarations are interesting to me as a researcher, because I have not seen them described in process-centric methodolo-

gies, which focus on process entry and exit criteria. They are easier to discuss when we consider software development as a cooperative game. In a cooperative game, the project team's web of interrelationships, and the promises holding them together, are more apparent.

The role-deliverable-milestone chart (Figure 4-15) is a quick way to view the methodology in brief. It has an advantage over process diagrams in that it shows the parallelism involved in the project quite clearly. It also allows the team to see the key stages of completion the artifacts go through. This helps them manage their actions according to the intermediate states of the artifacts, as recommended in some modern methodologies (Highsmith 2000).

SCOPE

The *scope* of a methodology consists of the range of roles and activities that it attempts to cover (Figure 4-2).

The earliest object-oriented methodologies presented the designer as having the key role and discussed the techniques, deliverables, and standards for the design activity of that role. These methodologies were considered inadequate in two ways:

- They were not as broad as needed. A real project involves more roles than just the OO designer, and each role involves more activities, more deliverables, and more techniques than these books presented.
- They were too constricting. Designers need more than one design technique in their toolbox.

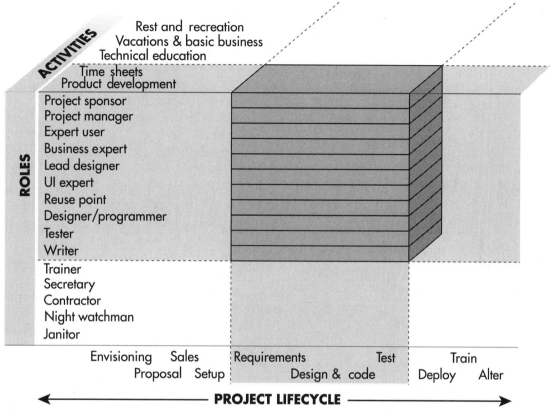

Figure 4-2 The three dimensions of scope. A methodology selects a subset of all three.

Groups with a long history of continuous experience, such as the U.S. Department of Defense, Andersen Consulting, James Martin and Associates, IBM, and Ernst & Young already had methodologies covering the standard lifecycle of a project, even starting from the point of project sales and project setup. Their methodologies cover every person needed on the project, from staff assistant through sales staff, designer, project manager, and tester.

The point is that both are "methodologies." The scope of their concerns is different.

The scope of a methodology can be characterized along three axes: *lifecycle coverage*, *role coverage*, and *activity coverage* (Figure 4-2).

- Lifecycle coverage indicates when in the lifecycle of the project the methodology comes into play, and when it ends.
- Role coverage refers to which roles fall into the domain of discussion.
- Activity coverage defines which activities of those roles fall into the domain of discussion. The methodology may take into account filling out time

sheets (a natural inclusion as part of the project manager's project monitoring and scheduling assignment) and may omit vacation requests (because it is part of basic business operations).

Clarifying a methodology's intended scope helps take some of the heat out of methodology arguments. Often, two seemingly incompatible methodologies target different parts of the lifecycle or different roles. Discussions about their differences go nowhere until their respective scope intentions are clarified.

In this light, we see that the early OO methodologies had a relatively small scope. They addressed typically only one role, the domain designer or modeler. For that role, only the actual domain modeling activity is represented, and only during the analysis and design stages. Within that very narrow scope, they covered one or a few techniques and outlined one or a few deliverables with standards. No wonder experienced designers felt they were inadequate for overall development.

The scope diagram helps us see where methodology fragments combine well. An example is the natural fit of Constantine and Lockwood's user interface design recommendations (Constantine 1999) with methodologies that omit discussion of UI design activities (leaving that aspect to authors who know more about the subject).

Without having these scoping axes at hand, people would ask Larry Constantine, "How does your *methodology* relate to the *other* Agile Methodologies on the market?" In a talk at Software Development 2001, Larry Constantine said he didn't know he was designing a *methodology*, he was just discussing good ways to design user interfaces.

Having the methodology scope diagram in view, we easily see how they fit. XP's scope of concerns is shown in Figure 4-3. Note that it lacks discussion of user interface design. The scope of concerns for *Design for Use* is shown in Figure 4-4. We see, from these figures, that the two fit together. The same applies for *Design for Use* and Crystal Clear.

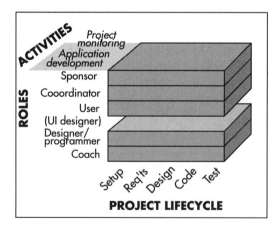

Figure 4-3 Scope of Extreme Programming.

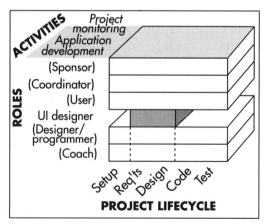

Figure 4-4 Scope of Constantine & Lockwood's *Design for Use* methodology fragment.

CONCEPTUAL TERMS

To discuss the *design* of a methodology, we need different terms: *methodology size, ceremony,* and *weight; problem size; project size; system criticality; precision; accuracy; relevance; tolerance; visibility; scale;* and *stability.*

Methodology size. The number of control elements in the methodology. Each deliverable, standard, activity, quality measure, and technique description is an element of control. Some projects and authors will wish for *smaller* methodologies; some will wish for *larger.*

Ceremony. The amount of precision and the tightness of tolerance in the methodology. Greater ceremony corresponds to tighter controls (Booch 1995). One team may write use cases on napkins and review them over lunch. Another team may prefer to fill in a three-page template and hold half-day reviews. Both groups write and review use cases, the former using low ceremony, the latter using high ceremony.

The amount of ceremony in a methodology depends on how life critical the system will be and on the fears and wishes of the methodology author, as we will see.

Methodology weight. The product of size and ceremony, the number of control elements multiplied by the ceremony involved in each. This is a conceptual product (because numbers are not attached to size and ceremony), but it is still useful.

Problem size. The number of elements in the problem and their inherent cross-complexity.

There is no absolute measure of problem size, because a person with different knowledge is likely to see a simplifying pattern that reduces the size of the problem. Some problems are clearly different enough from others that relative magnitudes can be discussed (launching a space shuttle is a bigger problem than printing a company's invoices).

The difficulty in deciding the problem size is that there will often be controversy over how many people are needed to deliver the product and what the corresponding methodology weight is.

Project size. The number of people whose efforts need to be coordinated: staff size. Depending on the situation, you may be coordinating only programmers or an entire department with many roles.

Many people use the phrase *project size* ambiguously, shifting the meaning from *staff size* to *problem size* even within a sentence. This causes much confusion, particularly because a small, sharp team often outperforms a large, average team.

The relationship between problem, staff, and methodology size are discussed in the next section.

System criticality. The damage from undetected defects. I currently classify criticality simply as one of loss of comfort, loss of discretionary money, loss of irreplaceable money, or loss of life. Other classifications are possible.

Precision. How much you care to say about a particular topic. Pi to one decimal place of precision is 3.1, to four decimal places is 3.1416. Source code contains more precision than a class diagram; assembler code contains more than its high-level source code. Some methodologies call for more precision earlier than others, according to the methodology author's wishes.

Accuracy. How correct you are when you speak about a topic. To say "Pi to one decimal place is 3.3" would be inaccurate. The final object model needs to be more accurate than the initial one. The final GUI description is more accurate than the low-fidelity prototypes. Methodologies cover the growth of accuracy as well as precision.

Relevance. Whether or not to speak about a topic. User interface prototypes do not discuss the domain model. Infrastructure design is not relevant to collecting user functional requirements. Methodologies discuss different areas of relevance.

Tolerance. How much variation is permitted. The team standards may require revision dates to be put into the program code—or not. The tolerance statement may say that a date must be found, either put in by hand or added by some automated tool. A methodology may specify line breaks and indentation, leave those to peoples' discretion, or state acceptable bounds. An example in a decision standard is stating that a working release must be available every 3 months, *plus or minus one month.*

Visibility. How easily an outsider can tell if the methodology is being followed. Process initiatives such as ISO9001 focus on visibility issues. Because achieving visibility creates overhead (cost in time, money, or both), agile methodologies as a group lower the emphasis on such visibility. As with ceremony, different amounts of visibility are appropriate for different situations.

Scale. How many items are rolled together to be presented as a single item. Booch's former "class categories" provided for a scaled view of a set of classes. The UML "package" allows for scaled views of use cases, classes, or hardware boxes. Project plans, requirements, and designs can all be presented at different scales.

Scale interacts somewhat with precision. The printer or monitor's dot density limits the amount of detail that can be put onto one screen or page. However, even if it could all be put onto one page, some people would not want to see all that detail. They want to see a rolled-up or high-level version.

Stability. How likely it is to change. I use only three stability levels: *wildly fluctuating,* as when a team is just getting started; *varying,* as when some development activity is in mid-stride; and *relatively stable,* as just before a requirements / design / code review or product shipment.

One way to find the stability state is to ask: "If I were to ask the same questions today and in two weeks, how likely would I be to get the same answers?"

In the *wildly fluctuating* state, the answer is "Are you kidding? Who knows what this will be like in two weeks!"

In the *varying* state, the answer is "Somewhat similar, but of course the details are likely to change."

In the *relatively stable* state, the answer is "Pretty likely, although a few things will probably be different."

Other ways to determine the stability may include measuring the "churn" in the use case text, the diagrams, the code base, the test cases, and so on (I have not tried these).

Precision

Precision is a core concept manipulated within a methodology. Every category of work product has low-, medium-, and high-precision versions.

Here are the low-, medium-, and high-precision versions of some key work products.

The project plan. The low-precision view of a project plan is the *project map* (Figure 4-5). It shows the fundamental items to be produced, their dependencies, and which are to be deployed together. It may show the relative magnitudes of effort needed for each item. It does not show who will do the work or how long the work will take (which is why it is called a *map* and not a *plan*).

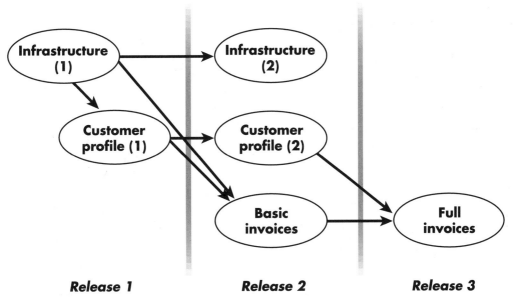

Figure 4-5 A project map: a low-precision version of a project plan.

Those who are used to working with PERT charts will recognize the project map as a coarse-grained PERT chart showing project dependencies, augmented with marks showing where releases occur.

This low-precision project map is very useful in organizing the project before the staffing and time lines are established. In fact, I use it to derive time lines and staffing plans.

The medium-precision version of the project plan is a project map expanded to show the dependencies between the teams and the due dates.

The high-precision version of the project plan is the well-known, task-based GANTT chart, showing task times, assignments, and dependencies.

The more precision in the plan, the more fragile it is, which is why constructing GANTT charts is so feared: It is time-consuming to produce and gets out of date with the slightest surprise event.

The user interface design. The low-precision description of the user interface is the screen flow diagram, which states only the purpose and linkage of each screen.

The medium level of precision description consists of the screen definitions with field lengths and the various field or button activation rules.

The highest-precision definition of the user interface design is the program's source code.

Behavioral requirements / use cases. Behavioral requirements are often written with use cases.

The lowest-precision view of a set of use cases is the Actors-Goals list, the list of primary actors and the goals they have with respect to the system (Figure 4-6). This lowest-precision view is useful at the start of the project when you are prioritizing the use cases and allocating work to teams. It is useful again whenever an overview of the system is needed.

Actor	Goal
Customer	Buy a product
Customer	Get a refund
Mktg. Dept.	Set up a promotion
Manager	Check statistics

Figure 4-6 An *Actors-Goals* list: the lowest-precision view of behavioral requirements.

The medium level of precision consists of a one-paragraph brief synopsis of the use case, or the use case's title and main success scenario.

The medium-high level of precision contains extensions and error conditions, named but not expanded.

The final, highest level of precision includes both the extension conditions and their handling.

These levels of precision are further described in Cockburn (2001c).

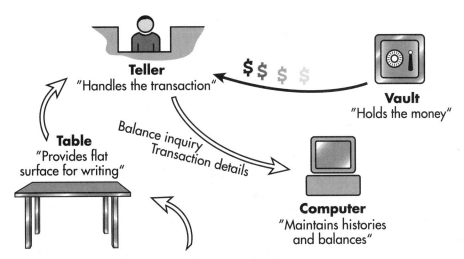

Figure 4-7 A Responsibility-Collaborations diagram: the low-precision view of an object-oriented design.

The program design. The lowest level of precision in an object-oriented design is a Responsibility-Collaborations diagram, a very coarse-grained variation on the UML object collaboration diagram (Figure 4-7). The interesting thing about this simple design presentation is that people can already review it and comment on the allocation of responsibilities.

A medium level of precision is the list of major classes, their major purpose, and primary collaboration channels.

A medium-high level is the class diagram, showing classes, attributes, and relationships with cardinality.

A high level of precision is the list of classes, attributes, relations with cardinality constraints, and functions with function signatures. These often are listed on the class diagram.

The final, highest level of precision is the source code.

These levels for design show the natural progression from Responsibility-Driven Design (Beck 1989, Wirfs-Brock 1990) through object modeling with UML, to final source code. The three are not in opposition, as some imagine, but rather occur along a very natural progression of precision.

As we get better at generating final code from diagrams, the designers will add precision and code-generation annotations to the diagrams. As a consequence, the diagrams plus annotations become the "source code." The C++ or Java stops being source code and becomes generated code.

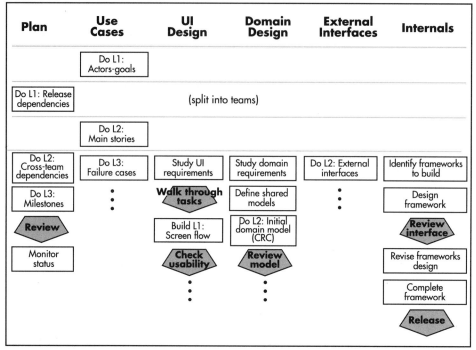

Figure 4-8 Using low levels of precision to trigger other activities.

Working with "Precision"

People do a lot with these low-precision views. During the early stages of the project, they plan and evaluate. At later stages, they use the low-precision views for training.

I currently think of a level of precision as being reached when there is enough information to allow another team to start work. Figure 4-8 shows the evolution of six types of work products on a project: the project plan, the use cases, the user interface design, the domain design, the external interfaces, and the infrastructure design.

In looking at Figure 4-8, we see that having the actor-goal list in place permits a preliminary project plan to be drawn up. This may consist of the project map

along with time and staffing assignments and estimates. Having those, the teams can split up and capture the use-case briefs in parallel. As soon as the use-case briefs—or a significant subset of them— are in place, all the specialist teams can start working in parallel, evolving their own work products.

One thing to note about precision is that the work involved expands rapidly as precision increases. Figure 4-9 shows the work increasing as the use cases grow from actors, to actors and goals, to main success scenarios, to the various failure and other extension conditions, and finally to the recovery actions. A similar diagram could be drawn for each of the other types of work products.

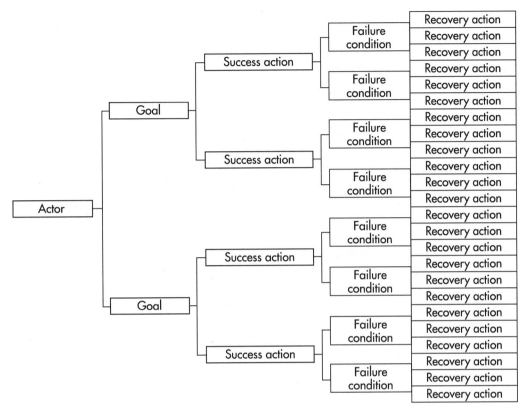

Figure 4-9 Work expands with increasing precision level (shown for use cases).

Because higher-precision work products require more energy and also change more often than their low-precision counterparts, a general project strategy is to defer, or at least carefully manage, their construction and evolution.

Stability and Concurrent Development

Stability, the "likelihood of change," varies over the course of the project (Figure 4-10).

A team starts in a situation of *instability*. Over time, team members reduce the fluctuations and reach a *varying* state as the design progresses. They finally get their work *relatively stable* just prior to a design review or publication. At that point, the reviewers and users provide new information to the development team, which makes the work less stable again for a period.

On many projects, instability jumps unexpectedly on occasions, such as when a supplier suddenly announces that he will not deliver on time, a product does not perform as predicted, or an algorithm does not scale as expected.

You might think that you should strive for maximum stability on a project.

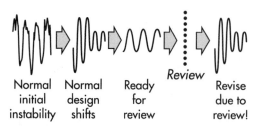

| Normal initial instability | Normal design shifts | Ready for review | Review | Revise due to review! |

Figure 4-10 Reducing fluctuations over the course of a project.

However, the appropriate amount of stability to target varies by topic, by project priorities, and by stage in the project. Different experts have different recommendations about how to deal with the varying rates of changes across the work products and the project stages.

The simplest approach is to say, "Don't start designing until the requirements are Stable (with a capital 'S'); don't start programming until the design is Stable," and

so on. This is serial development. Its two advantages make it attractive to many people. It is, however, fraught with problems.

The first advantage is its simplicity. The person doing the scheduling simply sequences the activities one after the other, scheduling a downstream activity to start when an upstream activity is finished.

The second advantage is that, if no major surprises force a change to the requirements or the design, a manager can minimize the number of work-hours spent on the project by carefully scheduling when people arrive to work on their particular tasks. There are three problems, though.

The first problem is that the *elapsed* time needed for the project is the straight sum of the times needed for requirements, design, programming, test, and so on.

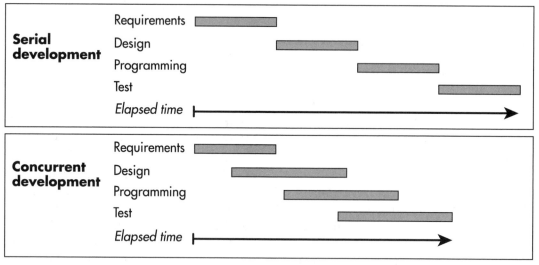

Figure 4-11 Successful serial development takes longer (but fewer workdays) compared to successful concurrent development.

This is the longest time that can be required for the project. With the most careful management, the project manager will get the longest elapsed time at the minimum labor cost. For projects on which reducing elapsed time is a top priority, this is a bad trade-off.

The second problem is that surprises usually *do* crop up during the project. When one does, it causes unexpected revisions of the requirements or design and raises the development cost. In the end, the project manager minimizes neither the labor cost nor the development time.

The third problem is the absence of feedback from the downstream activities to the upstream activities.

In rare instances, the people doing the upstream activity can produce high-quality results without feedback from the downstream team. On most projects, though, the people who are creating the requirements need to see a running version of what they ordered so that they can correct and finalize their requests.

Usually, after seeing the system in action, they change their requests. This forces changes in the design, coding, testing, and so on. Incorporating these changes lengthens the project's elapsed time and increases total project costs.

Selecting the serial-development strategy really only makes sense if you can be sure that the team will be able to produce good, final requirements and design on the first pass. Few teams can do this.

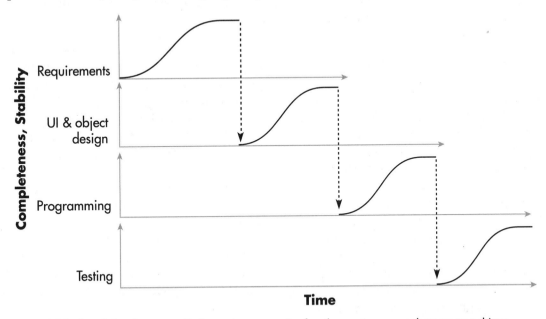

Figure 4-12 Serial development. Each workgroup waits for the upstream workgroup to achieve complete stability before starting.

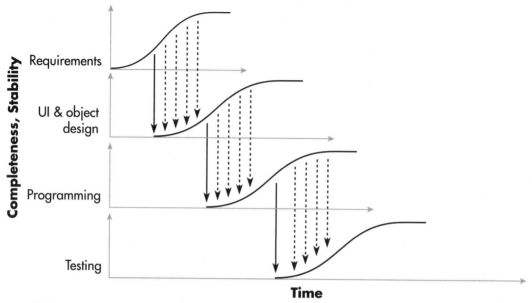

Figure 4-13 Concurrent development. Each group starts as early as its communications and rework capabilities indicate. As it progresses, the upstream group passes update information to the downstream group in a continuous stream (the dashed arrows).

A different strategy, concurrent development, shortens the elapsed time and provides feedback opportunities at the cost of increased rework. Figure 4-11 and Figure 4-13 illustrate it, and "Principle 7. Efficiency is expendable in nonbottleneck activities." on page 156 analyzes it further.

In concurrent development, each downstream activity starts at some point judged to be appropriate with respect to the completeness and stability of the upstream team's work (different downstream groups may start at different moments with respect to their upstream groups, of course). The downstream team starts operating with the available information, and as the upstream team continues work, it passes new information along to the downstream team.

To the extent that the downstream team guesses right about where the upstream team is going and the upstream team does not encounter major surprises, the downstream team will get its work approximately right. The team will do some rework along the way, as new information shows up.

The key issue in concurrent development is judging the completeness, stability, rework capability, and communication effectiveness of the teams.

The advantages of concurrent development are twofold, the exact opposites of the disadvantages of serial development:

• The upstream teams get feedback from the downstream teams. The designers can indicate how difficult the requirements are to implement.

The programmers may produce code soon enough for the requirements group to get feedback on the desirability of the requirements.

- Although each downstream activity takes longer than it would if done serially and the upstream team never changed its mind, the downstream activity starts much earlier. The net effect is that the downstream team finishes sooner than it otherwise would, possibly just a few days or weeks after the upstream work is finished.

Such concurrent development is described as the Gold Rush strategy in *Surviving Object-Oriented Projects* (Cockburn 1998). The Gold Rush strategy presupposes both good communication and rework capacity. The Gold Rush strategy is suited to situations in which the requirements gathering is predicted to go on for longer than can be tolerated in the project plan, so there would simply not be enough time for proper design if the next team had to wait for the requirements to settle.

Actually, many projects fit this profile.

Gold-Rush-type strategies are not risk free. There are three pitfalls to watch out for:

- The first pitfall is overdoing the strategy; for example, allowing the design team to get ahead of the requirements team (Figure 4-14). One such team announced one day that its design was already stable and ready for review. The team was just waiting for the requirements people to hurry up and generate the requirements!

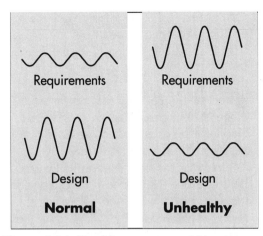

Figure 4-14 Keeping upstream activities more stable than downstream activities. The wavy lines show the instability of work products in requirements and design. In the healthy situation (left) both fluctuate at the same time, but the requirements fluctuation is smaller than the design. In the unhealthy situation, the design is already stable before the requirements have even started settling down!

- The second pitfall is when the communications path between the teams is not rich enough. If the teams are geographically separated, for example, it is harder for the upstream team to pass along its changing information. As the communications cost rises, it eventually becomes more effective to wait for greater stability in the upstream work before triggering the downstream team.
- The third pitfall is making a mistake in estimating a team's rework capacity. Where a team has little or no spare capacity, it must be given much more stable inputs to work from.

16 Smalltalkers, 2 Database Designers

One project had 16 Smalltalk programmers and only two database designers.

In this situation, we could let the Smalltalk programmers start working as soon as the requirements were starting to shape up. At the same time, we could not afford to trigger the database designers to start their work until the object model had been given passing marks in its design review.

Only *after* the object model had passed "stable enough for review" and actually been reviewed, with the DBAs in the review group, could the DBAs take the time to start their design work.

The complete discussion about when and where to apply concurrent development is presented in "Principle 7. Efficiency is expendable in nonbottleneck activities." on page 156.

The point to understand now is that stability plays a role in methodology design.

Both XP and Adaptive Software Development suggest maximizing concurrency (Highsmith 2000). This is because both are intended for situations with strong time-to-market priorities and requirements that are likely to change *as a consequence of* producing the emerging system.

Fixed-price contracts often benefit from a mixed strategy: In those situations, it is useful to have the requirements quite stable before getting far into design. The mix will vary by project. Sometimes, the company making the bid may do some designing or even coding just to prepare its bid.

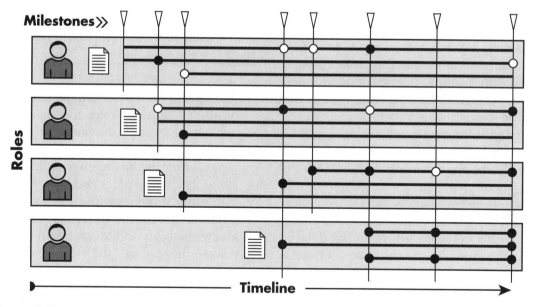

Figure 4-15 Role-deliverable-milestone view of a methodology.

PUBLISHING A METHODOLOGY

Publishing a methodology has two components: the pictorial view and the text itself.

The Pictorial View

One way to present the design of a methodology is to show how the roles interact across work products (Figure 4-15). In such a "Role-Deliverable-Milestone" view, time runs from left to right across the page, roles are represented as broad bands across the page, and work products are shown as single lines within a band. The line of a work product shows critical events in its life: its birth event (what causes someone to create it), its review events (who examines it), and its death event (at what moment it ceases to have relevance, if ever).

Although the Role-Deliverable-Milestone view is a convenient way to capture the work-product dependencies within a methodology, it evidently is also good for putting people to sleep:

METHODOLOGY CHART AS SLEEPING AID

I once created the proverbial wall chart of the methodology for a large project, meticulously showing the several hundred interlocking parts of the group's methodology using the Role-Deliverable-Milestone view to condense the information.

Many people had been asking to see the entire methodology, so I printed the chart, several feet on each side, and put it on a large wall.

It was interesting to watch people's eyes glaze over whenever I was pointing to the time line for another project role, such as the project managers or technical writers, and only come back into focus when I got to their own section.

It turned out that most people really only wanted to see the section of the methodology that affected them and not what everyone in the organization was doing.

The pictorial view misses the practices, standards, and other forms of collaboration so important to the group. Those don't have a convenient graphical portrayal and must be listed textually.

The Methodology Text

In published form, a methodology is a text that describes the techniques, activities, meetings, quality measures, and standards of all the job roles involved. You can find examples in *Object-Oriented Methods: Pragmatic Considerations* (Martin 1998), and *The OPEN Process Specification* (Graham 1997). The Rational Unified Process has its own Web site with thousands of Web pages.

Methodology texts are large. At some level there is no escape from this size. Even a tiny methodology, with four roles, four work products per role, and three milestones per work product has 68 (4 + 16 + 48) interlocking parts to describe, leaving out any technique discussions. And even XP, which initially weighed in at only about 200 pages (Beck 2000), now approaches 1,000 pages when expanded to include additional guidance about each of its parts (Jeffries 2001, Beck 2000, Auer 2002, Newkirk 2001).

There are two reasons why most organizations don't issue a thousand-page text describing their methodology to each new employee:

- The first is what Jim Highsmith neatly captures with the distinction, "documentation versus understanding."

The real methodology resides in the minds of the staff and in their habits of action and conversation. Documenting chunks of the methodology is not at all the same as providing understanding, and having understanding does not presuppose having documentation. Understanding is faster to gain, because it grows through the normal job experiences of new employees.

- The second is that the needs of the organization are always changing. It is impractical, if not impossible, to keep the thousand-page text current with the needs of the project teams.

As new technologies show up, the teams must invent new ways of working to handle them, and those cannot be written in advance.

An organization needs ways to evolve new variants of the methodologies on the fly and to transfer the good habits of one team to the next team. You will learn how to do that as you proceed through this book.

Reducing Methodology Bulk

There are several ways to reduce the physical size of the methodology publication:

Provide examples of work products. Provide work examples rather than templates.

Take advantage of people's strengths in working with tangibles and examples, as discussed earlier.

Collect reasonably good examples of various work products: a project plan, a risk list, a use case, a class diagram, a test case, a function header, a code sample.

Place them online, with encouragement to copy and modify them. Instead of writing a standards document for the user interface, post a sample of a good screen for people to copy and work from. You may need to annotate the example showing which parts are important.

Doing these things will lower the work effort required to establish the standards and will lower the barrier to people using them.

One of the few books to show deliverables and their standards is *Developing Object-Oriented Software* (IBM OOTC 1997), which was prepared for IBM by its Object-Oriented Technology Center in the late 1990s and was then made public.

Remove the technique guides. Rather than trying to teach the techniques by providing detailed descriptions of them within the methodology document, let the methodology simply name the recommended techniques in the methodology, along with any known books and courses that teach them.

Techniques-in-use involve tacit knowledge. Let people learn from experts, using apprenticeship-based learning, or let them learn from a hands-on course in which they can practice the technique in a learning environment.

Where possible, get people up to speed on the techniques before they arrive on the project, instead of teaching the technique as part of a project methodology on project time. The techniques will then become skills owned by people, who simply do their jobs in their natural ways.

Organize the text by role. It is possible to write a low-precision but descriptive paragraph about each role, work product, and milestone, linking the descriptions with the Role-Deliverable-Milestone chart. The sample role descriptions might look something like these:

Sample Role Descriptions	
Executive Sponsor	A person who acts in the capacity to support and monitor the progress of an approved project. Responsible for scoping, prioritizing, and funding at the project level.
Cross-team Lead	A person who is responsible for the progress of multiple teams, for uniting the efforts of these teams, for establishing priorities across teams, and for allocating resources (people) across teams.
Team Lead	A person who is responsible for the direction and progress of one team.

Sample Role Descriptions (cont'd)	
Developer	A technical person who develops the software product. This may include UI, business classes, infrastructure, or data.
Writer	A person who publishes technical communication about various subjects through media such as manuals, white papers, shared drives, intranet, or Internet.
Rollout	One or more persons who communicate and coordinate field technicians and customer representatives and who roll out the products.
External Tester	One or more persons who perform QA-related test functions outside of the development groups.
Maintainer	A person who makes necessary changes to the product after it ships.

For the work products, you need to record who writes them, who reads them, and what they contain. A fuller version would contain a sample, noting the tolerances permitted and the milestones that apply. Here are a few simple descriptions:

Overall Project Plan	
Writer	Cross-team Lead
Readers	Executive Sponsor, Team Leads, newcomers
Contains	Across all teams, what is planned to be in the next several releases, the cross-team dependencies between their contents, the planned timing of development

Dependency Table	
Writer	Team Lead
Readers	Team Leads, Cross-team Leads
Contains	What this team needs from every other team, and the date each item is needed. May include a fallback plan in case the item is not delivered on time.

Team Status Sheet	
Writer	Team Lead
Readers	Cross-team Lead, Developers
Contains	The current state of the team: rolled-up list of things being worked on, next milestone, what is holding up progress, and stability level for each

For the review milestones, record what is being reviewed, who is to review it, and what the outcome is. For example:

Release Proposal Review	
Reviewers	Application Team Lead, Cross-team Lead, and Executive Sponsor
Purpose	Basically a scope review
Reviewing	Use case summary, use cases, actors, external system description, development plan
Outcome	Modifications to scope, priorities, dates, possibly corrections to actor list or external systems

Application Design Review	
Reviewers	Team Lead, related Cross-team Leads, Cross-Team Mentors, Business experts
Purpose	Check quality, correctness, and conformance of the application design
Reviewing	Use cases, actors, domain class diagram, screen flows, screen designs, class tables (if any), and interaction diagrams (if any)
Outcome	Factual corrections to the domain model, to the screen details. Suggestions or requirements for improved UI or application design, based on either quality or conformance considerations

With these short paragraphs in place, the methodology can be summarized by role (as the following two examples show). The written form of the methodology, summarized by role, is a checklist for each person that can be fit onto one sheet of paper and pinned up in the person's workspace. That sheet of paper contains no surprises (after the first reading) but serves to remind team members of what they already know.

Here is a slightly abridged example for the programmers:

Designer-Programmer	
Writes	Weekly status sheet Source code Release notes (etc.)
Reads	Actor descriptions UI style guide (etc.)
Reviews	Application design review (etc.)
Publishes	Application configuration Test cases (etc.)
Declares	UI Stable

You can see that this is not a methodology used to stifle creativity. To a newcomer, it is a list outlining how he is to participate on the team. To the ongoing developer, it is a reminder.

Using the Process Miniature

Publishing a methodology does not convey the visceral understanding that forms tacit knowledge. It does not convey the *life* of the methodology, which resides in the many small actions that accompany teamwork. People need to see or personally enact the methodology.

My current favorite way of conveying the methodology is through a technique I call the *process miniature*.

In a process miniature, the participants play-act one or two releases of the process in a very short period of time

On one team I interviewed, new people were asked to spend their first week developing a (small) piece of software all the way from requirements to delivery. The purpose of the week-long exercise was to introduce the new person to the people, the roles, the standards, and the physical placement of things in the company.

More recently, Peter Merel invented a one-hour process miniature for Extreme Programming, giving it the nickname *Extreme Hour*. The purpose of the Extreme Hour is to give people a visceral encounter with XP so that they can discuss its concepts from a base of almost-real experience.

In the Extreme Hour, some people are designated "customers." Within the first 10 minutes of the hour, they present their requests with developers and work through the XP planning session.

In the next 20 minutes, the developers sketch and test their design on overhead transparencies. The total length of time for the first iteration is 30 minutes.

In the next 30 minutes, the entire cycle is repeated so that two cycles of XP are experienced in just 60 minutes.

Usually, the hosts of the Extreme Hour choose a fun assignment, such as designing a fish-catching device that keeps the fish alive until delivering them to the cooking area at the end of the day and also keeps the beer cold during the day. (Yes, they do have to cut scope during the iterations!)

We used a 90-minute process miniature to help the staff of a 50-person company experience a new development process we were proposing (you might notice the similarity of this process miniature experience to the *informance* described on page 57).

In this case, we were primarily interested in conveying the programming and testing rules we wanted people to use. We therefore could not use a drawing-based problem such as the fish trap but had to select a real programming problem that would produce running, tested code for a Web application.

A PROCESS MINIATURE EXPERIENCE

We wanted to demonstrate two full iterations of the process in 90 minutes.

We wanted to show people negotiating over requirements and then creating and testing production of code, using the official five-layer architecture, execution database, configuration-management system, official Web style sheets, and fully automated regression test suites.

We therefore had to choose a tiny application. We elected to construct a simple up-down counter that would stick at 0 and 20 and could be reset to 0. The counter would use a Web browser interface and store its value in the official company database.

To meet the constraint of 45 minutes per iteration, we choreographed the show to a small extent. The marketing analysts were told to ask for more than the team could possibly deliver in 30 minutes of programming ("Could we please have a graphical, radial dial for the counter, in three colors?"). We did this in order to let the audience experience scope negotiation as they would encounter it in real life.

We also rehearsed how much the programmers would bid to complete the first iteration and how they might cut scope during the middle of the iteration so that the audience could see this in action.

The point of scripting these pieces was to give the entire company a view of what we wanted to establish as the social conventions for normal scope negotiation during project runs.

We left the actual programming as live action. Even though the team members knew the assignment, they still had to type it all in, in real time, as part of the experience. The audience, sitting through all of the typing, came to appreciate the amount of work that went into even such a trivial system.

Whatever form of process miniature you use, plan on replaying it from time to time in order to reinforce the team's social conventions. Many of these conventions, such as the scope negotiation rules just described, won't find a place in the documentation but can be partially captured in the play.

METHODOLOGY DESIGN PRINCIPLES

Designing a methodology is not at all like designing software, hardware, bridges, or factories. Four things, in particular, get in the way:

- Variations in people. People are not the reliable components that designers count on when designing the other systems.
- Variations across projects. The appropriate methodology varies by project, nationality, and local culture.
- Long debug cycles. The test and debug cycle for a methodology is on the order of months and years.
- Changing technologies. By the time the methodology designer debugs one methodology design, the technologies, techniques, and cultures have changed and the design needs updating.

COMMON DESIGN ERRORS

People who come freshly to their assignment of designing a methodology make a standard set of errors:

One Size for All Projects

Here is a conversation that I have heard all too often over the years:

"Hi, Alistair. We have projects in many technologies all over the globe. We desperately need a common methodology for all of them. Could you please design one for us?"

"I'm afraid that would not be practical: The different technologies, cultures, and project priorities call for different ways of working."

"Right, got that. Now, please do tell us what our common methodology will be."

"...!!?"

This request is so widespread that I spend most of the next chapter on methodology tailoring.

The need for localized methodologies may be clear to you by now, but it will not be clear to your new colleague who is given the assignment to design the corporation's common methodology.

Intolerant

Novice methodology designers have this notion that they have *the* answer for software development and that everyone really ought to work that way.

Software development is a fluid activity. It requires that people notice small discrepancies wherever they lie and that they communicate and resolve the discrepancies in whatever way is most practical. Different people thrive on different ways of working.

A methodology is, in fact, a straightjacket. It is exactly the set of conventions and policies the people agree to use: It is the size and shape of straightjacket they choose for themselves.

Given the varying characteristics of different people, though, that straightjacket should not be made any tighter than it absolutely needs to be.

Techniques are one particular section of the methodology that usually can be made tolerant. Many techniques work quite well, and different ones suit different people at different times.

The subject of how much tolerance belongs in the methodology should be a conscious topic of discussion in the design of your methodology.

Heavy

We have developed, over the years, an assumption that a heavier methodology, with closer tracking and more artifacts, will somehow be "safer" for the project than a lighter methodology with fewer artifacts.

The opposite is actually the case, as the principles in this section should make clear. However, that initial assumption persists, and it manifests itself in most methodology designs.

The heavier-is-safer assumption probably comes from the fear that project managers experience when they can't look at the code and detect the state of the project with their own eyes. Fear grows with the distance from the code. So they quite naturally request more reports summarizing various states of affairs and more coordination points. The alternative is to . . . trust people. This can be a truly horrifying thought during a project under intense pressure. Being a Smalltalk programmer, I felt this fear first-hand when I had to coordinate a COBOL programming project.

Fear or no fear, adding weight to the methodology is not likely to improve the team's chance of delivering. If anything, it makes the team less likely to deliver, because people will spend more time filling in reports than making progress. Slower development often translates to loss of a market window, decreased

morale, and greater likelihood of losing the project altogether.

Part of the art of project management is learning when and how to trust people and when not to trust them. Part of the art of methodology design is to learn what constraints add more burden than safety. Some of these constraints are explored in this chapter.

Embellished

Without exception, every methodology I have ever seen has been unnecessarily embellished with rules, practices, and ideas that are not strictly necessary. They may not even belong in the methodology. This even applies to the methodologies I have designed. It is so insidious that I have posted on the wall in front of me, in large print: "Embellishment is the pitfall of the methodologist."

EMBELLISHING A METHODOLOGY

I detected this tendency in myself while designing my first methodology.

I asked a programmer colleague, a very practical person freshly returned from a live project, to double-check, edit, and trim my design. He indeed found the embellishments I was worried about. However, he then added one chapter to the methodology, calling for the production of contract-based design and deliverables he had just read about.

I phoned him. "Surely you don't mean to say you used these on your last project?" I asked.

He replied, "Well, no, not on that project. But it's a really good idea and I think we *ought to* do it."

From this experience, I learned that the words "ought to" and "should" indicate embellishment. If someone says that people "should" do something, it probably means that they have never done it yet, they have successfully delivered software without it, and there probably is no chance of getting people to use it in the future.

Here is a sample story about that.

DISCOVERING "SHOULD"

TESTER: "And then the developers have a meeting with the testers in which they describe the basic design."

ME: "Really, do they do that?"

TESTER: "What do you mean? Of course they do."

ME: "Oh, yeah. They really do that, do they?"

TESTER: "They've got to, or else the testers can't do their job!"

ME: "Right. Um . . . In that case, there was such a meeting, and I can interview those people to find out what happened in the meeting. Can you tell me the date of such a meeting, and who was in the room?"

TESTER: "Well, we were going to have it. I mean, you really *should* have that meeting, it's really valuable . . ."

We didn't have to go much farther than that. Of course, no such meeting had taken place. Further, it was doubtful that we could enforce such a meeting in that company at that time, however useful it might have been.

There is another side to this embellishment business. Typically, the process owner has a distorted view of how developers really work. In my interviews, I rarely ever find a team of people who work the way the process owner says they work. This is so pervasive that I have had to mark as unreliable any interview in which I only got to speak with the manager or process designer.

The following is a sample, and typical, conversation from one of my interviews. At the time, I was looking for successful implementations of Object Modeling Technique (OMT). The person who was both process and team lead told me that he had a successful OMT project for me to review, and so I flew to California to interview this team.

UNCOVERING PROCESS SHORTCUTS

ME: "These are samples of the work products? . . . This is a state diagram?"

LEADER: "Well, it's not really one. It's more of a flow diagram. I have to teach them how to make state diagrams properly."

ME: "But these are actual samples of the work products produced. Did you use an iterative and incremental process?"

Developer nods.

LEADER: "We used a modification of Boehm's spiral model."

ME: "OK. And did the requirements or the design change in the second iteration?"

DEVELOPER: "Of course."

ME: "OK. . . . How did you manage to update all these diagrams in the second iteration?"

DEVELOPER: "Oh, we didn't. We just changed the code . . ."

Extreme Programming stands in contrast to the usual, deliverable-based methodologies. XP is based around activities. The rigor of the methodology resides in people carrying out their activities properly.

Not being aware of the difference between deliverable-based and activity-based methodologies, I was unsure how to investigate my first XP project. After all, the team has no drawings to keep up to date, so obviously there would be no out-of-date work products to discover!

An activity-based methodology relies on activities in action. XP relies on programming in pairs, writing unit tests, refactoring, and the like.

When I visit a project that claims to be an XP project, I usually find pair programming working well (or else they wouldn't declare it an XP project). Then, while they are pair programming, the people are more likely to write unit tests, and so I usually see some amount of test-writing going on.

The most common deviation from XP is that the people do not refactor their code often, which results in the code base becoming cluttered in ways that properly developed XP code shouldn't.

In general, though, XP has so few rules to follow that most of the areas of embellishment have been removed. XP is a special case of a methodology, and I'll analyze it separately at the end of the chapter.

Personally, I tend to embellish around design reviews and testing. I can't seem to resist sneaking an extra review or an extra testing activity through the "should" door ("Of course they should do that testing!" I hear you cry. Shouldn't they?!).

The way to catch embellishment is to have the directly affected people review the proposal. Watch their faces closely to discover what they know they won't do but are afraid to say they won't do.

Untried

Most methodologies are untried. Many are simply proposals created from nothing. This is the full-blown "should" in action: "Well, this really looks like it *should* work."

After looking at dozens of methodology proposals in the last decade, I have concluded that nothing is obvious in methodology design. Many things that look like they *should* work don't (testing and keeping documentation up to date, for example), and many things that look like they *shouldn't* work actually do work (pair programming and test-first development, for example).

The late Wayne Stevens, designer of the IBM Consulting Group's Information Engineering methodology in the early 1990s, was well aware of this trap.

Whenever someone proposed a new object-centered / object-based / object-hybrid methodology for us to include in the methodology library, he would say, "Try it on a project, and tell us afterwards how it worked." They would typically object, "But that will take years! It is *obvious* that this is great!" To my recollection, not one of these *obvious* new methodologies was ever used on a project.

Since that time, I have used Wayne Stevens' approach and seen the same thing happen.

How are new methodologies made? Here's how I work when I am personally involved in a project:

- I adjust, tune, and invent whatever is needed to take the project to success.
- After the project, I extract those things I would repeat again under similar circumstances and add them to my repertoire of tactics and strategies.
- I listen to other project teams when they describe their experiences and the lessons they learned.

But when someone sends me a methodology *proposal*, I ask him to try it on a project first and report back afterwards.

Used Once

The successor to "untried" is "used once." The methodology author, having discovered one project on which the methodology works, now announces it as a general solution. The reality is that different projects need different methodologies, and so any one methodology has limited ability to transfer to another project.

I went through this phase with my Crystal Orange methodology (Cockburn 1998), and so did the authors of XP. Fortunately, each of us had the good sense to create a "truth-in-advertising" label describing our own methodology's area of applicability.

We will revisit this theme throughout the rest of the book: How do we identify the area of applicability of a methodology, and how do we tailor a methodology to a project in time to benefit the project?

METHODOLOGICALLY SUCCESSFUL PROJECTS

You may be wondering about these project interviews I keep referring to. My work is based on looking for "methodologically successful" projects. These have three characteristics:

- The project was delivered. I don't ask if it was completed on time and on budget, just that the software went out the door and was used.
- The leadership remained intact. They didn't get fired for what they were doing.
- The people on the project would work the same way again.

The first criterion is obvious. I set the bar low for this criterion, because there are so many strange forces that affect how people refer to the "successfulness" of a project. If the software is released and gets used, then the methodology was at least that good.

The second criterion was added after I was called in to interview the people involved with a project that was advertised as being "successful." I found, after I got there, that the project manager had been fired a year into the project because no code had been developed up to that time, despite the mountains of paperwork the team had produced. This was not a large military or life-critical project, where such an approach might have been appropriate, but it was a rather ordinary, 18-developer technical software project.

The third criterion is the difficult one. For the purpose of discovering a successful methodology, it is essential that the team be willing to work in the prescribed way. It is very easy for the developers to block a methodology. Typically all they have to say is, "If I do that, it will move the delivery date out two weeks." Usually they are right, too.

If they don't block it directly, they can subvert it. I usually discover during the interview that the team subverted the process, or else they tolerated it once but wouldn't choose to work that way again.

Sometimes, the people follow a methodology because the methodology designer is present on the project. I have to apply this criterion to myself and disallow some of my own projects. If the people on the project were using my suggestions just to humor me, I couldn't know if they would use them when I wasn't present.

The pertinent question is, "Would the developers continue to work that way if the methodology author was no longer present?"

So far, I have discovered three methodologies that people are willing to use twice in a row. They are

- Responsibility-Driven Design (Wirfs-Brock 1990)
- Extreme Programming (Beck 1999)
- Crystal Clear (Cockburn, forthcoming)

(I exclude Crystal Orange from this list, because I was the process designer and lead consultant. Also, as written, it deals with a specific configuration of technologies and so needs to be reevaluated in a different, newly adapted setting.)

Even if you are not a full-time methodology designer, you can borrow one lesson from this section about project interviews. Most of what I have learned about good development habits has come from interviewing project teams. The interviews are so informative that I keep on doing them.

This avenue of improvement is also available to you. Start your own project interview file, and discover good things that other people do that you can use yourself.

AUTHOR SENSITIVITY

A methodology's principles are not arrived at through an emotionally neutral algorithm but come from the author's personal background. To reverse the saying from *The Wizard of Oz*, "Pay great attention to the man behind the curtain."

Each person has had experiences that inform his present views and serve as their anchor points. Methodology authors are no different.

In recognition of this, Jim Highsmith has started interviewing methodology authors about their backgrounds. In *Agile Software Development Ecosystems*, he will present not only each author's methodology but also his or her background.

A person's anchor points are not generally open to negotiation. They are fixed in childhood, early project experiences, or personal philosophy. Although we can renormalize a discussion with respect to vocabulary and scope, we cannot do that with personal beliefs. We can only accept the person's anchor points or disagree with them.

When Kent Beck quipped, "All methodology is based on fears," I first thought he was just being dismissive. Over time, I have found it to be largely true. One can almost guess at a methodology author's past experiences by looking at the methodology. Each element in the methodology can be viewed as a prevention against a bad experience the methodology author has had.

- Afraid that programmers make many little mistakes? Hold code reviews.
- Afraid that users don't know what they really want? Create prototypes.
- Afraid that designers will leave in the middle of the project? Have them write extensive design documentation as they go.

Of course, as the old saying goes, just because you are paranoid doesn't mean that they *aren't* after you. Some of your fears may be well founded. We found this to be the case in one project, as told to us over time by an adventuresome team leader. Here is the story as we heard it in our discussion group:

DON'T TOUCH MY PRIVATE VARIABLES

A team leader wanted to simplify the complex design surrounding the use of not-quite-private methods that wrote to certain local variables.

Someone in our group proposed making all methods public. This would simplify the design tremendously.

The team leader thought for a moment and then identified that he was operating on a fear that the programmers would not follow the necessary programming convention to keep the software safe. He wanted the programmers to use those public methods *only* for the particular programming situation that was causing trouble.

He was afraid that in the frenzy of deadlines, they would use them all the time, which would cause maintenance problems. He was willing to try the experiment of making them public and just writing on the team's whiteboard the very simple rule restricting their use.

I said, "Maybe your fears are well founded. How about if you don't just *trust* the people to behave well, but also write a little script to check the *actual* use of those methods over time? This way you will discover whether your fears are well founded or not."

The team leader agreed.

The team leader went on vacation for two weeks.

When he returned, he ran the script and found that the programmers had, in fact, been using the new, public methods, ignoring the note on the whiteboard.

(One person at the table chimed in here, "Well, sure, those were the only documented methods!")

This story raises an interesting point about trust: As much as I love to trust people, a weakness of people is being careless. Sometimes it is important to simply trust people, but sometimes it is important to install a mechanism to find out whether people can be trusted on a particular topic.

The final piece of personal baggage of the methodology authors is their individual philosophy. Some have a laissez-faire philosophy, some a military control philosophy. The philosophy comes with the person, shaping his experiences and being shaped by his experiences, fears, and wishes.

It is interesting to see how much of an author's methodology philosophy is used in his personal life. Does Watts Humphrey use a form of the Personal Software Process when he balances his checkbook? Does Kent Beck do the simplest thing that will work, getting incremental results and feedback as soon as he can? Do I travel light, and am I tolerant of other people's habits?

Here are some key bits of my background that either drive my methodology style or at least are consistent with it.

I travel light, as you might guess. I use a small laptop, carry a small phone, drive a small car, and see how little luggage I need when traveling. In terms of the eternal tug-of-war between mobility and armor, I am clearly on the side of mobility.

I have lived in many countries and among many cultures and keep finding that each works. This perhaps is the source of my sensitivity to development cultures and why I encourage tolerance in methodologies.

I also like to think very hard about consequences, so that I can give myself room to be sloppy. Thus, I balance the checkbook only when I absolutely have to, doing it in the fastest way possible, just to make sure checks don't bounce. I don't care about absolute accuracy. Once, when I built bookshelves, I worked out the fewest places where I had to be accurate in my cutting (and the most places where I could be sloppy) to get level and sturdy bookshelves.

When I started interviewing project teams, I was prepared to discover that process rigor was the secret to success. I was actually surprised to find that it wasn't. However, after I found that using light methodologies, communicating, and being tolerant were effective, it was natural that I would capitalize on those results.

Beware the methodology author. Your experiences with a methodology may have a lot to do with how well your personal habits align with those of the methodology author.

SEVEN PRINCIPLES

Over the years, I have found seven principles that are useful in designing and evaluating methodologies:

1. Interactive, face-to-face communication is the cheapest and fastest channel for exchanging information.
2. Excess methodology weight is costly.
3. Larger teams need heavier methodologies.
4. Greater ceremony is appropriate for projects with greater criticality.
5. Increasing feedback and communication reduces the need for intermediate deliverables.
6. Discipline, skills, and understanding counter process, formality, and documentation.
7. Efficiency is expendable in nonbottleneck activities.

Following is a discussion of each principle.

Principle 1. Interactive, face-to-face communication is the cheapest and fastest channel for exchanging information.

The relative advantages and appropriate uses of warm and cool communication channels were discussed in the last chapter. Generally speaking, we should prefer to use warmer communication channels in software development, because we are interested in reducing the cost of detecting and transferring information.

Principle 1 predicts that people sitting near each other with frequent, easy contact will find it easier to develop software, and the software will be less expensive to develop. As the project size increases and interactive, face-to-face communications become more difficult to arrange, the cost of communication increases, the quality of communication decreases, and the difficulty of developing the software increases.

The principle does not say that communication quality decreases to zero, nor does it imply that all software can be developed by a few people sitting in a room. It implies that a methodology author might want to emphasize small groups and personal contact if productivity and cost are key issues. The principle is supported by management research (Plowman 1995 and Sillince 1996, among others).

We also used Principle 1 in the story "Videotaped Archival Documentation" on page 95, which describes documenting a design by videotaping two people discussing that design at a whiteboard.

The principle addresses one particular question: "How do forms of communication affect the cost of detecting and transferring information?"

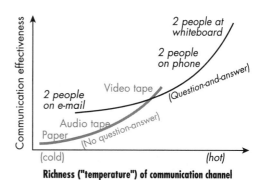

Figure 4-16 Effectiveness of different communication channels (repeat of Figure 3-14).

One could ask other questions to derive other, related principles. For example, it might be interesting to uncover a principle to answer this question: "How do forms of communication affect a sponsor's evaluation of a team's conformance to a contract?" This question would introduce the issue of *visibility* in a methodology. It should produce a very different result, probably one emphasizing written documents.

Principle 2. Excess methodology weight is costly.

Imagine six people working in a room with osmotic communication, drawing on the printing whiteboard. Their communication is efficient, the bureaucratic load low. Most of their time is spent developing software, the usage manual, and any other documentation artifacts needed with the end product.

Now ask them to maintain additional intermediate work products, written plans, GANTT charts, requirements documents, analysis documents, design documents, and test plans. In the imagined situation, they are not truly needed by the team for the development. They take time away from development.

Productivity under those conditions decreases. As you add elements to the methodology, you add more things for the team to do, which pulls them away from the meat of software development.

In other words, a small team can succeed with a larger problem by using a lighter methodology (Figure 4-17).

Methodology elements add up faster than people expect. A process designer or manager requests a new review or piece of paperwork that should "only take a half hour from time to time." Put a few of these together, and suddenly the designers lose an additional 15–20 percent of their already cramped week. The additional work items disrupt design flow. Very soon, the designers are trying to get their design thinking done in one- or two-hour blocks which, as you saw earlier, does not work well.

This is something I often see on projects: designers unable to get the necessary quiet time to do their work because of the burden of paperwork and the high rate of distractions.

This principle contains a catch, though. If you try to increase productivity by removing more and more methodology elements, you eventually remove those that address code quality. At some point the strategy backfires, and the team spends more time repairing bad work than making progress.

What size problem can a given number of people attack, using various methodology weights?

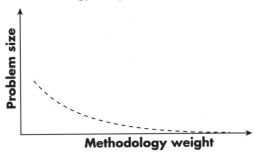

Figure 4-17 Effect of adding methodology weight to a small team.

The key word, of course, is *excess*. Different methodology authors produce different advice as to where "excess" methodology begins. I find that a team operating from people's strengths—communication and citizenship—can do with a lot less methodology than most managers expect. Jim Highsmith is more explicit about this. His suggestion would be that you start lighter than you think will possibly work!

There are two points to draw from this discussion:

- Adding a "small" amount of bureaucratic burden to a project adds a large cost.
- Some part of the methodology should address the quality of the output.

Principle 3. Larger teams need heavier methodologies.

With only four or six people on the team, it is practical to put them together in a room with printing whiteboards and allow the convection currents of information to bind the ongoing conversation in their cooperative game of invention and communication.

After the team size exceeds 8 or 12 people, though, that strategy ceases to be so effective. As it reaches 30 to 40 people, the team will occupy a floor. At 80 or 100 people, the team will be spread out on multiple floors, in multiple buildings, or in multiple cities.

With each increase in size, it becomes harder for people to know what others are doing and how not to overlap, duplicate, or interfere with each other's work. As the team size increases, so does the need for some form of coordination and communication.

Figure 4-18 shows the effect of adding methodology to a large team. With very light methodologies, they work without coordination. As they start to coordinate their work, they become more effective (this is the left half of the curve). Eventually, for any size group, diminishing returns set in and they start to spend more time on the bureaucracy than on developing the system (the right half of the curve).

The right half of the curve is described in Principle 2, "Excess methodology weight is costly." Principle 3 describes the left half of the curve: "Larger teams need heavier methodologies."

What size problem can a given number of people attack, using various methodology weights?

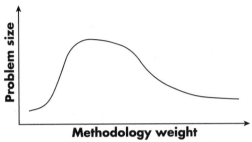

Figure 4-18 Effect of adding methodology weight to a large team.

Principle 4. Greater ceremony is appropriate for projects with greater criticality.

This principle addresses ceremony and tolerance, as discussed in the second section of this chapter.

A PORTFOLIO OF PROJECTS

In the IT department of the Central Bank of Norway, we worked on many kinds of projects.

One was to allow people to order dinners from the cafeteria when they worked late.

One was to provide SQL programming support for staff who were investigating financial investments.

A third was to track all the bank-to-bank transactions in the country.

A fourth was to convert the entire NB system to be Year-2000 safe.

The cost of leaving a fault in the third and fourth systems was quite different from the cost of leaving a fault in the first two. I use the word *criticality* for this distinction. It was more critical to get the work correct in the latter two than in the former two projects.

Just as communications load affects the appropriate choice of methodology, so does criticality. I have chosen to divide criticality into four categories, according to the loss caused by a defect showing up in operation:

• Loss of comfort.

The cafeteria produces lasagne instead of a pizza. At the worst, the person eats from the vending machine.

• Loss of discretionary monies.

Invoicing systems typically fall into this category. If a phone company sends out a billing mistake, the customer phones in and has the bill adjusted.

Many project managers would like to pretend that their project causes more damage than this, but in fact, most systems have good human backup procedures, and mistakes are generally fixed with a phone call. I was surprised to discover that the bank-to-bank transaction tracking system actually fit into this category. Although the numbers involved seemed large to me, they were the sorts of numbers that the banks dealt with all the time, and they had human backup mechanisms in place to repair computer mistakes.

• Loss of essential monies.

Your company goes bankrupt because of certain errors in the program. At this level of criticality, it is no longer possible to patch up the mistake with a simple phone call.

Very few projects really operate at this level. I was recently surprised to discover two.

One was a system that offered financial transactions over the Web. Each transaction could be repaired by phone, but there were 50,000 subscribers, estimated to become 200,000 in the following year, and a growing set of services was being offered. The call-in rate was going to increase by leaps and bounds. The time cost of repairing mistakes already fully consumed the time of one business expert who should have been working on other things and took up almost half of another business expert's time. This company decided that it simply could not keep working as though mistakes were easily repaired.

The second was a system to control a multi-ton, autonomous vehicle. Once again, the cost of a mistake was not something to be fixed with a phone call and some money. Rather, every mistake of the vehicle could cause very real, permanent, and painful damage.

• Loss of life.

Software to control the movement of the rods in a nuclear reactor fall into this category, as do pacemakers, atomic power plant control, and the space shuttles. Typically, members of teams whose programs can kill people know they are working on such a project and are willing to take more care.

As the degree of potential damage increases, it is easy to justify greater development cost to protect against mistakes. In keeping with the second principle, adding methodology adds cost, but in this case, the cost is worth it. The cost goes into defect reduction rather than communications load.

Principle 4 addresses the amount of ceremony that should be used on a project. Recall that ceremony refers to the tightness of the controls used in development and the tolerance permitted. More ceremony means tighter controls and less tolerance.

Consider a team-building software for the neighborhood bowling league. The people write a few sentences for each use case, on scraps of paper or a word processor. They review the use cases by gathering a few people in a room and asking what they think.

Consider, in contrast, a different team, which is building software for a power plant. These people use a particular tool, fill in very particular fields in a common template, keep versions of each use case, and adhere to strong writing style conventions. They review, baseline, change control, and sign off the use cases at several stages in the lifecycle.

The second set of use cases is more expensive to develop. The team works that way, though, expecting that fewer mistakes will be made. The team justifies being less tolerant of variation by the added safety of the final result.

Principle 5. Increasing feedback and communication reduces the need for intermediate deliverables.

Recall that a deliverable is a work product that crosses decision boundaries. An intermediate deliverable is one that is passed across decision boundaries *within* the team. These might include the detailed project plan, refined requirement documents, analysis and design documents, test plans, inter-team dependencies, risk lists, and so on.

I refer to them also as "promissory notes," as in:

"I promise that the system will look like these requirements describe."

"I promise that this analysis model will work as the core for the system's design."

"I promise that this design will work well over time."

There are two ways to reduce the need for promissory notes:

1. Deliver a working piece of the system quickly enough that the sponsor can tell whether the team understood the requirements properly.

Delivering a working piece of the system quickly leads to these other benefits:

- The requirements writers will be able to tell whether the requirements they wrote are actually going to meet the user's needs.

- The team needs fewer requirements reviews and can often simplify the requirements process in other ways.
- The designers can see the effects of their decisions early rather than after many other decisions have been built on top of a mistake.
- Test planning becomes much simpler. Sometimes another intermediate work product, the Test Plan, can be replaced by the running test cases.

2. Reduce the team size, putting everyone close enough together that they can simply tell each other what they are doing instead of writing internal documents to each other.

Note the word *internal*. The sponsors may still require written documentation of different sorts as part of the external communication needs.

Principle 6. Discipline, skills, and understanding counter process, formality, and documentation.

When Jim Highsmith says, "Don't confuse documentation with understanding," he means that much of the knowledge that binds the project is *tacit* knowledge, knowledge that people have inside them, not on paper anywhere.

The knowledge base of a project is immense, and much of that knowledge consists of knowing the team's rituals of negotiation, which person knows what information, who contributed heavily in the last release, what pieces of discussion went into certain design decisions, and so on. Even with the best documentation in the world, a new team cannot necessarily just pick up where the previous team left off. The new team will not start making progress until the team members build up their tacit knowledge base.

When referring to "documentation" for a project, be aware that the knowledge that becomes documentation is only a small part of what there is to know. People who specialize in technology transfer know this. As the one IBM Fellow put it, "The way to get effective technology transfer is not to transfer the technology itself but to transfer the *heads* that hold the technology!" ("Jumping Gaps across Time," on page 99.)

Highsmith continues, "Process is not discipline." Discipline involves a person *choosing* to work in a way that requires consistency. Process involves a person following instructions. Of the two, discipline is the more powerful. A person who is choosing to act with consistency and care will have a far better effect on the project than a person who is just following instructions.

The common mistake is in thinking that somehow a process will impart discipline.

Highsmith's third distinction is, "Don't confuse formality with skill."

Insurance companies are in an unusual situation. We fill in forms, send them to the insurance back office, and receive insurance policies. This is quite amazing. Probably as a consequence of their living in this unusual realm, I have several times been asked by insurance companies to design use case and object-oriented design forms. Their goal, I was told on each occasion, was to make it foolproof to construct high-quality use cases and OO designs.

Sadly, our world is not built that way. A good designer will read a set of use cases and create an OO design directly, one that improves as he reworks the design over time. No amount of form filling yet replaces this skill. Similarly, a good user interface designer creates much better programs than a mediocre interface designer can create.

Figure 4-19 shows a merging of Highsmith's and my thoughts on these issues.

Highsmith distinguishes *exploratory* or *adapting* activities from *optimizing* activities. The former, he says, is exemplified by the search for new oil wells. In searching for a new oil well, one cannot predict what is going to happen. After the oil well is functioning, however, the task is to keep reducing costs in a predictable situation.

In software development, we become more like the optimizing oil company as we become more familiar with the problem to be solved, the team, and the technologies being used. We are more like the exploratory company, operating in an adaptive mode, when we don't know those things.

Light methodologies draw on understanding, discipline, and skill more than on documentation, process, and formality. They are therefore particularly well suited for exploratory situations. The typical heavy methodology, drawing on documentation, process, and formality, is designed for situations in which the team will not have to adapt to changing circumstances but can optimize its costs.

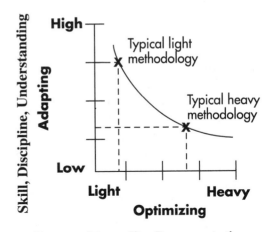

Process, Formality, Documentation

Figure 4-19 Documentation is not understanding, process is not discipline, formality is not skill.

Of the projects I have seen, almost all fit the profile of *exploratory* situations. This may explain why I have only once seen a project succeed using an *optimizing* style of methodology. In that exceptional case, the company was still working in the same problem domain and was using the same basic technology, process, and architecture as it had done for several decades.

The characteristics of exploratory and optimizing situations run in opposition to each other. Optimizing projects try to reduce the dependency on tacit knowledge, personal skill, and discipline and therefore rely more on documentation, process, and formality. Exploratory projects, on the other hand, *allow* people to reduce their dependency on paperwork, processes, and formality by relying more on understanding, discipline, and skill. The two sets draw away from each other.

Highsmith and I hypothesize that any methodology design will live on the track shown in the figure, drawing either to one set or the other, but not both.

Principle 7. Efficiency is expendable in nonbottleneck activities.

Principle 7 provides guidance in applying concurrent development and is a key principle in tailoring the Crystal methodologies for different teams in different situations. It is closely related to Elihu Goldratt's ideas as expressed in *The Goal* (Goldratt 1992) and *The Theory of Constraints* (Goldratt 1990).

To get a start on the principle, imagine a project with five requirements analysts, five Smalltalk programmers, five testers, and one relational database designer (DBA), all of them good at their jobs. Let us assume, for the sake of this example, that the group cannot hire more DBAs. Figure 4-20 shows the relevant part of the situation, the five programmers feeding work to the single DBA.

The DBA clearly won't be able to keep up with the programmers. This has nothing to do with his skills, it is just that he is overloaded. In Goldratt's terms, the DBA's activity is the *bottleneck* activity. The speed of this DBA determines the speed of the project.

To make good progress, the team had better get things lined up pretty well for the DBA so that he has the best information possible to do his work. Every slowdown, every bit of rework he does, costs the project directly.

That is quite the opposite story from the Smalltalk programmers. They have a huge amount of excess capacity compared with the DBA.

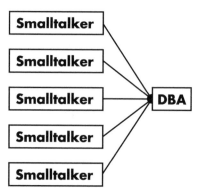

Figure 4-20 The five Smalltalk programmers feeding work to the one DBA.

Faced with this situation, the project manager can do one of two things:

- Send four of the programmers home so that the Smalltalk programmers and the DBA have matched capacities.
- Make use of the programmers' extra capacity.

If he is mostly interested in saving money, then he sends four of the programmers home and lives with the fact that the project is going to progress at the speed of these two solo developers.

If he is interested in getting the project done as quickly as possible, he doesn't send the four Smalltalk programmers home. He takes advantage of their spare capacity.

He has them revise their designs several times, showing the results to users, *before* they hand over their designs to the DBA. This way, they get feedback that enables them to change their designs before, not after, the DBA goes through his own work.

He also has them start *earlier* in the requirements-gathering process, so that they can show intermediate results to the users sooner, again getting feedback earlier. He has them spend a bit more time drawing their designs so that the DBA can read them easily.

He does this knowing that he is causing them extra work. He is drawing on their spare capacity.

Figure 4-21 diagrams this second work strategy. In that figure you see only one requirements person submitting information to one Smalltalk programmer, who is submitting work to the one DBA. The top two curves are used five times, for the five requirements writers and the five programmers.

Notice in Figure 4-21 that the Smalltalker starts work as soon as the requirements person has something to hand him, but the DBA waits until the Smalltalker's work is almost complete and quite stable before starting.

Notice also that the DBA is completing work faster than the others. This is a reflection of the fact that the other groups are doing more rework, and hence reaching completeness and stability more slowly. This is necessary because four other groups are submitting work to the DBA. In a balanced situation, the DBA reaches completion five times as fast as the others.

People on a bottleneck activity need to work as efficiently as possible and cannot afford to do much rework. (I say "much rework" because there is always rework in software development; the goal is to reduce the amount of rework.)

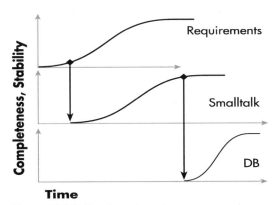

Figure 4-21 Bottleneck station starts work higher on the completeness and stability curve than do nonbottleneck stations.

Principle 7 has three consequences.

Consequence 1. Do whatever you can to speed up the work at the bottleneck activity. That result is fairly obvious, except that people often don't do it.

Every project has a bottleneck activity. It moves during the project, but there is always one. In the above example, it is the DBA's work. There are four ways to improve a bottleneck activity. Principle 7 addresses the fourth.

1. Get better people doing that work.
2. Get more people to do that work.
3. Get better tools for the people doing that work.
4. Get the work that feeds that activity to a more complete and stable state before passing it along.

Consequence 2. People at the nonbottleneck activities can work inefficiently without affecting the overall speed of the project! This is not obvious.

Of course, one way for people to work inefficiently is to take long smoking breaks, surf the Web, and spend time at the water cooler. Those are relatively uninteresting for the project and for designing methodologies.

More interesting is the idea of *spending* efficiency, trading it for stability.

The nonbottleneck people can spend some of their extra capacity by starting earlier, getting results earlier, doing more rework and doing it earlier, and doing other work that helps the person at the bottleneck activity.

Spending excess capacity for rework is significant for software development because rework is one of the things that causes software projects to take so much time. The users see the results and change their requests; the designers see their algorithm in action and change the design; the testers break the program; and the programmers change the code. In the case of the above example, all of these will cause the DBA rework.

Applying Principle 7 and the diagram of concurrent development (Figure 4-13) to the problem of the five Smalltalkers and one DBA, the project manager can decide that the Smalltalk programmers can work "inefficiently," meaning "doing more rework than they might otherwise," in exchange for making their work more stable earlier. This means that the DBA, to whom rework is expensive, will be given more stable information at the start.

Principle 7 offers a strategy for when and where to use early concurrency, and when and where to delay it. Most projects work from a given amount of money and an available set of people. Principle 7 helps the team members adjust their work to make the most of the people available.

Principle 7 can be used on every project, not just those that are as out of balance as the sample project. Every project has a bottleneck activity. Even when the bottleneck moves, Principle 7 applies to the new configuration of bottleneck and nonbottleneck activities.

Consequence 3. Applying the principle of expendable efficiency yields different methodologies in different situations, even keeping the other principles in place. Here is a first story, to illustrate:

WINIFRED AND PRINCIPLE 7

Project Winifred did resemble the sample project above. It was the project on which I learned to apply the principle.

In the middle of the project, there were about a dozen Smalltalk programmers, four COBOL programmers, and two DBAs. The Smalltalk programmers could revise their designs faster than any of the others. The two DBAs were overloaded, as in the example story.

We arranged for the Smalltalkers to work very closely with the requirements writers, getting started as soon as there was information to work from. Applying osmotic and face-to-face communication, rather than documents between them, the Smalltalkers worked by word of mouth, changing their designs as they heard new information from the requirements writers.

The DBAs and COBOL programmers started their work only after the Smalltalkers had a "relatively stable" design that had passed its design review.

I described this use of the principle as the Gold Rush strategy in *Surviving Object-Oriented Projects* (Cockburn 1998). That book also describes the related use of the Holistic Diversity strategy and examines project Winifred more extensively.

Here is a second story, with a different outcome:

eBucks.com and Principle 7

The company eBucks.com had 15 developers and a dozen business specialists. They also had a backlog of six dozen work initiatives.

The programmers were being distracted away from their work several times each day and consequently were making little headway against their backlog.

Gold Rush was exactly the wrong strategy to use in this situation. The programmers had no spare capacity. In fact, programming was the bottleneck activity.

We first took several steps to reduce the distractions hitting the programmers. That was still not enough, given their backlog.

We decided, therefore, that the business specialists would write use cases, business rules, and data descriptions to hand to the programmers.

Note that this strategy appears at first glance to go against a primary idea of this book: maximizing face-to-face communication. However, in this situation, these programmers could not keep information in their heads. They needed the information to reach them in a "sticky" form, so they could refer to it after the conversations.

After the programmers work through the backlog, the bottleneck activity will move, and the company may find it appropriate to move to a more concurrent, conversation-based approach.

Just what they do will depend on where the next bottleneck shows up.

Here is a third story:

Udall and Principle 7

Project Udall had become stuck, with dozens of developers and a large, unworkable design.

Four of the senior developers decided to ignore all the other developers and simply restarted their work. They added people to their private workgroup slowly, inviting only the best people to join them.

They reasoned (correctly, as it turns out) that the two bottleneck activities were getting political alignment on design decisions and transferring information from the senior designers' heads to the others.

They decided that it would be more effective for them to let the others do *anything* other than program on the system than to spend key design resources convincing and training the others.

This was a most surprising and effective application of the principle of expendable efficiency.

When I interviewed one of the team leads, I asked, "What about all those other people? What did they do?"

The team lead answered, "We let them do whatever they wanted to. Some did nothing, some did small projects to improve their technical skills. It didn't matter, because they wouldn't help the project more by doing anything else."

The restarted project did succeed. In fact, it became a heralded success at that company.

Consequences of the Principles

The above principles work together to help you choose an appropriate size for the team when given the problem, and to choose an appropriate size for the methodology when given the team. Look at some of the consequences of combining the principles:

Consequence 1. Adding people to a project is costly. People who are supposed to know this sometimes seem unaware of it, so it is worth reviewing.

Imagine 40 or 50 people working together. You create teams and add meetings, managers, and secretaries to orchestrate their work.

Although the managers and secretaries protect the programming productivity of the individual developers, their salaries add cost to the project. Also, adding these people adds communication needs, which call for additional methodology elements and overall lowered productivity for the group (Figure 4-22).

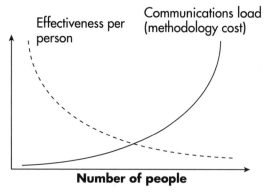

Figure 4-22 Reduced effectiveness with increasing communication needs (methodology size).

Consequence 2. Team size increases in large jumps. The effects of adding people and adding methodology load combine, so that adding "a few" people is not as effective an approach as it might seem. Indeed, my experience hints that to double a group's output, one may need to almost square the number of people on the project! Here is a story to illustrate:

MYTHICAL MAN-MONTH REVISITED

Fred Brooks, in *The Mythical Man-Month*, writes that one may have a project that cannot be delivered in time by even the 10 best people in the world. As a consequence, he writes, one may have to use 200 or 300 people.

He explains that there are two effects driving the need for extra people. One is that more people are needed to handle the communications load on the project. The other is that it will not be possible to hire 200 people of the same caliber as the proposed 10. The communications load is compounded by a decrease in talent.

Here is a second, more recent story, with a similar outcome:

SIX TO 24 PROGRAMMERS

At the start of one fixed-priced project, we estimated that we could deliver the project with six good Smalltalk programmers.

That wasn't an option, though. At that time, we couldn't get our hands on six good Smalltalk programmers. To make matters worse, we were given 10 novices to train and only two expert programmers to both train them and create code.

During our estimation process, we concluded we would need a staff of 24 programmers of mixed abilities.

Over the course of the project, we eventually had four experts and 20 other programmers with mixed experience. We got our 24 programmers.

We reviewed our assessment at several times during the project, and at the end. Yes, six good Smalltalk programmers would have been sufficient. No, 12 programmers, even 16 programmers of the mixed experience levels we were seeing would not have been sufficient.

The correct jump was from six good programmers to 24 programmers of mixed ability.

Consequence 3. Teams should be improved, not enlarged. Here is a common problem: A manager has a 10-person team that sits close together and achieves high communication rates with little energy.

The manager needs to increase the team's output. He has two choices: add people or keep the team the same size and do something different within the team.

If he increases the team size from 10 to 15, the communications load, communications distances, training, meeting, and documentation needs go up. Most of the money spent on this new group will get spent on communications overhead, without producing more output.

This group is likely to grow again, to 20 people (which will add a heavier communications burden but will at least show improvement in output).

The second strategy, which seems less obvious, is to lock the team size at 10 people (the maximum that can be coordinated through casual coordination) and improve the people on the team.

To improve the individuals on the team, the manager can do any or all of the following:

- Send them to courses to improve their skills.
- Seat them closer together to reduce communications cost.
- Improve their amicability and teamwork.
- Replace some of the people on the team with more talented (and more highly paid) people.

Repeating the strategy over time, the manager will keep finding better and better people who work better and better together.

Notice that in the second scenario, the communications load stays the same, while the team becomes more productive. The organization can afford to pay the people more for their increased contribution. It can, in fact, afford to double their salaries, considering that these 10 are replacing 20! This makes sense. If the pay is good, bureaucratic burden is low, and team members are proud of their output, they will enjoy the place and stay, which is exactly what the organization wants them to do.

FEWER AND BETTER

Kent Arett, CEO of the gift catalog company The Popcorn Factory, has applied the above strategy for years. He used it successfully at both Fingerhut and Sears.

Fingerhut had morale and staff turnover problems when he arrived ("It was a revolving door," as he describes it). The 80 or so people in the IS department he inherited were completely busy just supporting old applications and had no time for new development.

He did two things: He reduced staff by about 25 percent, keeping only the better people, and he raised their salaries. With this, their output increased enough that only about 15 people were needed for support, and the rest could work on new development. At that point, he raised salaries even higher for those people doing support work!

He was most proud, though, that a number of future department heads came from these programmers.

As VP of Operations at Sears, he converted an $800 million annual operating loss to a $100 million operating profit in five years. He says that a key part of this success was simultaneously reducing and improving the staff: They kept only the best 80 out of 300 developers and at the same time raised their salaries.

He adds, "There's one more thing: Paint the vision. Paint the vision and get motivated people, and it's 'Game Over.'"

Consequence 4. Different methodologies are needed for different projects.

Figure 4-23 shows one way to examine projects to select an appropriate methodology. The attraction of using a grid in this figure is that it works from fairly objective indices:

- The number of people being coordinated
- The system criticality
- The project priorities

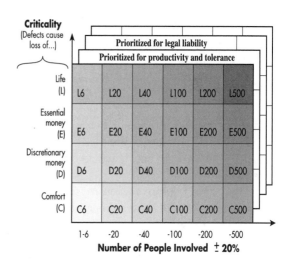

Figure 4-23 Characterizing projects by communication load, criticality, and priorities.

You can walk into a project work area, count the people being coordinated, and ask for the system criticality and project priorities.

In the figure, the lettering in each box indicates the project characteristics. A "C6" project is one that has six people and may cause loss of comfort; a "D20" project is one that has 20 people and may cause the loss of discretionary monies.

In using this grid, you should recognize several things:

Communication load rises with the number of people. At certain points, it becomes incorrect to run the project in the same way: Six people can work in a room, 20 in close proximity, 40 on a floor, 100 in a building. The coordination mechanisms for the smaller-sized project no longer fit the larger-sized project.

- A project that may cause a company to go out of business or may cause loss of life needs more careful checking than a project that may only cause loss of comfort or discretionary monies.

- Projects that are prioritized with legal liability concerns will require more care and tracking of the work.

Here is how I once used the grid:

CHANGING GRID CELLS MID-PROJECT

The banking project I was asked to coordinate at the Central Bank of Norway started as a three-person effort, using the same three people who had done the previous system. I characterized it as a D6 type of project and planned to more or less just trust the programmers to do a good job.

After a month or so, though, it became clear that we were coordinating large amounts of money and that we should perhaps be more careful about the mistakes we let slip. I moved the project rating to E6, and we spent a week or two fixing the design with respect to fault tolerance, recovery, and race conditions.

After the architect and lead programmer went on paternity leave, we got two new programmers and two testers. At this point, we had seven people, two in Lillehammer, two on the first floor, and one each on the second, third, and fourth floors in Oslo (remember the cost of communicating across floors?). It turned out that this system was actually being developed by two companies, and our team was coordinating its work with a group of 35 developers at a different location in Oslo who were using a different (waterfall) methodology.

It was at this moment that the grid came in handy. I reclassified our project as an E20 project (some mix of the number of people and the geographic dispersion).

Paying attention to the methodology principles, I did not add more paperwork to the project but stepped up personal communications, using phone calls and the video link, and increased personal study of the issues affecting the outcome of the project.

The grid characteristics can be used in reverse to help discuss the range of projects for which a particular methodology is applicable.

This is what I do with the Crystal methodology family in Chapter 6. I construct one methodology that might be suitable for projects in the D6 category (Crystal Clear), another that might be suitable for projects in the D20 range (Crystal Yellow), another for D40 category projects (Crystal Orange), and so on. Looking at methodologies in this way, you would say that Extreme Programming is suited for projects in the C4 to E14 categories.

Consequence 5. Lighter methodologies are better, until they run out of steam.

What we should be learning is that a small team with a light methodology can sometimes solve the same problem as a larger team with a heavier methodology. From a project cost point of view, as long as the problem can be solved with 10 people in a room, that will be more effective than adding more people.

At some point, though, even the 10 best people in the world won't be able to deliver the needed solution in time, and then the team size must jump drastically. At that point, the methodology size will have to jump also (Figure 4-24).

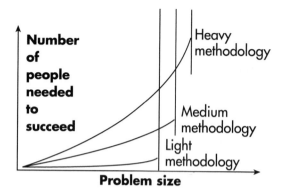

Figure 4-24 Small methodologies are good but run out of steam.

There is no escaping the fact that larger projects require heavier methodologies. What you can escape, though, is using a heavy methodology on a small project. What you can work toward is keeping the methodology as light and nimble as possible for the particular project and team.

Agile is a reasonable goal, as long as you recognize that a large-team agile methodology is heavier than a small-team agile methodology.

Consequence 6. Methodologies should be stretched to fit. Look for the lightest, most "face-to-face"-centric methodology that will work for the project. Then stretch the methodology. Jim Highsmith summarizes this with the phrase, "A little less than enough is better than a little more than enough."

A manager of a project with 50 people and the potential for "expensive" damage has two choices:

I. He can choose a larger-category methodology (say, E100) and remove the excess weight from it. This is attractive to some managers, because it gives them bragging rights: "Yeah, we had to use an E100 methodology for our project!" However, it is unlikely that the team will remove as much as it can, and so the project will go slower and be more expensive than it needs to be.

2. He should choose a smaller-category methodology (say, D40) and adapt it up to the project. Although this gives him fewer bragging rights, the team is likely to add fewer irrelevant items to the methodology, and as a consequence, the project is more likely to go faster and be less expensive.

XP was first used on D8 types of projects. Over time, people found ways to make it work successfully for more and more people. As a result, I now rate it for E14 projects.

More Principles
We should be able to uncover other principles.

One of the more interesting candidates I recently encountered is the "real options evaluation" model (Sullivan 1999).

In considering the use of financial options theory in software development, Sullivan and his colleagues highlight the "value of information" (VOI) against the "value of flexibility" (VOF).

VOI deals with this choice: *"Pay to learn, or don't pay if you think you know."* The concept of VOI applies to situations in which it is possible to discover information earlier by paying more.

An application of the VOI concept is deciding which prototypes to build on a project.

VOF deals with this choice: *"Pay to not have to decide or don't pay, either because you are sure enough the decision is right, or because the cost of changing your decision later is low."* The concept of VOF applies to situations in which it is *not possible* to discover information earlier.

An application of the VOF concept is deciding how to deal with competing (potential) standards, such as COM versus CORBA.

A second application, which they discuss in their article, is evaluating the use of a spiral development process. They say that using spiral development is a way of betting on a favorable future. If conditions improve at the end of the first iteration, the project continues. If the conditions worsen, the project can be dropped at a controlled cost.

I haven't yet seen these concepts tried explicitly, but they certainly fit well with the notion of software development as a resource-limited cooperative game. They may provide guidance to some process designer and yield a new principle for designing methodologies.

XP UNDER GLASS

Extreme Programming (XP) is an *agile* methodology that illustrates the ideas in this book very well. Additionally, it is effective, well documented, and controversial. Thus, it makes a wonderful sample methodology to examine. At this point, we finally have enough vocabulary to put it under the methodology microscope.

The short story is that XP scores very high within its area of applicability. It (like all others) needs to be adjusted when applied outside its sweet spot.

XP IN A NUTSHELL

The briefest of reviews of XP is in order, although much has been written about it elsewhere (Beck 2000, Jeffries 2001, XP URL).

Following is a summary, as brief as it would be if given as instructions over the phone or e-mail:

Use only 3 to 10 programmers. Arrange for one or several customers to be on site to provide ongoing expertise. Everyone works in one room or adjacent rooms, preferably with the workstations clustered, monitors facing outward in a circle, half as many workstations as programmers.

Do development in three-week periods, or *iterations*. Each iteration results in running, tested code that is of direct use to the customers. The compiled system is rolled out to its end users at the end of each release period, which may be every two to five iterations.

The unit of requirements gathering is the "user story," user-visible functionality that can be developed within one iteration. The customers write the stories for the iteration onto simple index cards. The customer(s) and programmers negotiate what will get done in the next iteration in the following way:

- The programmers estimate the time to complete each card.
- The customers prioritize, alter, and de-scope as needed so that the most valuable stories are most likely to get done in the allotted time period.

The programmers write the tasks for each story on flipcharts on the wall or a whiteboard, estimating the time they will need for each task. Over time, the customers and programmers can reprioritize or de-scope the tasks or stories.

Development on a story starts with the programmers discussing the story with the expert customer. Because this discussion is guaranteed to take place, the text written on the story card can be very brief, just enough to remind everyone of what the conversation is going to be about. The understanding of the requirements grow through those conversations and any pictures or documents the people decide they need.

Programmers work in pairs. They follow strict coding standards that they set up at the beginning of the project. They create unit tests for everything they write and make sure that those tests run at 100 percent every time they check in their code to the mandatory versioning and configuration-management system. They develop in tiny increments of 15 minutes to a few hours long, integrating their code several times a day. At the end of each of these integrations, they ensure that the entire code base passes all unit tests.

At any time, any two programmers sitting together may change any line of code in the system. In fact, they are supposed to. Anytime the two find a section of code that appears hard to understand or overly complex, they are to revise it, constantly simplifying and improving it. At all times, they are to keep the overall design as simple as they can and the code as clear as they can. This constant refactoring is possible because of the extensive unit test suites in place. It is also possible because the programmers rotate pair assignments every day or so, and so knowledge of the changes in the code structure passes through the group through the shifting partnerships.

While the programmers are working, the customers are doing three things: They visit with the programmers to clarify ideas, they write system acceptance tests to be run during and at the end of the iteration, and they select stories to be built for the next iteration. They may be on the project full time or not, as they decide.

The team holds a stand-up meeting every day, in which they describe what they are working on, what is working well for them, and what they might need help with. The meeting is held standing up to keep it short. At the end of each iteration, they hold another meeting in which they review what they did well and what they want to work on next time. They post this list for all to see during the next iteration.

XP prizes four values: communication, simplicity, testing, and courage. The "courage" value is intended as courage to go ahead and make improvements to the system at any time.

One person on the team is designated the "coach" for the team. This person reviews with the team members their use of the key practices: use of pair programming and testing, pair rotation, keeping design simple, communicating, and so on.

DISSECTING XP

An XP team makes great use of osmotic communication, face-to-face communication, convection currents of information flow, and information radiators on the wall.

The consistent availability of experts means that the delay from question to answer is short. The time and energy cost to discover a needed piece of information is low; the rate of information dispersion is high.

Feedback is rapid. The customers get quick feedback as to the implementation implications of their requirements requests during the planning session. They see running code within days and can adjust accordingly their views on what should really be programmed. The programmers get immediate correction on the code they enter, because another person sitting next to them is watching what they type and because there are unit tests for each function they write. When changing the design, they get rapid feedback from the extensive unit and acceptance tests. They get fairly rapid feedback on their process, about every few weeks, through the iteration cycles.

XP uses human strength of communication. Through pair work and rapid feedback, it compensates for the human tendency to make mistakes.

XP is a high-discipline methodology. It calls for tight adherence to strict coding and design standards, strong unit test suites that must pass at all times, good acceptance tests, constant working in pairs, vigilance in keeping the design simple, and aggressive refactoring.

These disciplines are protected through two mechanisms and are exposed in three places.

It turns out (much to the surprise of many) that most people like working in pairs. It provides pride-in-work, because they get more done in less time, with fewer errors, and usually end up with a better design than if they were working alone. They like this. As a result, they do it voluntarily. While in pairs, they help each other write tests and follow coding standards. Thus, pair programming helps hold unit-testing in place.

Having a coach helps keep the other disciplines in place. Reports from various groups indicate to me that even better than having a coach is having several very enthusiastic XP practitioners on the team. This is because the coach is an *external* force, while enthusiastic teammates create peer pressure—an *internal*, and hence more powerful, force.

The places where XP is still exposed with respect to being high-discipline are coding standards, acceptance tests, and aggressive refactoring. Of those, aggressive refactoring probably will remain the most difficult, because it requires consistency, energy, and courage, and no mechanisms in the methodology reinforce it.

There are some high-ceremony (low-tolerance) standards. The policy standards include the use of iterations. Design and programming are done in tiny increments of hours or a few days. Planning and development cycles are two to four weeks, releases one to four months. The testing policy standard is that all unit tests run at 100 percent for all checked-in code. A policy standard states that the team is to be colocated, with a strong recommendation toward the "caves and common" seating (Auer 2002).

XP includes within its definition a selection of techniques that the people need to learn: the planning game, the daily stand-up meeting, refactoring, and test-first development.

XP is designed for small, colocated teams aiming to get quality and productivity as high as possible. It does this through the use of rich, short, informal communication paths with emphasis on skill, discipline, and understanding at the personal level, minimizing all intermediate work products.

Adjusting XP

Two traits of XP are controversial: absence of documentation and the restriction to small teams.

Absence of Documentation

We can explore the documentation issue in terms of the cooperative game. XP targets success at the primary goal: delivering software.

It targets succeeding at the secondary goal, setting up for the next game, solely through the tacit knowledge built up within the project team.

The knowledge that binds the group and the design is tacit knowledge: the sum of knowledge of all the people on the team. The tacit knowledge is communicated through osmotic communication, rotation in the pair programming, clear, simple code, and extensive unit tests. People joining the team gain this tacit knowledge by pair programming with experienced people in rotation.

While the attention to tacit knowledge is good, sometimes the sponsors want other deliverables besides the system in operation. They may want usage manuals or paperwork describing the system's design. Even if the customers don't need these things, the organization's executives are likely to want to protect themselves against the eventual disappearance of the team's tacit knowledge.

Although it is not likely that everyone will quit at one time, it is likely that the organization will reduce staff size after the main development period of the project. At that point the tacit knowledge starts to be in jeopardy: If several people leave in quick succession, the new people will not have had enough time to absorb the project details adequately. At that point, the project has neither documents nor tacit knowledge.

XP actually contains a mechanism to deal with this situation: the planning game. It just happens that XP projects to date have not made use of the planning game for this purpose.

In the planning game, the sponsors can write story cards that call for creating documentation instead of new program features. During the planning game, the developers estimate the time it will take to generate the documentation, and the customers prioritize those stories against the stories specifying new features.

Using the planning game in this way, the sponsors can properly play the two competing subgames: that of delivering software quickly and that of protecting the group's knowledge.

The above discussion is hypothetical. I have not seen it used. The reason may be, and this is the hazard to the scheme, that the people who are requesting new functionality have great allegiance to the current project and little or no allegiance to future, possible projects. In other words, they don't have a *duration of accountability* that permits them to adequately balance the priority of new functionality against documentation. Resolving this problem will probably remain difficult.

An XP team might consider less common and less expensive ways to document the system design, such as video documentation (as described in Chapter 3).

Restriction to Small Team

Many people exclaim: "XP doesn't scale!"

At this point, you should review, if you don't recall them, the graphs of problem size versus team size in the last section.

A well-structured, 10-programmer team using XP properly may be able to solve a larger problem than a 30-person team using a larger methodology. In fact, on the first official XP project, an 8-person XP team delivered in one year what the previous, 26-person team had failed to deliver in the previous year. So be aware of what the statement "XP doesn't scale" really means. XP scales quite well in problem size (up to its limit); at the same time, it does not scale in staff size.

- XP, as written, has been demonstrated on projects with up to 12 programmers and four onsite customers. It may have trouble with larger teams due to its reliance on tacit knowledge. It is difficult to build extensive tacit knowledge without good osmotic communication, and that is hard to do with more people than conveniently fit in a room. A larger project team trying XP will have to adjust the teaming structures, interfaces, and use of documentation to accommodate the greater coordination needs of the larger group and the thinner communication lines.

I leave it as an exercise to the inventive practitioner to experiment with these modifications to XP.

WHY METHODOLOGY AT ALL?

At this point it is appropriate to review the reasons for spending so much energy on methodologies at all, because they are the cause of so much argument and frustration the world over.

WHAT A METHODOLOGY ADDRESSES

A methodology addresses "how we work around here." As such, it can serve several uses:

1. Introducing new people to the process

"Hi, how do we work around here?" is a natural question for new team members to ask. It is helpful to have something available so they can learn their place in the organization.

METHODOLOGY IN A DRAWER

On my first hardware design project, my team leader told me,

"We draw the gates and ICs on these D-sized sheets of paper, name at the bottom left. We use only symmetric clocks, triggering on the rising edge. We put our drawings in the drafting department's cabinet, second drawer from the top. Let me know before you do that, though, and we'll schedule a design review . . ."

Even experienced people coming onto the project need to know how to play into the process in action.

2. Substituting people

Although people are not plug-replaceable, they often do need to be replaced.

METHODOLOGY ON THE JOB

A colleague was being hired by a contracting company he didn't know, to do some proposal work in a field he didn't know, for a client he didn't know.

The contract lead sat with him for two days reviewing the company's methodology: who produced what, how the work products were structured, what standards were needed, what his priorities should be, who he would talk to.

I found this an impressive use of methodology. My colleague will walk onto the project and be useful in less than four hours, even though so much of the work will be new to him. Contracting companies make the most use of this aspect of methodologies.

3. Delineating responsibilities

A methodology indicates what is *not* part of a person's job. Thus, XP states that decisions about a story's priority belong to the customer, not the programmer; design estimates are made by the programmers, not the customer.

4. Impressing the sponsors

This force drives construction of thick methodology manuals.

Consider two companies bidding to do work for you. The first says, "We have this carefully thought through and documented process that we have used many times. Here it is in these boxes of binders."

The second says, "We sit close together and trade notes, without writing anything down. In particular, we don't need to write down our methodology, because we are all responsible individuals."

Which would you hire?

The force plays on the natural assumption that a heavier and more precisely choreographed methodology is "safer." It is a nonnegligible factor in the awarding of contracts, even if the process used on the job is not the same as the one that is outlined in the manuals.

5. Demonstrating visible progress

Related to impressing the sponsors, the purpose of the methodology may be to allow the contractors to show their sponsors what they have been doing.

In the methodology my colleague was being taught, a key element was to produce something visible every single day so that the sponsors would *know* that they had been "making progress."

Exercise for the reader: Reconsidering XP in this light, ask yourself what an XP team could show every single day to demonstrate visible progress to the sponsors.

6. Curriculum for education

After a methodology names techniques and standards for people to use, courses can be found or designed that teach skills around those techniques and standards.

For example, the people can be sent, according to their job responsibilities, to develop skills in writing use cases, facilitat-

ing meetings, semantic modeling, programming, and the use of various tools.

People can be sent to learn standards that will be used. The organization might center a class on the subset parts of UML they expect to use or perhaps a variation for real-time systems.

HOW TO EVALUATE A METHODOLOGY

In light of the above, how might you evaluate a methodology?

You would first ask why the methodology exists, and then what game you are playing. Based on those you might evaluate the methodology for:

- How rapidly you can substitute or train people
- How great an effect it has on the sales process
- How much freedom it gives people (or how constraining it is)
- How fast it allows people to respond to changing situations
- How well it protects your organization from lawsuits or other damage

You have undoubtedly noticed that the principles of methodology design presented in this chapter are oriented toward designing methodologies whose priorities are being productive and responsive to change.

I leave as an exercise for another author to capture the principles for methodologies that enhance sales, substitutability, and safety from lawsuits.

WHAT SHOULD I DO TOMORROW?

Start by recognizing that no single methodology definition can possibly suit all projects. Don't even think that the Rational Unified Process, Unified Process, or the Something Else methodology will fit your project *out of the box*. If you follow a methodology out of the box, you will have one that fits some project in the world, but probably not yours.

Practice noticing how the seven principles of methodology design relate to your project:

- Look for where your team could benefit from using warmer communications channels and where cooler ones are needed.
- Identify the bottleneck activities on your project:
  — Track them as they change.
  — Invent ways to utilize some other group's excess capacity to streamline the bottleneck group's work or to reduce uncertainty.
- Reduce the internal deliverables on your project:
  — Arrange for higher-bandwidth communication channels between the developers and opportunities for rapid feedback, and you will find that some of the promissory notes are no longer really needed.
  — Find the bottleneck activities, and see if you can trade efficiency elsewhere for increased productivity at the bottleneck station.

- Find a place where lightening the methodology would actually cause damage. Think about what might be an alternative.
- Review the list of purposes of a methodology. Evaluate the purpose of your group's methodology, and then rank its effectiveness with respect to that purpose.
- Practice naming the scope and elements of your methodology and other methodologies. Observe how much they differ due to addressing different scopes or different priorities.
- Look at the different methodologies in use on different projects, and evaluate them according to how they address their different project sizes.
- Experiment with the difference between problem size and project size.
- Can you think of a project that had more people than it needed?
- Can you think of a difficult problem that was turned into an easy problem through the application of some particular point of view?

Level 2 readers:

- Add these ideas to your bag of tricks.
- Learn where to apply, adjust, and drop them.

Level 3 readers: See if you can explain these ideas to someone else.

5

Agile and Self-Adapting

The pieces of the puzzle are in place. We have seen

- Software development as a cooperative game of invention and communication
- People as funky but good at looking around and taking initiative, communicating particularly well informally, face to face
- Methodology as the set of conventions the team adopts, with different conventions suiting different sorts of projects
- Light methodologies as delivering more quickly but having to become heavier as the team size grows
- Projects as unique ecosystems and the need for a project's methodology to fit the project ecosystem

Everything fits together neatly, except . . . *How light is right for any one project, and how do we do this on our project?*

"Light but Sufficient" discusses how light is right for any one project, and in particular, what it means to be *too light*. The target is to balance lightness with sufficiency.

"Agile" discusses the significance of certain project "sweet spots": colocation, proximity to users, experienced developers, and so on. Less-agile mechanisms must be used as the project moves further away from those sweet spots. Virtual teams, in particular, lie far from the sweet spot and so make agile, distributed development more difficult.

"Becoming Self-Adapting" describes a technique for evolving a light-but-sufficient, project-personal methodology quickly enough to be useful to the project. The key idea is to reflect every few weeks on what works well and what should be changed.

Agile and Self-Adapting

LIGHT BUT SUFFICIENT

The theory so far seems to say that we should use a mostly oral tradition to bind the huge amount of information generated within the project.

Common sense tells us that oral tradition is insufficient.

LOOKING FOR DOCUMENTATION

A programmer told of his company rewriting their current core product because there is no documentation, no one is left who knows how the system was built, and they are unable to make their next changes. He said he hopes there will be documentation after the project, this time.

Another told of three projects, each of which will build on the previous project. The three are not at the same location. He said that they can't possibly work on a strictly oral basis.

It is possible to have too little stickiness in the information at hand. It is time to revisit the Cooperative Game principle:

The primary goal is to deliver software; the secondary goal is to set up for the following game.

Reaching the primary goal is clear: If you don't deliver the software, it won't matter how nicely you have set up for the following game.

If, on the other hand, you deliver the software and do a poor job of setting up for the following game, you jeopardize that game.

The two are competing activities. Balancing the two competing activities relies on two arts.

The first art is guessing how to allocate resources to each goal. Ideally, documentation activities are deferred as long as possible and then made as small as possible. Excessive documentation done too early delays the delivery of the software. If, however, too little documentation is done too late, the person who knows something needed for the next project has already vanished.

The second art is guessing how much can be bound in your group's oral tradition and how much has to be committed to archival documentation. Recall that it does not matter, past a certain point, whether the models and other documentation are complete, correctly match the "real" world (whatever that is), or are up to date with the current version of the code. What matters is whether the people receiving them find them useful for their specific needs.

The correct amount of documentation is exactly that needed for the receiver to make her next move in the game. Any effort to make the models complete, correct, and current past that point is a waste of money.

Usually, the people I have interviewed on the successful projects felt that they had succeeded *"despite* the obviously incomplete documents and sloppy processes" (their words, not mine). Viewed in our current light, however, we can guess that they succeeded exactly because the people made good choices in stopping work on certain communications as soon as they reached sufficiency and before diminishing returns set in. They made the paperwork adequate; they didn't polish it.

Adequate is a great condition if the team is in a race for an end goal and is short on resources.

Recall the programmer who said,

> "It is clear to me as I start creating use cases, object models, and the like that the work is doing some good. But at some point, it stops being useful and starts being both drudgery and a waste of effort. I can't detect when that point is crossed, and I have never heard it discussed. It is frustrating, because it turns a useful activity into a wasteful activity."

We are seeking that point, the one at which useful work becomes wasteful. That is the second art.

BARELY SUFFICIENT

I don't think I need to give examples of overly heavy or overly light methodologies. Most people have seen or heard enough of these.

"Just-barely-too-light" methodologies, on the other hand, are hard to find and are very informative. They are the ones that help us understand what *barely sufficient* means.

Two such project stories are given earlier in the book: "Just Never Documentation" on page 36, and "Sticking Thoughts onto the Wall" on page 98. In each, an otherwise well-run project ran below the level of sufficiency at a key moment.

JUST NEVER DOCUMENTATION (RECAPPED)

This team followed all of the XP practices and delivered software in a timely manner to a receptive customer. At the end of several years, the sponsoring executives slowed and eventually stopped new development.

After the team members dispersed, there was no archived documentation on the system and no team of people conversant with its structure. The formerly sufficient oral culture was now insufficient.

In this story, the team reached the first goal of the game, delivering a running system, but failed to set up for the next game, maintenance and evolution.

Using my own logic against me, one could argue that the documentation was exactly and perfectly sufficient for the needs of the company: The project was canceled, never to be restarted, and so the correct, minimal amount of documentation was *zero*!

However, drawing on Naur's "programming as theory building," we can see that the team members had successfully built up their own "theory" during the creation of the software, but they left insufficient tracks for the next team to benefit from the lessons they had learned.

STICKING THOUGHTS ONTO THE WALL (RECAPPED)

The analysts could not keep track of the domain in their heads, it was so complex. However, they had just switched from a heavy process to XP and thought they were forbidden from producing any paperwork.

As the months went by, they found it increasingly hard to decide what to develop next and to determine the implications of their decisions. They were running below the threshold of sufficiency for their portion of the game. Rather than less, they needed *more* documentation to make their project work.

They eventually recognized their situation and started inventing information holders so that their communications would reach sufficiency.

What we should see is that "insufficiency" lies not in the methodology but in the fit between the methodology and the project as ecosystem. What is barely sufficient for one team may be overly sufficient or insufficient for another. Insufficiency occurs when team members do not communicate well enough for other team members to carry out their work.

The ideal quantity, "barely sufficient," varies by time and place within any one project. The same methodology may be overly sufficient at one moment on a project and insufficient at another moment.

That second art mentioned above is finding the point of "barely sufficient," and then finding it again when it moves.

RECOMMENDATIONS FOR DOCUMENTATION

This leads us to a set of recommendations:

- Don't ask for requirements to be perfect, design documents to be up to date with the code, or the project plan to match the state of the project.
- Ask, instead, that the requirements gatherers capture just enough to communicate with the designers. Ask them to replace typing with faster communications media where possible, including visits in person or short video clips.
- If the designers happen all to be expert and sitting close by each other, ask to dispense with design documentation beyond whiteboard sketches, and then capture the whiteboard drawings with photos or printing whiteboards.
- Bear in mind that there will be other people coming after this design team, people who will, indeed, need more design documentation.
- Run that as a parallel and resource-competing thread of the project instead of forcing it into the linear path of the project's development process.
- Be as inventive as possible about ways to reach the two goals adequately, dodging the impracticalities of being perfect.
- Find (using exaggerated adjectives for a moment) the *lightest, sloppiest* methodology possible for the situation. Make sure it is just rigorous enough that the communication actually is sufficient.

AGILE

Agile implies being effective and maneuverable. An *agile* process is both light and sufficient. The lightness is a means of staying maneuverable. The sufficiency is a matter of staying in the game.

The question for using agile methodologies is not, "Can an agile methodology be used in this situation?" but "How can we remain agile in this situation?"

A 40-person team won't be as agile as a six-person colocated team. However, each team can maximize its use of the agile methodology principles and run as light and fast as circumstances allow. The 40-person team will use a heavier-agile methodology; the six-person team will use a lighter-agile one. Each team will focus on communications, community, frequent wins, and feedback.

If they are paying attention, they will reflect periodically about the fit of their methodology to their ecosystem and keep finding where the point "barely sufficient" has moved.

SWEET SPOTS

Part of getting to *agile* is identifying the sweet spots of effective software development and moving the project as close as possible to those sweet spots.

A team that can arrange to land on any of those sweet spots gets to take advantage of some extra-efficient mechanism. To the extent that the team can't arrange to land in a sweet spot, it must use less-efficient mechanisms. At that point, the team should think creatively to see how to get to the sweet spot and to deal with not being there.

Here are five sweet spots:

Two to Eight People in One Room

Information moves the fastest in this sweet spot.

The people ask each other questions without overly raising their voices. They are aware of when the other people are available to answer questions. They overhear relevant conversations without pausing in their work. They keep the design ideas and project plan on the board, in easy view.

People repeatedly tell me that although this environment can get noisy, their most effective projects have been those in which their small team sat in the same room.

When you leave this sweet spot, the cost of moving information increases very fast. Every doorway, corner, and elevator multiplies that cost.

The story "E-Presence and E-Awareness" on page 83 tells of one team not being able to land in this sweet spot. They used Web cams on their workstations to get some of the presence and awareness of sitting in the same room. They used chat boxes to get answers to the very many small questions that constantly arose. They were creative in mimicking the sweet spot in an otherwise "unsweet" situation.

Onsite Usage Experts

Having a usage expert available at all times means that the feedback time from imagined to evaluated solution is as short as possible, often just minutes to a few hours.

Such rapid feedback means that the development team gains a deeper understanding of the needs and habits of the users and makes fewer mistakes when coming up with new ideas. They try more ideas, which makes for a better final product. With a good sense of collaboration, the programmers will test the usage experts' ideas and offer counter-proposals. This will sharpen the customers' own ideas for how the new system should look.

The cost of missing this sweet spot is a lowered probability of making a really usable product and a much higher cost for running all the experiments.

There are many alternative, if less effective, mechanisms you can use when you can't land on this sweet spot. They have been well documented over the years: weekly interview sessions with the users; ethnographic studies of the user community; surveys; friendly alpha-test groups. There are certainly others.

Missing this sweet spot does not excuse you from getting good user feedback. It just means you have to work harder for it.

One-Month Increments

There is no substitute for rapid feedback, both on the product and on the development process itself. Incremental development is perfect for providing feedback points. Short increments help ensure that both the requirements and the process itself are repaired quickly. The question is, "How long should the delivery increments be?"

The correct answer varies, but project teams I have interviewed vote for one to three months, with a possible reduction to two weeks and a possible extension to four months.

It seems that people are able to focus their efforts for about three months, but not much longer. People tell me that with a longer increment period, they tend to get distracted and lose intensity and drive. In addition, increments provide the team with built-in opportunities to repair its process. The longer the increment, the longer the time between such repair points.

If this were the only consideration, then the ideal increment period might be one week. However, there is a cost to deploying the product at the end of an increment.

I place the sweet spot at around one month but have seen successful use of two- or three-month increments.

If the team cannot deliver to an end user every few months, for some reason, it should prepare a fully built increment in that period and get it ready for delivery (pretending, if necessary, that the sponsor will suddenly demand its delivery). The point of working this way is to exercise every part of the development process and to improve all parts of the process every few months.

Fully Automated Regression Tests

Fully automated regression tests (unit or functional tests, or both) offer two advantages:

- The developers can revise the code and retest it at the push of a button. People who have such tests report that they freely replace and improve awkward modules, knowing that the tests will help keep them from introducing subtle bugs.
- People report that they relax better on the weekends when they have automated regression tests. They run the tests every Monday morning and discover if someone has changed their system without their knowledge.

In other words, automated regression tests improve both the system design quality and the programmers' quality of life.

There are some parts of the system (and some systems) that are difficult to create automated tests for.

One of those is the graphical user interface. Experienced developers know this and allocate special effort to minimize the portions of the system that are not amenable to automated regression tests.

When the system itself does not have automated regression tests, experienced programmers find ways to create automated tests for their own portion of the system.

Experienced Developers

In an ideal situation—the sweet spot—the team consists of only experienced developers. Teams like this that I know

report much different, and better, results compared with the average, mixed team.

Because good, experienced developers may be two to ten times as effective as their colleagues, it is possible to shrink the number of developers drastically if the team consists entirely of experienced developers.

On project Winifred, we estimated before and after the project that six good Smalltalk programmers could develop the system in the needed time frame. Not being able to get six good Smalltalk programmers at that time, we used 24 programmers. The four experienced programmers built most of the difficult parts of the system and spent much of their time helping the inexperienced programmers.

If you can't land in this sweet spot, consider bringing in a half-time or full-time trainer or mentor to increase the abilities of the inexperienced people.

THE TROUBLE WITH VIRTUAL TEAMS

Virtual is a euphemism meaning *not sitting together*. With the current popularity of this word, project sponsors excuse themselves for imposing enormous communication barriers on their teams.

We have seen the damage caused to a project by having people sit apart. The speed of development is related to the time and energy cost per idea transfer, with large increases in transfer cost as the distance between people increases and large lost opportunity costs when some key question does not get asked. Splitting up the team is just asking for added project costs.

I categorize geographically distributed teams into three sorts, some of them more damaging than others. My terms for them are *multisite*, *offshore*, and *distributed* development.

Multisite Development

Multisite development occurs when a larger team works in relatively few locations, each location contains a complete development group developing a subsystem, and the subsystems are relatively well decoupled.

Multisite development has been performed successfully for decades.

The key in multisite development is to have full and competent teams in each location and to make sure that the leaders in each location meet often enough to share their vision and understanding.

Although many things can go wrong in multisite development, it has worked many times, and there are fairly standard rules about getting it to work (unlike the other two virtual team models).

Offshore Development

Offshore development is when "designers" in one location send specifications and tests to "programmers" in another location, usually in another country.

Because the offshore location lacks architects, designers, and testers, this is quite different from multisite development.

Here is how offshore development looks, using the words of cooperative games and convection currents:

The designers at the one site have to communicate their ideas over a thin communications channel to people who have a different vocabulary and sit several time zones away. The programmers need a thousand questions answered. When they find mistakes in the design, they have to do three expensive things: first, wait until the next phone or video meeting; second, convey their observations; and third, convince the designers of the possible mistake in the design. The cost in erg-seconds per meme is staggering, the delays enormous.

TESTING OFFSHORE CODING

One designer told me that his team had to specify the program to the level of writing the code itself and then had to write tests to make sure that the programmers had correctly implemented every line they had written. The designers did all the paperwork they considered unpleasant, without the reward of being able to do the programming.

In the time they spent specifying and testing, they could have written the code themselves, and they would have been able to discover their design mistakes much faster.

I have not been able to find methodologically successful offsite development projects. They fail the third test: The people I have interviewed have vowed not to do it again.

Fortunately, some offshore software houses are converting their projects into something more like multisite development, with architects, designers, programmers, and testers at the programming location. Although the communications line is still long and thin, the team members can at least gain some of the feedback and communication advantages of multisite development.

Distributed Development

Distributed development is when a team is spread across relatively *many* locations with relatively few, and often only one or two, people per location.

Distributed development is becoming more commonplace, but it is not becoming more effective. The cost of transferring ideas is great, and the lost opportunity costs of undetected questions is even greater. The distributed development model works when it mimics multisite development, with meaningful subteams of one or two people. In this scenario, each person's assignment is clear and contained.

However, the following is more common:

CRISS-CROSSED DISTRIBUTION

A company was developing four related products in four locations, each product having multiple subsystems.

A sweet spot would be to have all systems of one product developed at the same location, or one subsystem for all products. With either of these, the people would be physically proximate to the people they needed to exchange information with.

Instead, the dozens of people involved were arranged so that people working in the same city worked on different subsystems of different products. They were surrounded by people whose work had little to do with theirs and were separated from those with whom they needed to communicate!

Occasionally, people tell of developing software effectively with someone at a different location. This indicates that there is something new to discover: What permits these people to communicate so well over such a thin communications line? Is it just a lucky alignment of their personalities or thinking styles? Have they constructed a small multisite model? Or, are they drawing on something that most of us haven't learned to name yet?

SUCCESSFUL DISTRIBUTED DEVELOPMENT

I spent an evening talking with a couple of people who were successfully using four or five people who *never* met as a group.

They said that besides partitioning the problem carefully, they spent *a lot of time* on the phone, calling each person multiple times each day.

In addition to those obvious tactics, the team coordinator worked particularly hard to keep trust and amicability levels very high. She visited each developer every few weeks and made sure that they found her visits helpful (not blame sessions).

This coordinator was interested in replicating the successful development model.

We concluded, by the end of the evening, that she would need to find another development coordinator like herself—someone with a similar personal talent for developing trust and amicability.

Two aspects of their development struck me:

• Their attention to building trust among themselves
• The vast amount of energy they invested into communication on a daily basis, to achieve opportunistic learning, trust, and feedback

Open-Source Development

Open-source development, although similar in appearance to distributed development, differs in its philosophical, economic, and team structure models.

In contrast to the resource-constrained cooperative game most software development projects play, an open-source project is playing a *non-resource-constrained* cooperative game.

An industrial project aims to reach its goal in a given time frame with a given amount of money. The constraints of money and time limit how many people can work on it, and for how long. In these games we hear three phrases:

"Finish it before the market window closes!"

"Your job is to make the trade-off between quality and development time!"

"Ship it!"

An open-source development project, on the other hand, runs with the idea that with enough eyes, minds, fingers, and time, really good designs and really good-quality code will show up. There is, in principle, an unlimited number of people interested in contributing and no particular market window to hit. The project has its own life and existence. Each person improves the system where it is weak, at whatever rate that time and energy indicate.

The reward structure is also different, being based on intrinsic—as opposed to external—rewards. (See "Individuals" on page 41.) People develop open-source code for pleasure, as a service to a community they care about, and for peer recognition. The motivational model is discussed at length in "Homesteading the Noosphere" (Raymond URL).

A goal for an industrial developer would be to become the next Bill Gates. The corresponding goal for an open-source developer would be to become the next Linus Torvalds.

Finally, the open-source team structure of open-source development is different. Anyone can contribute code, but a designated gatekeeper protects the center, the code base. That gatekeeper does not need to be the best programmer but needs to be a good programmer with good people skills and a very good eye for quality. Over time, the best few contributors come to occupy the center, becoming intellectual owners of the design. Around these few people is an unlimited number of people who contribute patches and code suggestions, detect and report bugs, and write documentation.

It has been suggested, and is plausible, that one of the key aspects of open-source development is that *all communication is visible to anyone*. Consider the following comparison with industrial projects:

On an industrial project with a colocated team, trouble occurs if the team evolves into a society with an upper and a lower class. If analysts sit on one side of the building and programmers sit on the opposite side, an "us-them" separation easily builds that causes hostility between the groups (you could also say "factions"). In a well-balanced team, however, there is only "us"; there is not an "us-them" separation. A key role in the presence or absence of this split is the nature of the background chitchat within the group. When the seating forms enclaves of common specialists, that background chitchat almost inevitably contains comments about "them."

In open-source development, the equivalent situation would be that one subgroup, the colocated one, is thought to be having a set of discussions that the others cannot participate in. The people in the distributed group might be inclined to develop a sense of being second-class citizens, cut away from the heart of the community and cut off from relevant and interesting conversations.

When all communication is online, visible to everyone, there is no natural place for rumors to grow in hiding; once again, there is only "us."

I would like one day to see or do a decent investigation of this aspect of open-source development.

BECOMING SELF-ADAPTING

If you have been reading this book from the beginning, you should still see one mystery at this point.

Every person is different, every project is different, and each project differs internally across subject areas, subsystems, subteams, and time. Each situation calls for a different methodology (set of group conventions).

The mystery is how to construct a different methodology for each situation, without spending so much time designing the methodology that the team doesn't deliver software. You also don't want everyone on your project to have to become a methodology expert.

I hope you can guess what's coming.

BOTHER TO REFLECT

The trick to fitting your conventions to your ever-changing needs is to do two things, individually and as a team:

1. *Bother to think about what you are doing.*
2. *Have the team spend one hour together every other week reflecting on its working habits.*

If you do these two things, you can make your methodology effective, agile, and tailored to your situation. If you can't do that, well . . . you will stay where you are.

Although the magical ingredient is remarkably simple, it is quite difficult to pull off, given people's funky nature. People usually resist having the meeting. In some organizations, the distrust level is so high that people will not speak at such a get-together.

In this case, there is only one thing to do:

Do it once, post the results, and then see if you can do it again.

You may need to find someone within your organization who has the personal skills to make the meeting work. You may need to go outside your organization for the first few times, to get someone with the right personal skills and whom everyone in the room can accept.

A METHODOLOGY-GROWING TECHNIQUE

Here is a technique for on-the-fly methodology construction and tuning. I present it as what to do at five different times:

- Right now
- At the start of the project
- In the middle of the first increment
- After each increment
- In the middle of subsequent increments

After that, I describe a sample one-hour reflection workshop.

Right Now

Discover the strengths and weaknesses of your organization through short project interviews.

You can do this at the start of the project, but you can also do this right away, regardless of where you are in any project. The information will do you good in all cases, and you can start to build your own project interview collection.

Ideally, have several people interview several other people each, and start your collection with six to ten interview reports. It is useful but not critical to interview more than one person on one project. For example, you might talk to any two of the following: the project manager, the team lead, a user interface designer, and a programmer. Their different perspectives on the same project will prove informative. Even more informative, however, will be the common responses across multiple projects.

The important thing to keep in mind is that *whatever* the interviewee says is relevant. During an interview, I don't give my own opinions about any matter but use my judgement to select a next question to ask.

I suggest that you structure your interviews in this sequence as well:

1. Ask to see one sample of each work product produced.
2. Ask for a short history of the project.
3. Ask what should be changed next time.
4. Ask what should be repeated next time.
5. Identify priorities.
6. Find any holes.

Step 1. Ask to see one sample of each work product produced. Looking at these, you can detect how much bureaucracy was likely to be on the project and see what questions you should ask about the work products.

Look for duplicated work, places where the work products might have been difficult to keep up to date.

Ask whether iterative development was in use, and if so, how the documents were updated in following iterations.

Look, in particular, for ways in which informal communication was used to patch over inconsistencies in the paperwork.

WORK PRODUCT REDUNDANCY

On one project, the team lead showed me 23 work products.

I noticed a fair degree of overlap among them, and so I asked if the later ones were generated by tools from the earlier ones.

The team lead said no, the people had to reenter them from scratch.

So I followed up by asking how the people felt about this. He said they really hated it, but he made them do it anyway.

After looking at the work samples,

Step 2. Ask for a short history of the project. Record date started, staff changes (growing and shrinking), team structure, the emotionally high and low points of the project life.

Do this to calibrate the size and type of the project and to detect where there may be other interesting questions to ask.

DISCOVERING INCREMENTAL DEVELOPMENT

That is how I learned the fascinating story about the project I call "Ingrid" (Cockburn 1998).

During just the project inception phase, the team had hit most of the failure indicators I knew at the time. That their first four-month increment was a catastrophe came as no surprise to me. I even wondered why I had traveled so far just to hear about such an obvious failure.

The surprise was in what they did after that.

After that first increment, they changed almost everything about the project. I had never seen that done before.

Four months later, they rebuilt the project again—not as drastically, but enough to make a difference.

Every four months they delivered running, tested software, and then they sat down to examine what they were doing and how to get better (just as I am asking you to do).

The most amazing thing was that they didn't just talk about changing their way of working, they actually changed their way of working.

The value of this interview lay not in our discussing deliverables but in my hearing their phenomenal determination to succeed and their willingness to change—every four months—whatever was necessary to get the success they wanted.

After hearing the history of the project and listening for interesting threads of inquiry to pursue,

Step 3. Ask what should be changed next time. Ask, "What were the key things you did wrong that you wouldn't want to repeat on your next project?"

Write down whatever they say, and fish around for related issues to investigate.

After hearing the things not to repeat,

Step 4. Ask what should be repeated the next time. Ask, "What were the key things you did right that you would certainly like to preserve in your next project?"

Write down whatever they say. If the person says, "Well, the Thursday afternoon volleyball games were really good," write that down.

GETTING SERIOUSLY DRUNK TOGETHER

Once when I asked this question (in Scandinavia), a person said, "Getting seriously drunk together."

We went out and practiced that night, and I did, indeed, see improved teamwork between the people the next day.

In response to this question, people have named everything from where they sit, to having food in the refrigerator, to social activities, communication channels, software tools, software architecture, and domain modeling. Whatever you hear, write it down.

Step 5. Identify priorities. Ask, "What are your priorities with respect to the things you liked on the project? What is most critical to keep, and what is most negotiable?" Write those down.

It is useful to ask at this point, "Was there anything that surprised you about the project?"

Step 6. Find any holes. Finally, ask whether there is anything else you should hear about, and see where that goes.

At one company, we constructed a two-page interview template on which to write the results, so we could exchange them easily. That template contained the following sections:

1. Project name, job of person interviewed (the interviewee remains anonymous)
2. Project data (start/end dates, maximum staff, target domain, technology in use).
3. Project history
4. Did wrong/would not repeat

5. Did right/would preserve
6. Priorities
7. Other

Do this exercise, collect the filled-in templates, and look them over. Depending on your situation, you might have each interviewer talk about the interview, or you may just all read the notes.

Look for common themes across the projects.

THE COMMUNICATION THEME

At the company where we created the template, one theme showed up across the projects:

"When we have good communications with the customer sponsors and within the team, we have a good outcome. When we don't have good communications, we don't have good results."

Although that may seem trivially true, it seldom gets written down and attended to. In fact, within a year of that result, the following story occurred at that company:

THE COMMUNICATION THEME IN ACTION

Mine was one of three projects going on at the same time, each of which involved small teams with people sitting in several cities.

As you would expect I spent a great deal of energy on communications with the sponsors and programmers.

The three projects were completed at about the same time. The director of development asked me what the difference could be—why the project I was on was successful while the other two that ran at the same time were unsuccessful.

Recalling the project interviews, I suggested it might have something to do with the quality of communication between the development and sponsoring groups, and within the team.

He said this was an interesting idea. Both the programmers and the sponsors on the other projects had reported problems in communicating with their project leads. Both programmers and sponsors had felt isolated. The sponsors of my project, on the other hand, had been very happy with the communications.

The theme was different in another company. Here is what one interviewee told me:

THE CULTURAL GAP THEME

Our user interface designers all have Ph.D.s in psychology and sit together several floors above the programmers.

There is an educational, a cultural, and a physical gap between them and the programmers.

We have some difficulty due to the different approach of these people, and to the distance we sit from them.

This company will need extra mechanisms to increase contact between those two groups of people and extra reviews of their work.

The point of these stories is to highlight that what you learn in the interviews is likely to be relevant on your next project. Pay attention to the warnings that come up in the project interviews.

At the Start of the Project

Expect to do some tailoring to the corporate methodology standard. This will be needed whether the base methodology is ISO9001, XP, RUP, Crystal, or a local brew.

Stage 1: Base methodology to be tuned.

If possible, have two people work together on creating the base methodology proposal for the project. It will go faster, they will spot each other's errors, and they will help each other come up with ideas.

They have four steps to go through:

1. Determine how many people are going to be coordinated and identify their geographic distribution (see the grid in Figure 4-23). Decide what level of correctness is expected of this software and what degree of damage it could cause. Determine and write down the priorities for the project: time to market, correctness, or whatever they may be.
2. Using the methodology design principles from Chapter 4, select the basic parameters for the methodology: how tight the standards need to be, the extent of documentation needed, the ceremony in the reviews, the increment length (the time period until running code is delivered to real, even if sample, users).

If the increment length is longer than four months, they will have to find some way to create a tested, running version of the system every four months or less, to simulate having real increments.

3. Select a base for the methodology, one that is not too different from the way in which they would like to work.

Recall that it is easier to modify an existing methodology than to invent one from scratch. They may choose to start from the corporate standard, the published Unified Process, XP, Crystal Clear, Crystal Orange, or the last project's methodology.

4. Boil the methodology down to the basic work flow involved—who hands what to whom—and the conventions they think the group should agree to.

These steps could take between a day and a few days to complete for a small- or medium-sized project. If it looks like they will spend more than a week on it, then get one or two more people from the project team involved and drive it to completion in just two more days.

Stage 2: The starter methodology. Hold a team meeting to discuss the base methodology's work flow and conventions, and adjust it to become the starter methodology. For larger projects, where it is impractical to gather the whole team, gather the key representatives of each job role.

The purpose of the meeting is to

- Catch embellishments
- Look for ways to streamline the process and ways to communicate with less cost
- Detect other issues that were not spotted in the base methodology draft

Consider these questions in that meeting:
- How long are the iterations and increments to be (and what is the difference)?

- Where will people sit?
- What can be done to keep communication and morale high?
- Which work products and reviews will be needed, at what ceremony levels?
- Which standards for tools, drawings, tests, and code are mandatory, and which are just recommended?
- How will time reporting be done?
- Which other conventions should be set initially, and which might be evolved over time?

An important agenda item for the meeting is selecting a way for the team to detect morale and communication problems.

The meeting results will include:

- Basic work flow
- Hand-off criteria between roles, particularly including overlapped development and declaration milestones
- Draft standards or conventions to be followed
- Peculiarities of communication to be practiced

This is your starter methodology.

The meeting could take half a day but should not exceed one day.

In the Middle of the First Increment

Whether your increment length is two weeks or three months, run a small interview with the team members, individually or in a group meeting, at approximately the mid-point of the increment. Allow one to three hours.

The single question for resolution is,

"Are we going to make it, working the way we are working?"

In the first increment, you can't afford to change your group's whole way of working unless it is catastrophically broken. What you are looking for is to get safely to your first delivery. If the starter methodology will hold up that long, you will have more time, more insight, and a better moment to adjust it, *after* you have successfully made your first delivery.

Therefore, the purpose of this interview or meeting is to detect whether something is critically wrong and whether the first delivery will fail.

If you discover that the team's way of working isn't working, *first* consider reducing the scope of the first delivery.

Most teams overstate how much they can deliver in the first increment. This is simply normal and not a fault of the methodology. It is a result of over-ambitious management driving the schedule unrealistically and overly optimistic developers who overlook the learning to be done, the meetings to be held, and the normal bugs they put into the code. It comes from underestimating the learning curve of new technology and new teammates. Overstating how much can be delivered in the first increment is really quite normal.

Therefore, your first approach is to reduce scope.

You may, however, discover that reducing scope will not be sufficient. You may discover that the requirements are incomprehensible to the programmers or that the architects won't get their architecture specification finished in time.

If this is the case, then you need to react quickly and find a new way of working. This, combined with a drastically reduced functional scope, will allow you to meet that first delivery deadline.

You may introduce overlapped development or put people physically closer together, cut down the ambition level for the initial architecture or make greater use of informal communication channels. You may have to make emergency staff changes or introduce emergency training, consulting, or experienced contractors.

Your goal is to deliver *something*: some small, running, tested code in the first increment. This is a critical success factor on a project (Cockburn 1998). After you deliver this first release, you will have time to pause and consider what is happening.

After Each Increment

Hold a team reflection workshop after each increment.

Bothering to reflect is a critical success factor in evolving a successful methodology, just as incremental development is a critical success factor in delivering software.

The length of this reflection workshop may vary from company to company or country to country. Americans like to be always busy, short of money, and on the run. I see Americans allocating only two to four hours for this workshop. In other parts of the world, the workshop may be given more time.

I once participated in a two-day offsite version that combined reflection, team building, and planning for the next increment. It took place in Europe, not surprisingly.

The dominant reason for delaying this workshop until after the first increment is that you can only properly evaluate the effects of each element in your methodology after you have delivered running, tested software to a user. Only then can you see what was overdone and what was underdone.

There is a second reason for holding the workshop at the end of the increment: People are quite often exhausted after getting the software out the door. This meeting provides a chance to breathe and reflect. Done regularly, it becomes part of the project rhythm. After each increment, the team members benefit from a short shifting of mental and social gears.

Whether you take two hours or two days, the two questions you want to address are:

1. "What did we learn?"
2. "What can we do better?"

The responses may cross every boundary of the project, from management intervention to timecards, group communication, seating, project reviews, standards, and team composition.

Very often, teams tighten standards after the first increment, get more training, streamline the work flow, increase testing, and reorganize the teaming structures.

The changes will be much smaller after the second and subsequent increments, because by then the team will have already delivered several times.

In the Middle of the Subsequent Increments

After the first increment, the team has established one (barely) successful way of working. This is a methodology design to fall back on, if needed.

Having that as a fallback plan, you can be much more adventuresome in suggesting changes in the mid-increment meetings you hold in the second and later increments.

In those mid-increment meetings, and particularly after the second successful delivery, look to invent new and better ways of delivering.

See if you can do any of the following:

- Cut out entire sections of the methodology.
- Do more concurrent development.
- Use informal communications more to bind the project information.
- Introduce new and better testing frameworks.
- Introduce new and better test-writing habits.
- Get closer collaboration between the key groups in the project: between domain and usage experts, programmers, testers, training people, the customer care center, and the people doing field repair.

You might use interviews or a reflection workshop for these mid-increment adjustments. By this time, your team will have had quite a bit of practice with these meetings and will have an idea of how to behave.

You can omit the mid-increment workshops if the project is using increments of three weeks or less.

Why bother with mid-increment reviews, when the project is already delivering and you already have post-increment reviews in place?

In the middle of the development cycle, those things that are not working properly are right in people's faces. The details of the problems will not be as clear four or six weeks later, at the post-increment meeting. Therefore, you can pick up more details in the middle of the increment, get feedback immediately about the idea, and try out a new idea the same day instead of waiting several weeks or months.

What if a new idea doesn't work out?

Sometimes the team tries a new idea on the second or third increment and finds that the idea simply does not work well.

MID-PROJECT TEAM STRUCTURE CHANGES

On one project, we went through three different team structures during the third increment.

A short way into the third increment, we decided that the team structure we had been using was weak. So we chose a new team structure to use on increment three.

It was catastrophically bad. We knew within two weeks that we had to change it immediately.

Rather than revert to the original, awkward-but-successful team structure, we created a new suggestion and tried it out right away.

It turned out to be successful, and we kept it for the duration of the project.

In inventing new ways of working in these later increments, you create the opportunity to significantly improve your methodology. This is an opportunity not to be missed.

The Post-Project Review

Given the mid- and post-increment reflection workshops, I place less emphasis on having post-project reviews. I feel that the time to reflect is during the project, when the reflection and discussion will do the project some good. After the project, it is too late.

Usually, I find that teams that run post-project reviews did not bother to reflect during the project and suddenly want to know how to do better for the next project. If you find yourself in such a meeting, put forward the suggestion that next time you want to use incremental development and hold post-increment reviews instead.

Nonetheless, it may be that the post-project review is the only time you get to make statements regarding the staffing and project management used. If this is the case, I suggest getting and using the book *Project Retrospectives* (Kerth 2001), which describes how to run a two-day post-project review.

If you hold a post-project review, think about who is going to make use of the information and what they can really use as they run their next project. You might draft a short (two-page) set of notes for the next project team to read, outlining the lessons learned from this project.

Of course, you might write yourself a one-page "lessons learned" reminder after each of your own increments, as a normal outcome of your reflection workshop.

A REFLECTION WORKSHOP TECHNIQUE

The tangible output of a mid- or post-increment reflection workshop is a flipchart that is then posted on the wall in some prominently visible place and seen by the project participants as they go about their business.

I like to write directly on the flipchart that will be posted. It is the one that contains the group memories. Other people like to copy the list from the scratched-and scribbled-on flipchart to a fresh sheet for posting. The people who created the one shown in Figure 3-10 decided to use sticky notes instead of writing on the flipchart.

A Sample Reflection Workshop Technique

There are several different formats for running the workshop and for sharing the results (of course). I tend to run the simplest version I can think of. It goes approximately like this:

A REFLECTION WORKSHOP

Hi, welcome to this workshop to reflect on how we can get better at producing our software.

The purpose of this meeting is not to point fingers, to blame people, or to escape blame. It is to announce where we are getting stuck and nominate ideas for getting past that stuckness.

The outcome of this workshop will be a single flipchart on which we'll write the ideas we intend to try out during the next increment, the things we want to keep in mind as we work.

Let's break this flipchart into three pieces.

On the left side, let's capture the things we are doing well that we want to make sure we don't lose in the next increment.

On the right side, let's capture the new things we want to focus on doing.

On the supposition that the list of what we're doing right will be the shorter of the two, let's write down the major problems we're fighting with, halfway down the left side here (see Figure 5-1).

Let's start with what we're doing right. Is there anything that we're doing right, that we want to make sure we keep around for the next increment?

At this point some discussion ensues. It is possible that someone starts naming problem areas, instead of strong areas. If the problems are significant, write them down under the Problems section. Allow some time for people to reflect and discuss.

Keep These	Try These
Test lock-down	Pair testing
Quiet time	Fines for interruptions
Daily meetings	Programmers help testers
Problems	
Too many interruptions	
Shipping buggy code	

Figure 5-1 Sample poster from reflection workshop.

Eventually, move the discussion along:

> All right, what are some of the key problems we had the last time, and what can we do to improve things?

Write as little as possible in the Problems section: Write as few words as possible, and merge problems together if possible. The point of this poster is to post suggestions for improvement, not to focus on problems.

Collect the suggestions. If the list gets very long, question how many new practices or habits the group really wants to take on during this next period. It is sometimes depressing to see an enormous list of reminders. It is more effective to have a shorter list of things to focus on. Writing on a single flipchart with a fat flipchart pen is a nice, self-limiting way of handling this.

Periodically, see if someone has thought of more things the team is doing right that should be kept.

Toward the end of the workshop, review the list. See if people really are in agreement to try the new ideas or if they were just being quiet.

After the workshop, post the list where everyone can see it.

At the start of the next workshop, you might bring in the poster from the previous workshop and start by asking whether this way of writing and posting the workshop outcome was effective, or what else you might try.

Holding this meeting every two to six weeks will allow your team to track its local and evolving culture, to create its own, agile methodology.

The Value of Reflection

The article on *Shu-Ha-Ri* excerpted in the Introduction continues with the following very relevant discussion of reflection:

"As you learn a technique, and as it asymptotically approaches your mental model of the technique as you see others practicing it, you can begin to reason about the technique. It seems the important questions to ask are:

1. How does this technique work?
2. Why does this technique work?
3. How is this technique related to other techniques that I am practicing?
4. What are the necessary preconditions and postconditions to effectively apply this technique in the combative situation? . . .

As you develop a reasonable repertoire of techniques that you can perform correctly, you will need to expose yourself to as broad a range of practitioners as possible. As you watch others, you need to ask and answer at least three questions:

1. Which other practitioners do I respect and admire?
2. How is what they do different from what I do?
3. How can I change my practice (both mental model and attempts to correspond to it) to incorporate the differences that I think are most important? . . .

The questions you need to ask yourself about a competition in your post-mortems are:

1. Were you able to control the pace and actions of your opponents.
2. Were you able to keep calm and make your techniques effectively with an unhurried frame of mind.

3. Does your competition look like those of the practitioners you admire. . . .

Throughout all of this, you must honestly evaluate the results of each 'test'. Cycle back to Shu through Ha and then Ri as you go down dead end paths."

I couldn't say it better.

WHAT SHOULD I DO TOMORROW?

Consider *agile* as an attitude, not a formula. In that frame of mind, look at your current project and ask, "How can we, in this situation, work in an agile way?"

- Look for how far you are from the sweet spots in your development team. See how creative you can be in getting closer to or simulating them.
- Look for where your team can lighten its methodology. Look for where it is not yet sufficient.
- Perform one project interview as described.
- Get several people to perform one project interview each, and share the results. Find the common thread in your interview results.

- Hold a one-hour reflection workshop within your project. As you encounter difficulty in this, reflect on which aspects of people are showing up; compare them to the list in Chapter 3. Look for antidotes, and extend the list. Post the reflection workshop flipchart, and notice how many people ever look at it.
- See what it takes to hold a second reflection workshop. Learn how to get people to complain less and make more positive suggestions at these workshops.

Develop yourself into a Level 2 methodology designer. Yes, it is part of your profession.

6

The Crystal Methodologies

This chapter describes how I resolved the dilemmas involved in methodology design: the difficulty of communication, the need for people to be *people* within the methodology, and the need for multiple methodologies.

I chose to construct a *family* of methodologies, along with principles for tuning them. This is not a kit of methodology parts for you to assemble on your own but a set of samples that you adjust to your circumstances.

Crystal is the family name for the methodologies. As with geological crystals, each has a different color and hardness, corresponding to the project size and criticality: Clear, Yellow, Orange, Orange Web, Red, Magenta, Blue, and so on. Each one

- Is people- and communication-centric
- Gets adjusted to fit its particular setting
- Works from the project tolerance level and the bottleneck activities to an answer that matches the project ecosystem

This chapter describes three members of the Crystal family that have been put to use on live projects: Crystal Clear, Crystal Orange, and Crystal Orange Web. For each one, I

- Describe the project characteristics for which the methodology is appropriate
- Describe the methodology itself
- Reflect on the construction of the methodology

The reason for including this chapter is to show one way of working through the problems and principles surrounding methodology design and to give you something to copy and alter when you start on your own.

The Crystal Methodologies

SHAPING THE CRYSTAL FAMILY

Two plausible responses to the problem of needing multiple methodologies are to

- Create a kit of methodology parts that the project team assembles for its project
- Create a copy-and-alter family of specific methodologies that can be tailored on each project

Rational Corporation used the kit approach in the first generation of its methodology product, the Rational Unified Process (RUP) (Kruchten 1999). RUP is a framework for constructing methodologies for individual projects. It is centered on processes, work products, and tools and includes a collection of "best practices" to guide the practitioner along the way.

The assembling of a correct methodology for a RUP project hinges around creating a "development case" for the project and then assembling the parts from the RUP kit that fit the development case (Larman 2002).

The standard mistake managers make is not to do that assembling and tuning. They drop the library of work products on the development team and say, "Do that." The developers do one of two things:

- They recognize that producing all of those work products will damage the project, and so they ignore the manager's instructions.
- They do as they are told and produce all of those work products (and damage the project accordingly).

RUP is not incompatible with the principles developed in this book, but it doesn't naturally lead people to focus on the two key success factors: communication and community.

My hope is that after reading this book, managers who buy RUP will allocate time to get it tuned to their projects. I also hope that the people who do the tuning will cut down the required work products produced to the smallest possible set and augment RUP with attention to communication, community, concurrent development, and so on.

An alternative way of approaching methodology-per-project is to collect a set of concrete, sample methodologies that have been used on projects and let the people on the project use the tailoring techniques described in the last chapter to adjust them on the fly.

This is the approach Jim Highsmith and I are following. We are collecting examples of successfully used communication- and community-based agile methodologies that people can use as starting points.

By seeing one that is already written, the new project team can see how the communication and community issues were addressed in a real situation. By having a set of examples to choose from, the team can find the one that most closely matches its situation.

I call the methodologies I design *Crystal*.

The word *Crystal* serves two purposes:

First, it is just a pleasant name. In the book Crystal Clear, a protagonist called

Crystal personifies the methodology and argues for its design.

Second, it provides a metaphor that supports the first two degrees shown in the project grid in Figure 4-21.

Moving to the right in the grid means coordinating more people, which requires a heavier methodology. Using the crystal metaphor, moving right corresponds to choosing a darker color (clear quartz, topaz, ruby, sapphire).

Movement up in the grid corresponds to more potential damage from the system and the use of more rigor and ceremony. Using the crystal metaphor, moving up means increasing "hardness" (in the mineral hardness scale, the diamond—the hardest stone—receives hardness number 10).

Thus, according to the crystal metaphor, two people programming the overtime food menu are working on a project that calls for a soft, clear quartz crystal methodology. The two people programming the movement of boron rods in a nuclear reactor are working on a project that calls for a diamond-category methodology.

Of the two dimensions, I find the color dimension more useful as the project index. The hardness dimension can be more easily picked up in the methodology-tuning workshops.

I therefore index the Crystal methodologies by color: Clear, Yellow, Orange, Red, Magenta, Blue, Violet, and so on (Figure 6-1).

In Figure 6-1, I omit life-critical systems from the shaded areas. This is because I have not worked on or interviewed people about life-critical-system projects and so don't have enough information to say exactly how an agile life-critical project looks.

The E6 box, outside Crystal Clear, indicates that Crystal Clear does not explicitly address "essential monies" projects but that the team may be able to stretch Crystal Clear to such a situation.

The other restriction on Crystal methodologies is that they only address colocated teams. As discussed earlier, none of the distributed and offshore development projects I have seen would count as methodologically successful. The only recommendation I have for such projects is to put the team together at one location.

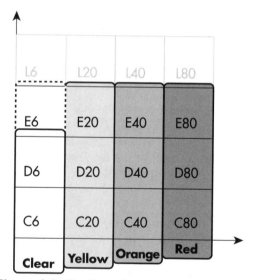

Figure 6-1 The Crystal methodologies are named by color.

Crystal does not aim to be upward or downward compatible. In using computer hardware, there are large financial consequences to changing hardware, which cause compatibility to be a key issue. I don't see similar consequences in moving up and down the methodology scale. People working on a four-person project that grows to become a 20-person project shouldn't ask, "How do I preserve our former working conventions?" They should ask, "What is a good way for 20 people to work together?"

CORE CRYSTAL ELEMENTS

The core Crystal philosophy is that software development is usefully viewed as a cooperative game of invention and communication, with a primary goal of delivering useful, working software and a secondary goal of setting up for the next game.

Two consequences of that philosophy are that different projects need to be run differently, and the amount of modeling and communication that people need to do is just the amount they need to jointly move the game forward.

Members of the Crystal family share

- Values and principles
- On-the-fly tuning

Two values are that Crystal methodologies are intrinsically

- People- and communication-centric
- Highly tolerant

The former means that tools, work products, and processes are there only to support the human component. The latter recognizes varying human cultures.

Within the tolerance of the Crystal family, though, the team can choose to work in a high-ceremony or high-discipline manner (adopting parts of PSP or XP, for example).

Seven principles were discussed in Chapter 4, "Methodologies." The principles are roughly summarized as follows:

- The team can reduce intermediate work products as it produces running code more frequently and as it uses richer communication channels between people.
- Because every project is different and evolves over time, the set of conventions the team adopts must also be shaped and must evolve.
- The shifting bottlenecks in the system determine the use of overlapped work and "sticky" information holders.

The two rules common to the Crystal family are:

- The project must use incremental development, with increments of four months or less (and a strong preference for one- to three-month increments).
- The team must hold pre- and post-increment reflection workshops (with a strong preference for holding mid-increment reflection workshops as well).

The two base techniques in Crystal are:

- The methodology-tuning technique: using project interviews and a team workshop to convert a base methodology to a starter methodology for the project
- The technique used to hold the reflection workshop

You are welcome to replace those two techniques with others if you have another way of accomplishing these goals.

Attending to the above issues creates a particular feeling. As someone wrote, it is possible to make another methodology *look* like a Crystal project without making it *feel* like a Crystal project. A visitor to a successful Crystal project will notice communications and community in action and will observe pragmatism in reaching the two goals of the cooperative game.

The following three sections describe the three Crystal methodologies I have so far constructed and seen used.

The structural differences between them are obvious. See if you can spot the commonalities.

CRYSTAL CLEAR

Crystal Clear is a methodology for D6-category projects. You should be able to stretch Crystal Clear to an E8 or D10 category project with some attention to communication and testing, respectively. I expect it to be difficult to extend beyond that, because Crystal Clear contains no communication structure for more people than can conveniently work in the same room and lacks the system-validation elements needed for life-critical systems.

BRIEF DESCRIPTION OF CRYSTAL CLEAR

There is only one team, seated in one office or in adjoining offices.

The roles needing separate people are

- Sponsor
- Senior designer-programmer
- Designer-programmer
- User (part-time at least)

One of those people may pick up the assignment of being project coordinator. Someone will be the business expert, and either one or many people will share the role of requirements gatherer.

The senior designer-programmer is the key person on the team. The other designer-programmers may comprise some mixture of novice and medium levels, depending on what the senior designer-programmer and the problem can support. Hiring people who know their jobs well helps.

The policy standards are that

- Software is delivered incrementally and regularly, every two to three months

- Progress is tracked by milestones consisting of software deliveries or major decisions, as opposed to written documents
- There is some amount of automated regression testing of application function
- There is direct user involvement
- There are two user viewings per release
- Downstream activities start as soon as upstream is "stable enough to review"
- Product- and methodology-tuning workshops are held at the start and middle of each increment

The policy standards are mandatory, but equivalent substitution is permitted as would be the case if Scrum work scheduling (Schwaber 2002), XP, or Adaptive Software Development (Highsmith 2000) policies were used.

The work products that are produced include:

- Release sequence
- Schedule of user viewings and deliveries
- Annotated use cases or feature descriptions
- Design sketches and notes as needed
- Screen drafts
- A common object model
- Running code
- Migration code
- Test cases
- User manual

The following are left as "local matters," to be set and maintained by the team:

- Templates for the work products
- Standards for coding and user interface
- Standards and details of regression testing

Crystal Clear *does* require project documentation to be created. Just what that documentation consists of is not spelled out by Crystal. That is left as a matter of local judgement. The combined team must decide how to present design notes to future team members.

The most important tools the team can own, besides a compiler, are these:

- A versioning and configuration-management system
- A printing whiteboard

You should be able to cost-justify several printing whiteboards on any project, based on just the time that people save in typing design documents and meeting summaries and in lost communications cost when people do not copy down whiteboard contents.

The techniques used by the individual roles are left entirely to the discretion of the individuals.

Substitution of elements from similar methodologies is permitted. For example, the team could decide to use Scrum or DSDM's timeboxing and dynamic prioritization policies, Scrum's daily stand-up meetings, pair programming from XP, and so on.

REFLECTION ABOUT CRYSTAL CLEAR

Crystal Clear is the most tolerant, low-ceremony, small-team methodology I can find that still works.

It contains those elements claimed by my interviewees to be the cause of their success:

- Focus on close seating and close communication
- Frequent delivery
- Information from real users
- Code-versioning tools

The printing whiteboard has proven more valuable than any of its higher-tech replacements, with the possible exception of the newest generation of whiteboard-capture software (www.pixid.com). People usually start a discussion thinking it won't be worthwhile to record. They discover *after* their discussion that it would be good to have a record of it.

Crystal Clear provides a place to fall back if you try, and give up on, XP. Any part of XP can be substituted for Clear, because XP meets all Crystal Clear standards except for documentation. If you move from XP to Crystal Clear, you will have to add documentation. I don't think you can get any sloppier than Crystal Clear and still plan on having better-than-even odds of completing a project successfully.

CRYSTAL ORANGE

Crystal Orange is a methodology for D40 category projects: up to 40 people, sitting in one building, working on a system that might cause loss of discretionary monies.

Crystal Orange calls out more team structures and more team coordination than is needed on a 20-person project. It is lacking in the subteaming structures that are needed on an 80-person project, and it is missing design- and code-verification activities as would be used on life-critical systems.

Crystal Orange is given 18 pages of description in *Surviving Object-Oriented Projects* (Cockburn 1998). It is characterized there as being useful "for a medium-sized production project in an industrial setting. The characteristics of such a project are:

- It is staffed by 10 to 40 people total.
- It is of 1 to 2 years in duration.
- Time-to-market is important.
- There is a need to communicate with present and future staff, and a need to keep time and costs down.
- It is not a life-critical system.

It is a common sort of project, requiring trade-offs between complete, extensive deliverables and rapid change in requirements and design. I have kept the number of deliverables low, to reduce the cost of maintaining them, yet included enough to keep the teams communicating. I tailored job assignments and teams to allow the fluidity usually needed on this kind of project. Many other sorts of projects also need provisions for fluidity and can take advantage of this methodology."

Recalling that lighter is better as long as it lasts, a team on an E50 type of project might extend Crystal Orange with some additional verification-testing elements rather than shift to a Red methodology targeted at 80 people.

BRIEF DESCRIPTION OF CRYSTAL ORANGE

The roles on the project include

- Sponsor
- Business expert
- Usage expert
- Technical facilitator
- Business analyst/designer
- Project manager
- Architect
- Design mentor
- Lead designer-programmer
- Other designer-programmers
- UI designer
- Reuse point
- Writer
- Tester

They are arranged in several teams:

- System planning
- Project monitoring
- Architecture
- Technology
- Functions
- Infrastructure
- External test

The larger functional team is split into cross-functional groups using the Holistic Diversity strategy (Cockburn 1998). Each such group contains a business analyst-designer, a UI designer, and one to three designer-programmers. Each group also contains a database designer and representatives of other technologies if several technologies are in use on the project. Each group may have a tester.

The structure of the teams has to be adjusted to account for possible shortages of certain specialists. The point of having a cross-functional group is to reduce deliverables and to enhance local communication. The people are evaluated as a single group so that each sees a purpose to contributing wherever he is needed, not just in his job description.

The work products include

- Requirements document
- Release sequence
- Schedule
- Status reports
- UI design document
- Common object model
- Inter-team specs
- User manual
- Source code
- Test cases
- Migration code

Each work product is developed until it is understandable by colleagues, to a level of precision and stability that permits peer review.

The policy standards are identical to those of Crystal Clear, except that the incremental delivery period may be extended to three or four months.

As with Crystal Clear, the policy standards are mandatory, but equivalent substitution is permitted as would be the case if Scrum, XP, or Adaptive Software Development policies were used.

Work product templates, coding style, user interface standards, and details of regression testing are left as local standards to be set and maintained by the team. The techniques used by the individual roles are left entirely to the discretion of the individuals.

REFLECTION ABOUT CRYSTAL ORANGE

Crystal Orange is not a structure to impose on a group of only 10 people. It is much too heavy. However, for 40 people working in three or four technologies, it is very light. It is held together by close communication within the Holistic Diversity functional groups and the frequent viewings by the users.

This methodology has been used successfully. That experience is described in the project Winifred report in *Surviving Object-Oriented Projects* (Cockburn 1998).

Although I would use the basics of the methodology again gladly, technology has shifted so that the specialists who show up on the project are different today than they were then, and their work products and needs for interaction are different. Also, the bottlenecks on the next project will probably be different than they were on project Winifred.

On a new project, I would use Crystal Orange as a base methodology and shape it using the methodology-tuning technique described earlier.

CRYSTAL ORANGE WEB

Crystal Orange Web is a methodology we created for eBucks.com, a company delivering code to the Web in a continual stream. It differs from Crystal Orange in that this methodology does not deal with a single project but with a continuous stream of initiatives that require programming and with each initiative's results being merged with the growing code base being used by the public.

This methodology is still in its trial run. I include it here because

- An increasing number of companies are finding themselves in this sort of situation
- It represents the most recent application of the ideas in this book
- It has a different shape than Crystal Orange

The eBucks.com situation was interesting for a second reason (the first being the continuous and criss-crossing web of demands from different customer groups). The company had already established a Web presence. It was no longer driven by time-to-market pressures but was beginning to feel pressures imposed by the cost of defects. Customer calls, arriving in exponentially increasing volumes, could easily negate profit margins. Thus, the company was shifting from productivity to defect freedom as its top priority.

There were about 50 people to coordinate in this situation: executives, business people, managers, analysts, programmers, and testers. I classified this as an E50 situation.

The group was relatively new, so some process definition was needed to make clear who made which decisions and who handed what information to whom. Otherwise, people generally knew who they had to talk to in order to get their jobs done.

I performed interviews, as called for in the methodology-tuning technique. I interviewed people in each job role, from marketing through testing and system operations. The interviews revealed the following facts:

- Convection currents of information were quite good. Everyone was on one floor. They had movable glass and whiteboard partitions as walls, so they could see and signal to each other while still having some privacy.
- Ongoing distractions were keeping people from having the quiet time they needed to make progress on their assignments (in all job roles). Each person was working on multiple initiatives, with frequent interruptions.
- Attitude, amicability, and morale were still quite good but were sinking because of the frequent interruptions and lack of progress. Also, the programmers sat on one side of the building while the business specialists sat on the other. This meant that the chit-chat in each group drove negative commentary about the other group.
- The company was less than a year old, meaning that old habits had not yet set in and that people were open to inventing new work habits and conventions.

BRIEF DESCRIPTION OF CRYSTAL ORANGE WEB

In keeping with the idea that a methodology is the set of conventions the group agrees to, we wrote the methodology as a set of conventions, in five categories. Here they are:

I. Regular Heartbeat, with Learning

The purpose of this category is to establish a core procedure for getting feedback on "how we work around here" and taking the time to reflect and improve on that. Every convention except the reflection workshop at the end of each cycle can be altered as an outcome of the reflection workshops.

I.I   *Two-week development cycles.* Overall production runs in fixed-length development cycles of two weeks. After each delivery, each team may opt for the next delivery to be either two or four weeks, depending on what the team can deliver of use to the public. Each team must deliver something useful to the public every four weeks.

1.2 *Post-cycle reflection workshop, suggestions visibly posted.* At the end of every cycle, the company meets to discuss what worked well, what didn't work so well, and which ideas to try out on the next cycle. The outcome of the meeting is a posted list of things to keep.

2. Basic Process

The purpose of this category is to organize who creates which pieces of work and who makes which decisions, in order to avoid duplication or gaps in the effort and to look far enough ahead to spot potential problems early. The process aims for delivery of business initiatives live to the Web.

2.1 A *business owner* writes a business use case and a system use case brief (Cockburn 2001c). The business use case illustrates the proposed new system features in operation, paying particularly close attention to the manual business processes that are invoked when things go wrong.

2.2 The brief is used by the technology group to estimate the work involved in creating the features. The *business executives* review the business use case, technology estimate, and value of the initiative before agreeing to further work. The *user interface designers* work with *marketing* and the *detail business analysts* to incorporate the features into the overall site flow and then produce screen designs and the XML for the screens.

2.3 The *detail business analysts* produce detailed use cases and data descriptions, which go to the *user interface designers*, the *server programmers*, and the *servlet programmers*. The *servlet programmers* work from the XML for the user interface, the use cases, the data descriptions, and the server interfaces to produce the servlets. The *server* and *servlet programmers* produce regression tests for their code and peer review the test cases. When the test cases are deemed good and the code passes the tests, the code is passed to the *integration testers*, who pester the *developers* to fix whatever remaining errors they find before the major deployment.

2.4 The *integration testers* post the changes going out in the new release to the internal group and also to the *call center*.

2.5 For live code, the *call center* returns bug reports to a special *SWAT team* whose sole purpose is to fix problems in production. The *SWAT team* is selected from the development group on a rotating basis every two cycles.

3. Maximum Progress, Minimum Distractions

The purpose of this category is to ensure that people are working on what is of greatest value to the company and have time to focus and make progress on that work.

3.1 The top corporate key initiatives are prioritized and visibly posted for each two-week production cycle. They are allocated to individual people so that each person knows his top two or three personal priority items for the cycle.

3.2 Work is broken into what can be completed and tested in the two-week cycles and is further broken down into things that can be accomplished in one to three workdays. Each person who is working on more than one initiative is guaranteed at least two consecutive days to work on any one initiative without being pulled onto another assignment.

3.3 The developers post on the whiteboards outside their office the current status of the work they plan to complete during a given week. Every morning, the developers meet with the business owner of the current work initiative. They conduct a short meeting to determine the current state of the work and the top work priorities and to discuss any questions. The business owner is not permitted to ask for status again the rest of the day. The period 10:00 to 12:00 each day is declared "focus time," in which no meetings take place, and everyone in the company is encouraged to turn off the phone.

4. Maximally Defect Free

The purpose of this category is to construct a culture of "Kill bugs here!"

4.1 Every server and servlet class will have a set of automated regression unit tests, written by the programmer for his own code, using JUnit and HttpUnit or the equivalent. Programmers only release code to integration test when the tests have passed the scrutiny of a peer developer. The integration tester therefore gets the code, the test cases, and a note from another programmer saying that he will vouch for the quality of the tests.

4.2 The server contains a loopback mechanism so that the integration testers can maintain their own, controlled test database (which other people can use).

4.3 A small, pidgin language will be used by business people to construct sample business transactions and name an expected response. This little language allows integration testers, business owners, and the servlet writers to construct a test scenario and add it to the test database.

4.4 Screen-click statistics from the call center are posted in a visible place so that everyone can see where the public is having difficulties (either navigation difficulties or problems due to programming defects).

5. A Community, Aligned in Conversation

The purpose of this category is to indicate the long-term target toward which the company is aiming.

5.1 Eventually, the programmers, user interface designers, testers, business owners, marketers, and so on should sit in cross-functional teams to maximize the effect of conversation around delivering initiatives across specialty boundaries and to minimize the effect of rumoring about others' specialties. This will have to be balanced with staffing levels and growing space needs.

REFLECTION ABOUT CRYSTAL ORANGE WEB

Two things strike me about this methodology.

The first is the reduced role of process and work products in expressing the methodology. They are present but occupy only a fragment of the space usually devoted to them.

The second is the general absence of concurrent development, which is one of my favorite development speed-up techniques. Concurrent development is missing because of the bottlenecks in the system.

The programmers had an enormous work backlog, no spare capacity, and were being interrupted constantly. The people were quite inexperienced in both developing software and in the business domain. These two points together meant that the programmers were not able to do overlapped development and hold the requirements in an oral culture. They needed stickiness in the information, which meant having specs written down for them.

With time, this should change; as it does, I hope they will reduce the paperwork and increase the conversation. In the meantime, they need the paper.

Six Months Later

I present this methodology as it was constructed as the starter methodology. We would expect to see some drift over time, both as people thought up new ways of working and as they drifted away from the high-discipline practices.

Michael Jordaan, CEO of eBucks.com, made these comments about the group's work habits six months later:

"Obviously, when you left some disciplines survived while others did not stand the test.

"The survivors include the fortnightly heartbeat with carefully planned cutoff times, which allows for developers and business owners to plan, testers to test rigorously, and customers to be informed upfront of scheduled upgrades.

"We discussed a three-week heartbeat, but this was considered too long. More complex issues than can be solved in two weeks are run at twice the heartbeat (four weeks), but we still encourage incremental rollouts.

"The post-heartbeat meeting is strictly enforced and it has become one of the few times that I get to speak to the entire team. I have made quite a point of paying tribute to those involved in successful upgrades.

Hopefully this public recognition is motivating. Mistakes are discussed and suggestions for improvements have been made at every meeting, supporting the learning culture we are creating.

"The quality of code going live has improved greatly as the testing team has a veto power, to prevent bad code from going live (and this can be embarrassing).

"The SWAT team, dedicated to eliminating live bugs, has also made great strides in responding to customer and call centre queries.

"Focus time is still adhered to (and we still ring a bell every morning at 10:00). If I go a single day without these two hours I now start panicking, so useful has it proven to be.

"Some things that did not survive were the habit of posting current priorities/work progress on a board. Maybe interruptions are less of an issue now, as people work from home or maybe relationships between business owners and developers have stabilised. Maybe people are just lazy.

"Most developers have a maximum of three tasks at any given time, except for the two key people working on the back end, who may easily have a list of 15 each. Moreover they are still interrupted by live issues, which interfere with their completion of tasks and lead to much frustration by other developers and business specialists.

"The issue here is lack of skilled resources. It is the age-old problem that training employees to assist, while undoubtedly the right medium-term solution, takes longer than simply doing it yourself."

In those comments, what I notice with some satisfaction is that the team still uses the core elements of the process: heartbeat with learning, and finding ways to modify even that heartbeat to fit their needs.

I notice the discussion of talent and skills as being critical to the project, and I notice them drifting away from what probably were embellishments in the methodology.

WHAT SHOULD I DO TOMORROW?

Whether you use Crystal or not, increase morale and communication on your project so that the people trade information a little bit better. This applies for any base methodology.

Get your experienced developers at Level 2 in methodology design. If your project doesn't have anyone at that level, do two things:

- Study your base methodology.
- Start holding reflection workshops so that *someone* gets up to Level 2 soon.

Compare what your team is doing with the three methodology samples given in this chapter. Choose a few ideas to apply on your own project.

APPENDIX A

The Agile Software Development Manifesto

"We are uncovering better ways of developing software by doing it and helping others do it. Through this work we have come to value:

Individuals and interactions over processes and tools
Working software over comprehensive documentation
Customer collaboration over contract negotiation
Responding to change over following a plan

That is, while there is value in the items on the right, we value the items on the left more."

Seventeen advocates of lightweight development processes gathered in Utah in early 2001 to discuss what they might have in common, or if they would just agree to disagree. I was one of them.

We agreed that the word *lightweight* was too much of a reaction against something and not enough of a belief in something. Agreeing on the importance of being able to respond to changing requirements within the project time frame, we chose the word *agile*.

We agreed on the above four values and on a dozen principles to support those values. We agreed that we were not interested in agreeing beyond that. We nicknamed the group the Agile Alliance.

This appendix discusses that meeting, the values, and the principles.

The Agile Software Development Manifesto

THE AGILE ALLIANCE

The meeting happened at Snowbird, Utah in February 2001.

The 17 people were Kent Beck, Mike Beedle, Arie van Bennekum, Alistair Cockburn, Ward Cunningham, Martin Fowler, James Grenning, Jim Highsmith, Andrew Hunt, Ron Jeffries, Jon Kern, Brian Marick, Robert C. Martin, Stephen J. Mellor, Ken Schwaber, Jeff Sutherland, and Dave "Pragmatic" Thomas. (If Dave A. Thomas from Object Technology International had been able to make it that week, we might have had two Dave Thomases as signatories!)

Each person there saw his own version of the meeting. What follows in this appendix is mine (but I did pass this text in front of the others).

The reason we met was to see whether there was anything in common among the various light methodologies: Adaptive Software Development, XP, Scrum, Crystal, Feature-Driven Development, Dynamic System Development Method (DSDM), and "pragmatic programming."

Kent Beck, Ward Cunningham, Ron Jeffries, James Grenning, and Robert Martin brought their views of XP, along with their considerable other experiences and their own personal wishes.

Martin Fowler brought long experience in both XP and methodology evaluation in general.

Jim Highsmith represented Adaptive Software Development and ideas around the emergent properties of complex, adaptive systems.

I was there, protecting my interests in methodology-per-project and just-in-time methodology construction.

Jeff Sutherland, Ken Schwaber, and Michael Beedle represented Scrum (Schwaber 2002).

Jon Kern of TogetherSoft represented Feature-Driven Development, the method described in *Java Modeling in Color with UML* (Coad 1999).

Arie van Bennekum, from the Netherlands, represented DSDM (Stapleton 1997).

Andy Hunt and Dave "Pragmatic" Thomas, authors of *The Pragmatic Programmer*, protected the interests of experienced programmers who have no affiliation to any one method.

Brian Marick represented the software-testing perspective.

Stephen J. Mellor was there to protect his interests in model-driven development. He was perhaps the most surprised to find himself able to agree with most of what was said and signed both the manifesto and the principles.

There were others who had been invited, and would certainly have contributed and signed, but those listed are the people who were there and who argued about, crafted, and signed the agreements.

We hoped against hope that we would actually agree on something.

None of us was interested in merging the practices to create a "Unified Light Methodology" (ULM). Given the individualism in the room, it was actually surprising that we agreed on anything.

We agreed on four things:

- We agreed at the first level, on the need to respond to change. We agreed that *agile* reflected our intent and permits discussion of heavier-agile methodologies for larger and life-critical projects.
- We agreed at the second level, on four core values as described in the manifesto.
- We agreed at the third level (just barely), on 12 more detailed statements consistent with those four values.
- It was clear that we would not agree on the fourth level, detailed project tactics. We did agree that this was healthy for the industry and that we should continue to innovate and compete in the world of ideas, to discover a larger set of agile software practices.

With those agreements and the adoption of the term *agile*, the 17 people created the Agile Alliance.

THE MANIFESTO

Let's look at the wording of the manifesto more closely.

> "We are uncovering better ways of developing software by doing it and helping others do it."

We (the people in the group) are software development practitioners, not merely onlookers making rules for others. We feel that we have "uncovered" practices more than invented them and want to be clear that we will continue to work by helping as well as by telling.

> "Through this work we have come to value . . ."

The ideas were not arrived at in a vacuum but rather are an outcome of our direct experience and reflection on that experience.

Before listing the four choices, I'll skip ahead and look at the closing sentence:

> "That is, while there is value in the items on the right, we value the items on the left more."

We are not interested in tearing down the house of software development. We recognize that tools, processes, documentation, contracts, and plans have value. What we wish to express is that when push comes to shove (which it usually does), something has to give. We feel that people who hang onto the right-hand choices in the list will not do as well as people who hang onto the left-hand choices.

We also want to recognize that some people disagree with one or all of our choices. One person said, on seeing our list: "I can agree with three of the four." We agreed that that sort of disagreement can lead to constructive conversations.

There is no "opposite" to *agile methodology,* just as there is no opposite to "Bengal tiger." There are alternatives to agile methodologies, phrased according to their own value systems: *repeatable, deliberate, predictable,* even *capricious* methodologies.

Understand, of course, that all of these denote the successful version of the practices. Perhaps better terms are *would-be-agile, would-be-predictable,* and *would-be-repeatable* development.

It is important to me, personally, to leave room for disagreement on these matters. Our industry still disagrees about what is critical to successful software development. The best approach for the time being is simply to say what one stands for. Evidently, this point is important to the other signatories, too.

With that in mind, let's look at the four choices:

"**Individuals and interactions** over processes and tools."

The first value is attending to the people on the team as opposed to roles in the process chart. Although a process description is needed to get a group of people started, people are not plug-replaceable, as we have seen.

The second choice being highlighted there is attending to the interactions between the individuals. New solutions and flaws in old solutions come to life in discussions between people. The quality of the interactions matters.

Actually, improved community benefits process-centric development just as much as it does chaotic development.

What this first value expresses is that we would rather use an undocumented process with good interactions than a documented process with hostile interactions.

"**Working software** over comprehensive documentation."

The working system is the only thing that tells you what the team *has* built. Running code is ruthlessly honest.

Documents showing the requirements, analysis, design, screen flows, object interaction sequence charts and the like are handy as hints. The team members use them as aids in reflecting on their own experience, to guess what the future will look like. The documents serve as markers in the game, used to build an image of the unreliable future.

On the other hand, the composite act of gathering requirements, designing, coding, and debugging the software reveals information about the development team, the development process, and the nature of the problem to be solved. Those things together with running final result provide the only reliable measure of the speed of the team, the shortcomings of the group, and a glimpse into what the team really should be building.

Documents can be very useful, as we have seen, but they should be used along with the words "just enough" and "barely sufficient."

"**Customer collaboration** over contract negotiation."

The third value describes the relationship between the people who want the software built and those who are building the software. The distinction is that in properly formed agile development, there is no "us" and "them," there is only "us."

Collaboration deals with community, amicability, joint decision-making, rapidity of communication, and connections to the interactions of individuals. Attention to customer collaboration indicates an amicable relationship (which does not preclude conflict, as explained in Chapter 3) across specialties and organizational boundaries. Saying "there is only us" refers to the fact that both are needed to produce good software.

Although contracts are useful at times, collaboration strengthens development both when a contract is in place and when no contract exists. Good collaboration can save a contract situation when it is in jeopardy. Good collaboration can sometimes make a contract unnecessary. Either way, collaboration is the winning element.

"**Responding to change** over following a plan."

The final value is about adjusting to fast-breaking project changes.

Building a plan is useful, and each of the agile methodologies contains specific planning activities. They also contain mechanisms for dealing with changing priorities.

Scrum, DSDM, and Adaptive Software Development call for timeboxed development with reprioritization *after* (not within) each timebox (XP allows reprioritization within the timebox). The timeboxed periods are in the two- to four-week range. The timeboxing guarantees that the team has the time and peace of mind to develop

working software. The relatively short development phases, what Scrum calls "sprints," allow the project sponsors to change priorities to match their needs.

Building a plan is useful. Referring to the plan is useful until it gets too far from the current situation. Hanging onto an outdated plan is not useful.

REFLECTING ON THE MANIFESTO

The need for different ways of working in different situations is not in the manifesto, but Jim Highsmith and I like to keep the point always in mind.

Being *agile* is different for a 100-person project than for a 10-person project. The agile 100-person project will use a heavier methodology than the agile 10-person project. This matches the methodology design principles presented in Chapter 4.

Of course, also in keeping with the methodology design principles, it might be possible to drop 90 people from the 100-person project, keep the 10 best people, and then run an agile 10-person project that delivers the same system in the same time frame.

The point is that we agree that methodologies do not come in ones or twos but in dozens, each tuned to the situation and project at hand, and each agile. This thought is not captured in the Manifesto.

Some of the people in the room recommend agile methodologies primarily for high-flux situations. My experience is that rude surprises pop up on even supposedly stable projects. I am still waiting to see an occasion when the agile value set is not appropriate.

SUPPORTING THE VALUES

The group of 17 quickly agreed on those value choices. Developing the next level of statements proved more than we could settle on in the time left in the meeting. The values included in this section make up the current working set.

These statements should evolve as we learn people's perceptions of our words and as we come up with more accurate words ourselves. I will be surprised if this particular version isn't out of date shortly after the book is published. For the latest version, check www.AgileAlliance.org.

We expect not to agree on the next level of recommendations, which relate to project tactics: how much architecture to develop at what times, what tools to use or avoid, and so on. We each still have our own experiences, fears, wishes, and philosophies, which color our practices and recommendations. We will differ at some specificity of recommendation.

These are the sentences we agreed on, and my commentary on each.

 I. Our highest priority is to satisfy the customer through early and frequent delivery of valuable software.

We are interested in delivering software that is fit for its purpose. Oddly, some of the companies I visit don't seem to value actually *delivering software*. Agile development is focused on delivering.

Delivering early allows for quick wins and early feedback about the requirements, the team, and the process, as we have seen throughout this book.

Delivering frequently allows for continued wins for the team, rapid feedback, and mid-project changes in project direction and priorities.

The duration used for deliveries needs to be negotiated on a project-by-project basis, because delivering updates on a daily or weekly basis can cause more disturbance to the users than it is worth. When users can't absorb changes to the system as often as every three months, then the project team needs to arrange some other way to get that feedback and to make sure that the process works all the way through test and integration.

This statement emphasizes the delivery of those items that have greatest value to the customers. With consumer mood changes, intensive competition, and stock-market swings, it is nearly impossible to guarantee a revenue stream for a project that takes a year or longer to deliver.

This statement indicates that value will be delivered early, so that in case the sponsors lose funding, they will not be left with a pile of promissory notes but with working software that delivers something of value to the buyers.

 2. Deliver working software frequently, from a couple of weeks to a couple of months, with a preference for the shorter timescale.

This half of the "early and frequent" delivery specifies the lengths of the work cycles. I have encountered the occasional project that can run incremental development with four-month cycles, but most use one-to three-month cycles. Using shorter cycles is rare, because the users usually can't take in more frequent changes than that.

On project Winifred (Cockburn 1998), a fixed-price contract involving 50 people over 18 months, we fixed our cycles for deliveries to users at three months. Knowing that this was really too long to wait for feedback, we made sure that some expert users came and had *two* chances to review running code inside each cycle. These two user viewings were scheduled flexibly, usually around the six-week and eight-week marks.

If the users can accept changes every month, and the development team can match the ongoing requests for changes, then the shorter feedback cycle is better.

3. Working software is the primary measure of progress.

This is the third reference to working software. This principle puts it firmly: Rely on the honesty that comes with running code rather than on promissory notes in the form of plans and documents. You are welcome to use other measures of progress as well, but working code is the one to bank on.

Agile methodologies place a premium on getting something up and running early and evolving it over time. Not all projects are equally amenable to tiny evolutionary steps. Deciding how to break up the giant architecture on a large project into smaller pieces that can be built and tested incrementally does take some

work. It can be done, however, and is worth the effort.

Stephen Mellor is careful to point out that in model-driven development, two pieces of working code must be demonstrated. One is the executable model, which is evaluated for fitness to the user needs. The other piece of working code to be demonstrated is the mapping algorithm that generates the final code. This one is more easily overlooked. A number of projects created a gorgeous executable model and then couldn't get the code-generation algorithm to work properly in time.

4. Welcome changing requirements, even late in development. Agile processes harness change for the customer's competitive advantage.

Agile processes can take on late-changing requirements exactly because of early and frequent delivery of running software, use of iterative and timeboxing techniques, continual attention to architecture, and willingness to update the design.

If your company can deliver quickly and respond to late-breaking information and your competitor's company can't, then your company can out-maneuver your competitors on the software front. This often translates to a major difference in the marketplace.

All of the agile methodologies have some mechanism to incorporate late-breaking changes in requirements, as already discussed. The details differ by methodology.

5. Business people and developers work together daily throughout the project.

The industry is littered with projects whose sponsors did not take the time to make sure they got what they needed. Frakes and Fox reported a study showing a strong correlation between links to users and project success or failure (Frakes 1995).

The best links are through onsite business expertise and daily discussions, which is what the statement calls for. The word "daily" refers to the sweet spot, where discussions are ongoing and occur on demand. Daily discussions are not practical on most projects, which means that the project is not sitting at the sweet spot. The statement indicates that the longer it takes to get information to and from the developers, the more damage will occur to the project.

6. Build projects around motivated individuals. Give them the environment and support they need, and trust them to get the job done.

We would rather see motivated, skilled people communicating well and using no process at all than a well-defined process used by unmotivated individuals. Dee Hock's story about the early VISA system gives an extreme example of this.

Individuals make projects work. Their motivation relates to the pride-in-work, amicability, and community on the project.

I first encountered the above statement in a project interview with Dave A. Thomas, then president of the very successful company, Object Technology International. He said, "We hire good people, give them the tools and training to get their work done, and get out of their way." I keep finding evidence supporting his recommendation.

7. The most efficient and effective method of conveying information to and within a development team is face-to-face conversation.

This falls directly out of Chapters 3 and 4 in this book. I won't repeat the discussion and caveats here. Review those chapters if you are just dipping into the book here.

8. The best architectures, requirements, and designs emerge from self-organizing teams.

We had some discussion around the choice of words in this principle. How self-organizing do we intend: completely self-organizing, or merely allowing good ideas to come from anyone on the project? Do we mean *emerge* mysteriously, *emerge* in small steps over time, or *emerge* as a logical consequence of the human-centric rules the team uses?

I prefer the middle of the three choices. Highsmith prefers the last of the three. None of us intends the first of the three, which comes from a misunderstanding of the word *emergent* as "lucky." Our common point is recognizing that the details of system design surprise even the most experienced designers.

We insist that the architecture be allowed to adjust over time, just as the requirements and process do. An architecture that is locked down too hard, too early, will not be able to adjust to the inevitable surprises that surface during implementation and with changing requirements. An architecture that grows in steps can follow the changing knowledge of the team and the changing wishes of the user community.

9. Continuous attention to technical excellence and good design enhance agility.

A tidy, well-encapsulated design is easier to change, and that means greater agility for the project. Therefore, to remain agile, the designers have to produce good designs to begin with. They also have to review and improve their designs regularly to deal with the better understanding of their design that comes with time and to clean up from when they cut corners to meet a short-term goal.

Managing Technical Debt

Ward Cunningham sometimes compares cleaning up the design with paying off debts. Going further, he discusses managing the technical debt on the project.

Making hasty additions to the system corresponds to borrowing against the future, taking on debt. Cleaning up the design corresponds to paying off the debt.

Sometimes, he points out, it is appropriate to take on debt and make hasty changes in order to take advantage of an opportunity. Just as debt accumulates interest and grows over time, though, so does the cost to the project of not cleaning up those hasty design changes.

Cut corners in the design, he suggests, when you are willing to take on the debt, and clean up the design to pay off the debt before the interest grows too high.

Given the deep experience present in the room, I found it interesting to see this attention to design quality at the same time as I saw the attention to short time scales, light documentation, and people.

The conflicting forces are resolved by designing as well as the knowledge at hand permits, but designing incrementally.

10. Agile processes promote sustainable development. The sponsors, developers, and users should be able to maintain a constant pace indefinitely.

There are two sides to this statement. One relates to social responsibility, the other to project effectiveness. Not everyone at the meeting was interested in signing onto the social responsibility platform, but we all agreed on the effectiveness issue.

People tire as they put in long hours. Their rate of progress slows, not just during their overtime hours but also during their regular hours. They introduce more errors into their work. Diminishing returns set in with extra hours. This is part of the nonlinearity of the human component.

An alert and engaged staff is more agile than a tired, plodding staff, even leaving aside all of the social responsibility issues. Long hours are a symptom that something has gone wrong with the project layout.

11. Simplicity—the art of maximizing the amount of work not done—is essential.

Simplicity is essential. That much is easy to agree on. The notion of simplicity is so subjective, though, that it is difficult to say anything useful about it. We were therefore pleased to find that we could all support this statement.

In the design of development processes, simplicity has to do with accomplishing while *not doing*, maximizing the work not done while producing good software. Jon Kern reminds us of Pascal's remark: "This letter is longer than I wish, for I had not the time to make it shorter." That comment reveals the difficulty of making things simple. A cumbersome model is easy to produce. Producing a simple design that can handle change effectively is more difficult.

In terms of methodology and people, Jim Highsmith likes to cite Dee Hock:

"Simple, clear purpose and principles give rise to complex, intelligent behavior.

"Complex rules and regulations give rise to simple, stupid behavior."

12. At regular intervals, the team reflects on how to become more effective, then tunes and adjusts its behavior accordingly.

It is fitting to end where we began. How light is right for any one project? Barely sufficient, and probably lighter than you expect.

How do we do this on our project? Bother to reflect on what you are doing. If your team will spend one hour together every other week reflecting on its working habits, you can evolve your methodology to be agile, effective, and fitting. If you can't do that, well . . . you will stay where you are.

REFLECTING ON THE SUPPORT STATEMENTS

Getting 17 people to agree on any set of words is difficult. The more detailed the advice, the more people's different backgrounds and philosophies come into play.

We hope that the four leading value choices and the 12 supporting statements will give you enough information to build your own agile work habits.

APPENDIX B

Naur, Ehn, Musashi

Peter Naur and Pelle Ehn wrote the two most compelling and accurate accounts of software development I have yet seen. Neither is as well known as it needs to be, and Ehn's book is out of print. I am happy, therefore, to present extracts from their articles, for wider readership.

Peter Naur's "Programming as Theory Building" neatly describes the mental activity of creating software and explains the "metaphor building" activity in Extreme Programming (XP).

Pelle Ehn wrote the wonderful book *Work-Oriented Design of Software Artifacts*, in which he considers how Wittgenstein's idea of language games informs our view of software development.

Miyamoto Musashi, the 17th-century samurai champion, never wrote software. The competing schools of sword fighting in his day sound painfully like today's schools of methodology. He admonishes people to avoid getting infatuated with tools and schools, to use different tools and strokes for different moments, and to just "cut off the opponent's arm." His admonitions apply directly to software development—if you realize that the opponent is the *problem*, and not your office mate.

Naur, Ehn, Musashi

PETER NAUR, PROGRAMMING AS THEORY BUILDING

Peter Naur, widely known as one of the authors of the programming language syntax notation "Backus-Naur Form" (BNF), wrote "Programming as Theory Building" in 1985. It was reprinted in his collection of works, *Computing: A Human Activity* (Naur 1992).

This article is, to my mind, the most accurate account of what goes on in designing and coding a program. I refer to it regularly when discussing how much documentation to create, how to pass along tacit knowledge, and the value of the XP's metaphor-setting exercise. It also provides a way to examine a methodology's economic structure.

In the article, which follows, note that the quality of the designing programmer's work is related to the quality of the match between his theory of the problem and his theory of the solution. Note that the quality of a later programmer's work is related to the match between his theories and the previous programmer's theories.

Using Naur's ideas, the designer's job is not to pass along "the design" but to pass along "the theories" driving the design. The latter goal is more useful and more appropriate. It also highlights that knowledge of the theory is tacit in the owning, and so passing along the theory requires passing along both explicit and tacit knowledge.

Here is Peter Naur's way of saying it.

"PROGRAMMING AS THEORY BUILDING"

Introduction

The present discussion is a contribution to the understanding of what programming is. It suggests that programming properly should be regarded as an activity by which the programmers form or achieve a certain kind of insight, a theory, of the matters at hand. This suggestion is in contrast to what appears to be a more common notion, that programming should be regarded as a production of a program and certain other texts.

Some of the background of the views presented here is to be found in certain observations of what actually happens to programs and the teams of programmers dealing with them, particularly in situations arising from unexpected and perhaps erroneous program executions or reactions, and on the occasion of modifications of programs. The difficulty of accommodating such observations in a production view of programming suggests that this view is misleading. The theory building view is presented as an alternative.

A more general background of the presentation is a conviction that it is important to have an appropriate understanding of what programming is. If our understanding is inappropriate we will misunderstand the difficulties that arise in the activity and our attempts to overcome them will give rise to conflicts and frustrations.

In the present discussion some of the crucial background experience will first be outlined. This is followed by an explanation of a theory of what programming is, denoted the Theory Building View. The subsequent sections enter into some of the consequences of the Theory Building View.

Programming and the Programmers' Knowledge

I shall use the word *programming* to denote the whole activity of design and implementation of programmed solutions. What I am concerned with is the activity of matching some significant part and aspect of an activity in the real world to the formal symbol manipulation that can be done by a program running on a computer. With such a notion it follows directly that the programming activity I am talking about must include the development in time corresponding to the changes taking place in the real world activity being matched by the program execution, in other words program modifications.

One way of stating the main point I want to make is that programming in this sense primarily must be the programmers' building up knowledge of a certain kind, knowledge taken to be basically the programmers' immediate possession, any documentation being an auxiliary, secondary product.

As a background of the further elaboration of this view given in the following sections, the remainder of the present section will describe some real experience of dealing with large programs that has seemed to me more and more significant as I have pondered over the problems. In either case the experience is my own or has been communicated to me by persons having firsthand contact with the activity in question.

Case 1 concerns a compiler. It has been developed by a group A for a Language L and worked very well on computer X. Now another group B has the task to write a compiler for a language L + M, a modest extension of L, for computer Y. Group B decides that the compiler for L developed by group A will be a good starting point for their design, and get a contract with group A that they will get support in the form of full documentation, including annotated program texts and much additional written design discussion, and also personal advice. The arrangement was effective and group B managed to develop the compiler they wanted. In the present context the significant issue is the importance of the personal advice from group A in the matters that concerned how to implement the extensions M to the language. During the design phase group B made suggestions for the manner in which the extensions should be accommodated and submitted them to group A for review. In several major cases it turned out that the solutions suggested by group B were found by group A to make no use of the facilities that were not only inherent in the structure of the existing compiler but were discussed at length in its documentation, and to be based instead on additions to that structure in the form of patches that effectively destroyed its power and simplicity. The members of group A were able to spot these cases instantly and could propose simple and effective solutions, framed entirely within the existing structure. This is an example of how the full program text and additional documentation is insufficient in conveying to even the highly motivated group B the deeper insight into the design, that theory which is immediately present to the members of group A.

In the years following these events the compiler developed by group B was taken over by other programmers of the same organization, without guidance from group A. Information obtained by a member of group A about the compiler resulting from the further modification of it after about 10 years made it clear that at that later stage the original powerful structure was still visible, but made entirely ineffective by amorphous additions of many different kinds. Thus, again, the program text and its documentation has proved insufficient as a carrier of some of the most important design ideas.

Case 2 concerns the installation and fault diagnosis of a large real-time system for monitoring industrial production activities. The system is marketed by its producer, each delivery of the system being adapted individually to its specific environment of sensors and display devices. The size of the program delivered in each installation is of the order of 200,000 lines. The relevant experience from the way this kind of system is handled concerns the role and manner of work of the group of installation and fault finding programmers. The facts are, first that these programmers have been closely concerned with the system as a full time occupation over a period of several years, from the time the system was under design. Second, when diagnosing a fault these programmers rely almost exclu-

sively on their ready knowledge of the system and the annotated program text, and are unable to conceive of any kind of additional documentation that would be useful to them. Third, other programmers' groups who are responsible for the operation of particular installations of the system, and thus receive documentation of the system and full guidance on its use from the producer's staff, regularly encounter difficulties that upon consultation with the producer's installation and fault finding programmer are traced to inadequate understanding of the existing documentation, but which can be cleared up easily by the installation and fault finding programmers.

The conclusion seems inescapable that at least with certain kinds of large programs, the continued adaptation, modification, and correction of errors in them, is essentially dependent on a certain kind of knowledge possessed by a group of programmers who are closely and continuously connected with them.

Ryle's Notion of Theory

If it is granted that programming must involve, as the essential part, a building up of the programmers' knowledge, the next issue is to characterize that knowledge more closely. What will be considered here is the suggestion that the programmers' knowledge properly should be regarded as a theory, in the sense of Ryle [1949]. Very briefly, a person who has or possesses a theory in this sense knows how to do certain things and in addition can support the actual doing with explanations, justifications, and answers to queries, about the activity of concern. It may be noted that

Ryle's notion of theory appears as an example of what K. Popper [Popper, and Eccles, 1977] calls unembodied World 3 objects and thus has a defensible philosophical standing. In the present section we shall describe Ryle's notion of theory in more detail.

Ryle [1949] develops his notion of theory as part of his analysis of the nature of intellectual activity, particularly the manner in which intellectual activity differs from, and goes beyond, activity that is merely intelligent. In intelligent behaviour the person displays, not any particular knowledge of facts, but the ability to do certain things, such as to make and appreciate jokes, to talk grammatically, or to fish. More particularly, the intelligent performance is characterized in part by the person's doing them well, according to certain criteria, but further displays the person's ability to apply the criteria so as to detect and correct lapses, to learn from the examples of others, and so forth. It may be noted that this notion of intelligence does not rely on any notion that the intelligent behaviour depends on the person's following or adhering to rules, prescriptions, or methods. On the contrary, the very act of adhering to rules can be done more or less intelligently; if the exercise of intelligence depended on following rules there would have to be rules about how to follow rules, and about how to follow the rules about following rules, etc., in an infinite regress, which is absurd.

What characterizes intellectual activity, over and beyond activity that is merely intelligent, is the person's building and having a theory, where theory is understood as the knowledge a person must have in order not only to do certain things intelligently but also to explain them, to answer queries about them, to argue about them, and so forth. A person who has a theory is prepared to enter into such activities; while building the theory the person is trying to get it.

The notion of theory in the sense used here applies not only to the elaborate constructions of specialized fields of enquiry, but equally to activities that any person who has received education will participate in on certain occasions. Even quite unambitious activities of everyday life may give rise to people's theorizing, for example in planning how to place furniture or how to get to some place by means of certain means of transportation.

The notion of theory employed here is explicitly *not* confined to what may be called the most general or abstract part of the insight. For example, to have Newton's theory of mechanics as understood here it is not enough to understand the central laws, such as that force equals mass times acceleration. In addition, as described in more detail by Kuhn [1970, p. 187ff], the person having the theory must have an understanding of the manner in which the central laws apply to certain aspects of reality, so as to be able to recognize and apply the theory to other similar aspects. A person having Newton's theory of mechanics must thus understand how it applies to the motions of pendulums and the planets, and must be able to recognize similar phenomena in the world, so as to be able to employ the mathematically expressed rules of the theory properly.

The dependence of a theory on a grasp of certain kinds of similarity between situations and events of the real world gives the reason why the knowledge held by someone who has the theory could not, in principle, be expressed in terms of rules. In fact, the similarities in question are not, and cannot be, expressed in terms of criteria, no more than the similarities of many other kinds of objects, such as human faces, tunes, or tastes of wine, can be thus expressed.

The Theory To Be Built by the Programmer

In terms of Ryle's notion of theory, what has to be built by the programmer is a theory of how certain affairs of the world will be handled by, or supported by, a computer program. On the Theory Building View of programming the theory built by the programmers has primacy over such other products as program texts, user documentation, and additional documentation such as specifications.

In arguing for the Theory Building View, the basic issue is to show how the knowledge possessed by the programmer by virtue of his or her having the theory necessarily, and in an essential manner, transcends that which is recorded in the documented products. The answers to this issue is that the programmer's knowledge transcends that given in documentation in at least three essential areas:

1) The programmer having the theory of the program can explain how the solution relates to the affairs of the world that it helps to handle. Such an explanation will have to be concerned with the manner in which the affairs of the world, both in their overall characteristics and their details, are, in some sense, mapped into the program text and into any additional documentation. Thus the programmer must be able to explain, for each part of the program text and for each of its overall structural characteristics, what aspect or activity of the world is matched by it. Conversely, for any aspect or activity of the world the programmer is able to state its manner of mapping into the program text. By far the largest part of the world aspects and activities will of course lie outside the scope of the program text, being irrelevant in the context. However, the decision that a part of the world *is* relevant can only be made by someone who understands the whole world. This understanding must be contributed by the programmer.

2) The programmer having the theory of the program can explain *why* each part of the program is what it is, in other words is able to support the actual program text with a justification of some sort. The final basis of the justification is and must always remain the programmer's direct, intuitive knowledge or estimate. This holds even where the justification makes use of reasoning, perhaps with application of design rules, quantitative estimates, comparisons with alternatives, and such like, the point being that the choice of the principles and rules, and the decision that they are relevant to the situation at hand, again must in the final analysis remain a matter of the programmer's direct knowledge.

3) The programmer having the theory of the program is able to respond constructively to any demand for a modification of

the program so as to support the affairs of the world in a new manner. Designing how a modification is best incorporated into an established program depends on the perception of the similarity of the new demand with the operational facilities already built into the program. The kind of similarity that has to be perceived is one between aspects of the world. It only makes sense to the agent who has knowledge of the world, that is to the programmer, and cannot be reduced to any limited set of criteria or rules, for reasons similar to the ones given above why the justification of the program cannot be thus reduced.

While the discussion of the present section presents some basic arguments for adopting the Theory Building View of programming, an assessment of the view should take into account to what extent it may contribute to a coherent understanding of programming and its problems. Such matters will be discussed in the following sections.

Problems and Costs of Program Modifications

A prominent reason for proposing the Theory Building View of programming is the desire to establish an insight into programming suitable for supporting a sound understanding of program modifications. This question will therefore be the first one to be taken up for analysis.

One thing seems to be agreed by everyone, that software will be modified. It is invariably the case that a program, once in operation, will be felt to be only part of the answer to the problems at hand. Also the very use of the program itself will inspire ideas for further useful services that the

program ought to provide. Hence the need for ways to handle modifications.

The question of program modifications is closely tied to that of programming costs. In the face of a need for a changed manner of operation of the program, one hopes to achieve a saving of costs by making modifications of an existing program text, rather than by writing an entirely new program.

The expectation that program modifications at low cost ought to be possible is one that calls for closer analysis. First it should be noted that such an expectation cannot be supported by analogy with modifications of other complicated manmade constructions. Where modifications are occasionally put into action, for example in the case of buildings, they are well known to be expensive and in fact complete demolition of the existing building followed by new construction is often found to be preferable economically. Second, the expectation of the possibility of low cost program modifications conceivably finds support in the fact that a program is a text held in a medium allowing for easy editing. For this support to be valid it must clearly be assumed that the dominating cost is one of text manipulation. This would agree with a notion of programming as text production. On the Theory Building View this whole argument is false. This view gives no support to an expectation that program modifications at low cost are generally possible.

A further closely related issue is that of program flexibility. In including flexibility in a program we build into the program certain operational facilities that are not immediately demanded, but which are likely to turn out to be useful. Thus a flexible program is able to handle certain classes of changes of external circumstances without being modified.

It is often stated that programs should be designed to include a lot of flexibility, so as to be readily adaptable to changing circumstances. Such advice may be reasonable as far as flexibility that can be easily achieved is concerned. However, flexibility can in general only be achieved at a substantial cost. Each item of it has to be designed, including what circumstances it has to cover and by what kind of parameters it should be controlled. Then it has to be implemented, tested, and described. This cost is incurred in achieving a program feature whose usefulness depends entirely on future events. It must be obvious that built-in program flexibility is no answer to the general demand for adapting programs to the changing circumstances of the world.

In a program modification an existing programmed solution has to be changed so as to cater for a change in the real world activity it has to match. What is needed in a modification, first of all, is a confrontation of the existing solution with the demands called for by the desired modification. In this confrontation the degree and kind of similarity between the capabilities of the existing solution and the new demands has to be determined. This need for a determination of similarity brings out the merit of the Theory Building View. Indeed, precisely in a determination of similarity the shortcoming of any view of programming that ignores the central requirement for the direct participation of persons who possess the appropriate insight becomes evident. The point is that the kind of similarity that has to be recognized is accessible to the human beings who possess the theory of the program, although entirely outside the reach of what can be determined by rules, since even the criteria on which to judge it cannot be formulated. From the insight into the similarity between the new requirements and those already satisfied by the program, the programmer is able to design the change of the program text needed to implement the modification.

In a certain sense there can be no question of a theory modification, only of a program modification. Indeed, a person having the theory must already be prepared to respond to the kinds of questions and demands that may give rise to program modifications. This observation leads to the important conclusion that the problems of program modification arise from acting on the assumption that programming consists of program text production, instead of recognizing programming as an activity of theory building.

On the basis of the Theory Building View the decay of a program text as a result of modifications made by programmers without a proper grasp of the underlying theory becomes understandable. As a matter of fact, if viewed merely as a change of the program text and of the external behaviour of the execution, a given desired modification may usually be realized in many different ways, all correct. At the same time, if viewed in relation to the theory of the program these ways may look very different, some of them perhaps conforming to that theory or extending it in a natural way, while others may be wholly inconsistent with that theory, perhaps having the character of unintegrated patches on the main part of the program. This difference of character of various changes is one that can only make sense to the programmer who possesses the theory of the program. At the same time the character of changes made in a program text is vital to the longer term viability of the program. For a program to retain its quality it is mandatory that each modification is firmly grounded in the theory of it. Indeed, the very notion of qualities such as simplicity and good structure can only be understood in terms of the theory of the program, since they characterize the actual program text in relation to such program texts that might have been written to achieve the same execution behaviour, but which exist only as possibilities in the programmer's understanding.

Program Life, Death, and Revival

A main claim of the Theory Building View of programming is that an essential part of any program, the theory of it, is something that could not conceivably be expressed, but is inextricably bound to human beings. It follows that in describing the state of the program it is important to indicate the extent to which programmers having its theory remain in charge of it. As a way in which to emphasize this circumstance one might extend the notion of program building by notions of program life, death, and revival. The building of the program is the same as the building of the theory of it by and in the team of programmers. During the program life a programmer team possessing its theory remains in active control of the program, and in particular retains control over all modifications. The death of a program happens when the programmer team possessing its theory is dissolved. A dead program may continue to be used for execution in a computer and to produce useful results. The actual state of death becomes visible when demands for modifications of the program cannot be intelligently answered. Revival of a program is the rebuilding of its theory by a new programmer team.

The extended life of a program according to these notions depends on the taking over by new generations of programmers of the theory of the program. For a new programmer to come to possess an existing theory of a program it is insufficient that he or she has the opportunity to become familiar with the program text and other documentation. What is required is that the new programmer has the opportunity to work in close contact with the programmers who already possess the theory, so as to be able to become familiar with the place of the program in the wider context of the relevant real world situations and so as to acquire the knowledge of how the program works and how unusual program reactions and program modifications are handled within the program theory. This problem of education of new programmers in an existing theory of a program is quite similar to that of the educational problem of other activities where the knowledge of how to do certain things dominates over the knowledge that certain things are the case, such as writing and playing a music instrument. The most important educational activity is the student's doing the relevant things under suitable supervision and guidance. In the case of programming the activity should include discussions of the relation between the program and the relevant aspects and activities of the real world, and of the limits set on the real world matters dealt with by the program.

A very important consequence of the Theory Building View is that program revival, that is reestablishing the theory of a program merely from the documentation, is strictly impossible. Lest this consequence may seem unreasonable it may be noted that the need for revival of an entirely dead program probably will rarely arise, since it is hardly conceivable that the revival would be assigned to new programmers without at least some knowledge of the theory had by the original team. Even so the Theory Building View suggests strongly that program revival should only be attempted in exceptional situations and with full awareness that it is at best costly, and may lead to a revived theory that differs from the one originally had by the program authors and so may contain discrepancies with the program text.

In preference to program revival, the Theory Building View suggests, the existing program text should be discarded and the new-formed programmer team should be given the opportunity to solve the given problem afresh. Such a procedure is more likely to produce a viable program than program revival, and at no higher, and possibly lower, cost. The point is that building a theory to fit and support an existing program text is a difficult, frustrating, and time consuming activity. The new programmer is likely to feel torn between loyalty to the existing program text, with whatever obscurities and weaknesses it may contain, and the new theory that he or she has to build up, and which, for better or worse, most likely will differ from the original theory behind the program text.

Similar problems are likely to arise even when a program is kept continuously alive by an evolving team of programmers, as a result of the differences of competence and background experience of the individual programmers, particularly as the team is being kept operational by inevitable replacements of the individual members.

Method and Theory Building

Recent years [have] seen much interest in programming methods. In the present section some comments will be made on the relation between the Theory Building View and the notions behind programming methods.

To begin with, what is a programming method? This is not always made clear, even by authors who recommend a particular method. Here a programming method will be taken to be a set of work rules for programmers, telling what kind of things the programmers should do, in what order, which notations or languages to use, and what kinds of documents to produce at various stages.

In comparing this notion of method with the Theory Building View of programming, the most important issue is that of actions or operations and their ordering. A method implies a claim that program development can and should proceed as a sequence of actions of certain kinds, each action leading to a particular kind of documented result. In building the theory there can be no particular sequence of actions, for the reason that a theory held by a person has no inherent division into parts and no inherent ordering. Rather, the person possessing a theory will be able to produce presentations of various sorts on the basis of it, in response to questions or demands.

As to the use of particular kinds of notation or formalization, again this can only be a secondary issue since the primary item, the theory, is not, and cannot be, expressed, and so no question of the form of its expression arises.

It follows that on the Theory Building View, for the primary activity of the programming there can be no right method.

This conclusion may seem to conflict with established opinion, in several ways, and might thus be taken to be an argument against the Theory Building View. Two such apparent contradictions shall be taken up here, the first relating to the importance of method in the pursuit of science, the second concerning the success of methods as actually used in software development.

The first argument is that software development should be based on scientific manners, and so should employ procedures similar to scientific methods. The flaw of this argument is the assumption that there is such a thing as scientific method and that it is helpful to scientists. This question has been the subject of much debate in recent years, and the conclusion of such authors as Feyerabend [1978], taking his illustrations from the history of physics, and Medawar [1982], arguing as a biologist, is that the notion of scientific method as a set of guidelines for the practising scientist is mistaken.

This conclusion is not contradicted by such work as that of Polya [1954, 1957] on problem solving. This work takes its illustrations from the field of mathematics and leads to insight which is also highly relevant to programming. However, it cannot be claimed to present a method on which to proceed. Rather, it is a collection of suggestions aiming at stimulating the mental activity of the problem solver, by pointing out different modes of work that may be applied in any sequence.

The second argument that may seem to contradict the dismissal of method of the Theory Building View is that the use of particular methods has been successful, according to published reports. To this argument it may be answered that a methodically satisfactory study of the efficacy of programming methods so far never seems to have been made. Such a study would have to employ the well established technique of controlled experiments (cf. [Brooks, 1980] or [Moher and Schneider, 1982]). The lack of such studies is explainable partly by the high cost that would undoubtedly be incurred in such investigations if the results were to be significant, partly by the problems of establishing in an operational fashion the concepts underlying what is called methods in the field of program development. Most published reports on such methods merely describe and recommend certain techniques and procedures, without establishing their usefulness or efficacy in any systematic way. An elaborate study of five different methods by C. Floyd and several co-workers [Floyd, 1984] concludes that the notion of methods as systems of rules that in an arbitrary context and mechanically will lead to good solutions is an illusion. What remains is the effect of methods in the education of programmers. This conclusion is entirely compatible with the Theory Building View of programming. Indeed, on this view the quality of the theory built by the programmer will depend to a large extent on the programmer's familiarity with model solutions of typical problems, with techniques of description and verification, and with principles of structuring systems consisting of many parts in complicated interactions. Thus many of the items of concern of methods are relevant to theory building. Where the Theory Building View departs from that of the methodologists is on the question of which techniques to use and in what order. On the Theory Building View this must remain entirely a matter for the programmer to decide, taking into account the actual problem to be solved.

Programmers' Status and the Theory Building View

The areas where the consequences of the Theory Building View contrast most strikingly with those of the more prevalent current views are those of the programmers' personal contribution to the activity and of the programmers' proper status.

The contrast between the Theory Building View and the more prevalent view of the programmers' personal contribution is apparent in much of the common discussion of programming. As just one

example, consider the study of modifiability of large software systems by Oskarsson [1982]. This study gives extensive information on a considerable number of modifications in one release of a large commercial system. The description covers the background, substance, and implementation, of each modification, with particular attention to the manner in which the program changes are confined to particular program modules. However, there is no suggestion whatsoever that the implementation of the modifications might depend on the background of the 500 programmers employed on the project, such as the length of time they have been working on it, and there is no indication of the manner in which the design decisions are distributed among the 500 programmers. Even so the significance of an underlying theory is admitted indirectly in statements such as that 'decisions were implemented in the wrong block' and in a reference to 'a philosophy of AXE'. However, by the manner in which the study is conducted these admissions can only remain isolated indications.

More generally, much current discussion of programming seems to assume that programming is similar to industrial production, the programmer being regarded as a component of that production, a component that has to be controlled by rules of procedure and which can be replaced easily. Another related view is that human beings perform best if they act like machines, by following rules, with a consequent stress on formal modes of expression, which make it possible to formulate certain arguments in terms of rules of formal manipulation. Such views agree well with the notion, seemingly common among persons working with computers, that the human mind works like a computer. At the level of industrial management these views support treating programmers as workers of fairly low responsibility, and only brief education.

On the Theory Building View the primary result of the programming activity is the theory held by the programmers. Since this theory by its very nature is part of the mental possession of each programmer, it follows that the notion of the programmer as an easily replaceable component in the program production activity has to be abandoned. Instead the programmer must be regarded as a responsible developer and manager of the activity in which the computer is a part. In order to fill this position he or she must be given a permanent position, of a status similar to that of other professionals, such as engineers and lawyers, whose active contributions as employers of enterprises rest on their intellectual proficiency.

The raising of the status of programmers suggested by the Theory Building View will have to be supported by a corresponding reorientation of the programmer education. While skills such as the mastery of notations, data representations, and data processes, remain important, the primary emphasis would have to turn in the direction of furthering the understanding and talent for theory formation. To what extent this can be taught at all must remain an open question. The most hopeful approach would be to have the student work on concrete problems under guidance, in an active and constructive environment.

Conclusions

Accepting program modifications demanded by changing external circumstances to be an essential part of programming, it is argued that the primary aim of programming is to have the programmers build a theory of the way the matters at hand may be supported by the execution of a program. Such a view leads to a notion of program life that depends on the continued support of the program by programmers having its theory. Further, on this view the notion of a programming method, understood as a set of rules of procedure to be followed by the programmer, is based on invalid assumptions and so has to be rejected. As further consequences of the view, programmers have to be accorded the status of responsible, permanent developers and managers of the activity of which the computer is a part, and their education has to emphasize the exercise of theory building, side by side with the acquisition of knowledge of data processing and notations.

References

Brooks, R. E. Studying programmer behaviour experimentally. *Comm. ACM* 23(4): 207–213, 1980.

Feyerabend, P. *Against Method*. London, Verso Editions, 1978; ISBN: 86091-700-2.

Floyd, C. Eine Untersuchung von Software-Entwicklungs-Methoden. Pp. 248–274 in *Programmierumgebungen und Compiler*, ed H. Morgenbrod and W. Sammer, Tagung I/1984 des German Chapter of the ACM, Stuttgart, Teubner Verlag, 1984; ISBN: 3-519-02437-3.

Kuhn, T. S. *The Structure of Scientific Revolutions*, Second Edition. Chicago,

University of Chicago Press, 1970; ISBN: 0-226-45803-2.

Medawar, P. *Pluto's Republic*. Oxford, University Press, 1982: ISBN: 0-19-217726-5.

Moher, T., and Schneider, G. M. Methodology and experimental research in software engineering, *Int. J. Man-Mach. Stud.* 16: 65-87, 1. Jan. 1982.

Oskarsson, Ö Mechanisms of modifiability in large software systems *Linköping Studies in Science and Technology, Dissertations, no. 77*, Linköping, 1982; ISBN: 91-7372-527-7.

Polya, G. *How To Solve It* . New York, Doubleday Anchor Book, 1957.

Polya, G. *Mathematics and Plausible Reasoning*. New Jersey, Princeton University Press, 1954.

Popper, K. R., and Eccles, J. C. *The Self and Its Brain*. London, Routledge and Kegan Paul, 1977.

Ryle, G. The *Concept of Mind*. Harmondsworth, England, Penguin, 1963, first published 1949.

Applying "Theory Building"

Viewing programming as theory building helps us understand "metaphor building" activity in Extreme Programming (XP), and the respective roles of tacit knowledge and documentation in passing along design knowledge.

The Metaphor as a Theory

Kent Beck suggested that it is useful to a design team to simplify the general design of a program to match a single metaphor. Examples might be, "This program really looks like an assembly line, with things getting added to a chassis along the line," or "This program really looks like a restaurant, with waiters and menus, cooks and cashiers."

If the metaphor is good, the many associations the designers create around the metaphor turn out to be appropriate to their programming situation.

That is exactly Naur's idea of passing along a theory of the design.

If "assembly line" is an appropriate metaphor, then later programmers, considering what they know about assembly lines, will make guesses about the structure of the software at hand and find that their guesses are "close." That is an extraordinary power for just the two words, "assembly line."

The value of a good metaphor increases with the number of designers. The closer each person's guess is "close" to the other people's guesses, the greater the resulting consistency in the final system design.

Imagine 10 programmers working as fast as they can, in parallel, each making design decisions and adding classes as she goes. Each will necessarily develop her own theory as she goes. As each adds code, the theory that binds their work becomes less and less coherent, more and more complicated. Not only maintenance gets harder, but their own work gets harder. The design easily becomes a "kludge." If they have a common theory, on the other hand, they add code in ways that fit together.

An appropriate, shared metaphor lets a person guess accurately where someone else on the team just added code, and how to fit her new piece in with it.

Tacit Knowledge and Documentation

The documentation is almost certainly behind the current state of the program, but people are good at looking around. What should you put into the documentation?

That which helps the next programmer build an adequate theory of the program.

This is enormously important. The purpose of the documentation is to jog memories in the reader, set up relevant pathways of thought about experiences and metaphors.

This sort of documentation is more stable over the life of the program than just naming the pieces of the system currently in place.

The designers are allowed to use whatever forms of expression are necessary to set up those relevant pathways. They can even use multiple metaphors, if they don't find one that is adequate for the entire program. They might say that one section implements a fractal compression algorithm, a second is like an accounting ledger, the user interface follows the model-observer design pattern, and so on.

Experienced designers often start their documentation with just

- The metaphors
- Text describing the purpose of each major component
- Drawings of the major interactions between the major components

These three items alone take the next team a long way to constructing a useful theory of the design.

The source code itself serves to communicate a theory to the next programmer. Simple, consistent naming conventions help the next person build a coherent theory. When people talk about "clean code," a large part of what they are referring to is how easily the reader can build a coherent theory of the system.

Documentation cannot—and so need not—say everything. Its purpose is to help the next programmer build an accurate theory about the system.

PELLE EHN, WITTGENSTEIN'S LANGUAGE GAMES

In *Work-Oriented Development of Software Artifacts* (Ehn 1988), Pelle Ehn describes a series of projects that explored ways of making software more appropriate to its final use, easier to use, and made by both programmers and end users.

The high point of the book for me is the way in which he considers software development in the context of four philosophers: Descartes, Marx, Heidegger, and Wittgenstein.

A person working in the style of Descartes thinks of an external reality worth describing and turns her efforts toward capturing that reality. She is therefore interested in the match to reality of the requirements, models, and code. This Cartesian approach filled our field's first half-century.

A person working in the style of Marx first asks, "Whom does this new system benefit? How does its deployment change the social power structure?" This is a meaningful question to consider, whether you like Marx's political theories or not.

A person working in the style of Heidegger considers the efficacy of the system as a tool. Ideally, the user should not "see" the system at all. She should see through the system to the task being performed. When I am typing a document, for example, I see the page growing text; I don't "see" the word processor. An accomplished pianist sees the music being formed, not the piano; a good carpenter sees the nail going into the wood, not the hammering tool. Heidegger's frame of evaluation helps us produce systems more fit for use.

It is only the style of Wittgenstein that opposes the style of Descartes. A person working in this style views the unfolding of the software design as the unfolding of a language game, in which new words are added to the language over time.

This immediately links to software development as a cooperative game of invention and communication. I probably owe a good deal of my construction of the cooperative game model to Ehn's writings. I had read and forgotten the following article years before working out the cooperative game idea. As I started to write this book, I reviewed this article and was shocked to see how many of my words echoed Ehn's.

Ehn is concerned with the building of shared experience through shared practice, of using practice directly as a basis for discovering needs. In other words, he is working with tacit knowledge. More than that, he highlights the place of *skill* in carrying out practices (it is interesting to read Musashi's words pointing out much the same). Although skill is a topic I have mentioned, Ehn develops it much more thoughtfully and completely.

I took the game thinking in a different direction. I am concerned with playing a group game amicably, so that communication can take place at all. You will see that Ehn's ideas complement the rest of the ideas in this book.

Pelle Ehn expresses it much better in his own words than I can through summaries. *Work-Oriented Development of Software Artifacts* is out of print, sadly. However, this excerpt from "Scandinavian Design: On

Participation and Skill" (Ehn 1992) contains the line of thinking I feel is so important.

The article is longer than I can reproduce here. In this extract, I added italics to emphasize points relevant to the notion of cooperative games.

"ON PARTICIPATION AND SKILL"

. . .

In the following, I will propose that this new understanding can be buttressed by an awareness of language games and the ordinary language philosophy of Ludwig Wittgenstein. My focus is on the shift in design from language as description towards language as action.

Rethinking Systems Descriptions

A few years ago I was struck by something I had not noticed before. While thinking about how perspectives make us select certain aspects of reality as important in a description, I realized I had completely overlooked *my own presumption that descriptions in one way or another are mirror images of a given reality.* My earlier reasoning had been that because there are different interests in the world, we should always question the objectivity of design choices that claimed to flow from design as a process of rational decision making. Hence, *I had argued that we needed to create descriptions from different perspectives in order to form a truer picture.* I did not, however, question the Cartesian epis ontology of an inner world of experiences (mind) and an outer world of objects (external reality). Nor did I *question the assumption that language was our way of mirroring this outer world* of real objects. By focusing on

which objects and which relations should be represented in a systems description, I took for granted the Cartesian mind-body dualism that Wittgenstein had so convincingly rejected in Philosophical Investigations (1953). Hence, although my purpose was the opposite, my perspective blinded me to the subjectivity of craft, artistry, passion, love, and care in the system descriptions.

Our experiences with the UTOPIA project caused me to re-examine my philosophical assumptions. Working with the end users of the design, the graphics workers, some design methods failed while others succeeded. *Requirement specifications and systems descriptions based on information from interviews were not very successful.* Improvements came when we made joint visits to interesting plants, trade shows, and vendors and had discussions with other users; when we dedicated considerably more time to learning from each other, designers from graphics workers and graphics workers from designers; *when we started to use design-by-doing methods and descriptions such as mockups and work organization games;* and when we started to understand and use traditional tools as a design ideal for computer-based systems.

The turnaround can be understood in the light of two Wittgensteinian lessons. The first is not to underestimate the importance of skill in design. As Peter Winch (1958) has put it, "A cook is not a man who first has a vision of a pie and then tries to make it. He is a man skilled in cookery, and both his projects and his achievements spring from that skill." The second is not to mistake the role of description methods in design: Wittgenstein argues convincingly that what a picture describes is determined by its use.

In the following I will illustrate how our "new" UTOPIAN design methods may be understood from a Wittgensteinian position, that is, why design-by-doing and a skill-based participatory design process works. *More generally, I will argue that design tools such as models, prototypes, mockups, descriptions, and representations act as reminders and paradigm cases for our contemplation of future computer-based systems and their use. Such design tools are effective because they recall earlier experiences to mind.* It is in this sense that we should understand them as representations. I will begin with a few words on practice, the alternative to the "picture theory of reality".

Practice Is Reality

Practice as the social construction of reality is a strong candidate for replacing the picture theory of reality. In short, practice is our everyday practical activity. It is the human form of life. It precedes subject-object relations. Through practice, we produce the world, both the world of objects and our knowledge about this world. Practice is both action and reflection. But practice is also a social activity; it is produced in cooperation with others. To share practice is also to share an understanding of the world with others. However, this production of the world and our understanding of it take place in an already existing world. The world is also the product of former practice. Hence, as part of practice, knowledge has to be understood socially—as producing or reproducing social processes and structures as well as

being the product of them (Kosik, 1967; Berger & Luckmann, 1966).

Against this background, we can understand the design of computer applications as a concerned social- and historical-conditioned activity in which tools and their use are envisioned. This is an activity and form of knowledge that is both planned and creative.

Once struck by the "naive" Cartesian presumptions of a picture theory, what can be gained in design by shifting focus from the correctness of descriptions to intervention into practice? What does it imply to take the position that what a picture describes is determined by its use? Most importantly, *it sensitizes us to the crucial role of skill and participation in design*, and to the opportunity in practical design to transcend some of the limits of formalization through the use of more action-oriented design artifacts.

Language as Action

Think of the classical example of a carpenter and his or her hammering activity. In the professional language of carpenters, there are not only hammers and nails. If the carpenter were making a chair, other tools used would include a draw-knife, a brace, a trying plane, a hollow plane, a round plane, a bow-saw, a marking gauge, and chisels (Seymour, 1984). The materials that he works with are elm planks for the seats, ash for the arms, and oak for the legs. He is involved in saddling, making spindles, and steaming.

Are we as designers of new tools for chairmaking helped by this labeling of tools, materials, and activities? In a Wittgensteinian approach the answer would be: only if we understand the practice in which these names make sense. To label our experiences is to act deliberately. To label deliberately, we have to be trained to do so. Hence, the activity of labeling has to be learned. Language is not private but social. The labels we create are part of a practice that constitutes social meaning. We cannot learn without learning something specific. To understand and to be able to use is one and the same (Wittgenstein, 1953). Understanding the professional language of chairmaking, and any other language-game (to use Wittgenstein's term), is to be able to master practical rules we did not create ourselves. The rules are techniques and conventions for chairmaking that are an inseparable part of a given practice.

To master the professional language of chairmaking means to be able to act in an effective way together with other people who know chairmaking. To "know" does not mean explicitly knowing the rules you have learned, but rather recognizing when something is done in a correct or incorrect way. To have a concept is to have learned to follow rules as part of a given practice. Speech acts are, as a unity of language and action, part of practice. They are not descriptions but below I will elaborate on language-games, focusing on the design process descriptions in design, design artifacts, and knowledge in the design of computer applications.

Language-Games

To use language is to participate in language-games. In discussing how we in practice follow (and sometimes break) rules as a social activity, Wittgenstein asks us to think of games, how they are made up and played. We often think of games in terms of a playful, pleasurable engagement. I think this aspect should not be denied, but a more important aspect for our purpose here is that games are activities, as are most of the common language-games we play in our ordinary language.

Language-games, like the games we play as children, are social activities. To be able to play these games, we have to learn to follow rules, rules that are socially created but far from always explicit. *The rule-following behavior of being able to play together with others is more important to a game than the specific explicit rules.* Playing is interaction and cooperation. *To follow the rules in practice means to be able to act in a way that others in the game can understand.* These rules are embedded in a given practice from which they cannot be distinguished. To know them is to be able to "embody" them, to be able to apply them to an open class of cases.

We understand what counts as a game not because we have an explicit definition but because we are already familiar with other games. There is a kind of family resemblance between games. Similarly, professional language-games can be learned and understood because of their family resemblance to other language-games that we know how to play.

Language-games are performed both as speech acts and as other activities, as meaningful practice within societal and cultural institutional frameworks. To be able to participate in the practice of a specific language-game, one has to share the form of life within which that practice is possible. This form of life includes our natural history as well as the social institutions and traditions into which we are born. This condition precedes agreed social conventions and rational reasoning. Language as a means of communication requires agreement not only in definitions, but also in judgments. Hence, intersubjective consensus is more fundamentally a question of shared background and language than of stated opinions (Wittgenstein, 1953).

This definition seems to make us prisoners of language and tradition, which is not really the case. Being socially created, the rules of language games, like those of other games, can also be socially altered. *There are, according to Wittgenstein, even games in which we make up and alter the rules as we go along. Think of systems design and use as language games. The very idea of the interventionistic design language-game is to change the rules of the language-game of use in a proper way.*

The idea of language-games entails an emphasis on how we linguistically discover and construct our world. However, language is understood as our use of it, as our social, historic, and intersubjective application of linguistic artifacts. As I see it, the language-game perspective therefore does not preclude consideration of how we also come to understand the world by use of other tools.

Tools and objects play a fundamental role in many language-games. A hammer is in itself a sign of what one can do with it in certain language-games. And so is a computer application. *These signs remind one of what can be done with them.* In this light, an important aspect in the design of computer applications is that its signs remind the users of what they can do with the application in the language-games of use (Brock, 1986). The success of "what-you-see-is-what-you-get" and "direct manipulation" user interfaces does not have to do with how they mirror reality in a more natural way, but with how they provide better reminders of the users' earlier experiences (Bødker, forthcoming). This is also, as will be discussed in the following, the case with the tools that we use in the design process.

Knowledge and Design Artifacts

As designers we are involved in reforming practice, in our case typically computer-based systems and the way people use them. Hence, the language-games of design change the rules for other language-games, in particular those of the application's use. What are the conditions for this interplay and change to operate effectively?

A common assumption behind most design approaches seems to be that the users must be able to give complete and explicit descriptions of their demands. Hence, the emphasis is on methods to support this elucidation by means of requirement specifications or system descriptions (Jackson, 1983; Yourdon, 1982).

In a Wittgensteinian approach, the focus is not on the "correctness" of systems descriptions in design, on how well they mirror the desires in the mind of the users, or on how correctly they describe existing and future systems and their use. Systems descriptions are design artifacts. In a Wittgensteinian approach, the crucial question is how we use them, that is, what role they play in the design process.

The rejection of an emphasis on the "correctness" of descriptions is especially important. In this, we are advised by the author of perhaps the strongest arguments for a picture theory and the Cartesian approach to design—the young Wittgenstein in Tractatus Logico-Philosophicus (1923). The reason for this rejection is the fundamental role of practical knowledge and creative rule following in language-games.

Nevertheless, we know that systems descriptions are useful in the language-game of design. The new orientation suggested in a Wittgensteinian approach is that we see such descriptions as a special kind of artifact that we use as "typical examples" or "paradigm cases." *They are not models in the sense of Cartesian mirror images of reality* (Nordenstam, 1984). *In the language-game of design, we use these tools as reminders for our reflection on future computer applications and their use. By using such design artifacts, we bring earlier experiences to mind, and they bend our way of thinking of the past and the future.* I think that this is why we should understand them as representations (Kaasboll, forthcoming). And this is how they inform our practice. *If they are good design artifacts, they will support good moves within a specific design language-game.*

The meaning of a design artifact is its use in a design language-game, not how it "mirrors reality." Its ability to support such use depends on the kinds of experience it evokes, its family resemblance to tools that the participants use in their everyday work activity. Therein lies a clue to why the breakthrough in the UTOPIA project was related to the use of prototypes and mockups. Since the design artifacts took the form of reminders or paradigm cases, they did not merely attempt to mirror a given or future practice linguistically. They could be experienced through the practical use of a prototype or mockup. This experience could be further reflected upon in the language-game of design, either in ordinary language or in an artificial one.

A good example from the UTOPIA project is an empty cardboard box with "desktop laser printer" written on the top. There is no functionality in this mockup. Still, it works very well in the design game of envisioning the future work of makeup staff. It reminded the participating typographers of the old "proof machine" they used to work with in lead technology. At the same time, it suggested that with the help of new technology, the old proof machine could be reinvented and enhanced.

This design language-game was played in 1982. At that time, desktop laser printers only existed in advanced research laboratories, and certainly typographers had never heard of them. To them, the idea of a cheap laser printer was "unreal."

It was our responsibility as professional designers to be aware of such future possibilities and to suggest them to the users. It was also our role to suggest this technical and organizational solution in such a way that the users could experience and envision what it would mean in their practical work, before the investment of too much time, money, and development work. Hence, the design game with the mockup laser printer. The mockup made sense to all participants—users and designers (Ehn & Kyng, 1991).

This focus on nonlinguistic design artifacts is not a rejection of the importance of linguistic ones. Understood as triggers for our imagination rather than as mirror images of reality, they may well be our most wonderful human inventions. Linguistic design artifacts are very effective when they challenge us to tell stories that make sense to all participants.

Practical Understanding and Propositional Knowledge

There are many actions in a language-game, not least in the use of prototypes and mockups, that cannot be explicitly described in a formal language. What is it that the users know, that is, what have they learned that they can express in action, but not state explicitly in language? Wittgenstein (1953) asks us to "compare knowing and saying: how many feet high Mont Blanc is—how the word 'game' is used—how a clarinet sounds. If you are surprised that one can know something you are perhaps thinking of a case like the first. Certainly not of one of the third."

In the UTOPIA project, we were designing new computer applications to be used in typographical page makeup. The typographers could tell us the names of the different tools and materials that they use such as knife, page ground, body text, galley, logo, halftone, frame, and spread. They could also tell when, and perhaps in which order, they use specific tools and materials to place an article. For example, they could say, "First you pick up the body text with the knife and place it at the bottom of the designated area on the page ground. Then you adjust it to the galley line. When the body text fits you get the headline, if there is not a picture," and so forth. What I, as designer, get to know from such an account is equivalent to knowing the height of Mont Blanc. What I get to know is very different from the practical understanding of really making up pages, just as knowing the height of Mont Blanc gives me very little of understanding the practical experience of climbing the mountain.

Knowledge of the first kind has been called propositional knowledge. It is what you have "when you know that something is the case and when you also can describe what you know in so many words" (Nordenstam, 1985). Propositional knowledge is not necessarily more reflective than practical understanding. It might just be something that I have been told, but of which I have neither practical experience nor theoretical understanding.

The second case, corresponding to knowing how the word game is used, was more complicated for our typographers. How could they, for example, tell us the skill they possess in knowing how to handle the knife when making up the page in pasteup technology? This is their practical experience from the language-games of typographic design. To show it, they have to do it.

And how should they relate what counts as good layout, the complex interplay of presence and absence, light and dark, symmetry and asymmetry, uniformity and variety? Could they do it in any other way than by giving examples of good and bad layouts, examples that they have learned by participating in the games of typographical design? As in the case of knowing how a clarinet sounds, this is typically sensuous knowing by familiarity with earlier cases of how something is, sounds, smells, and so on.

Practical understanding—in the sense of practical experience from doing something and having sensuous experiences from earlier cases—defies formal description. If it were transformed into propositional knowledge, it would become something totally different.

It is hard to see how we as designers of computer systems for page makeup could manage to come up with useful designs without understanding how the knife is used or what counts as good layout. For this reason we had to have access to more than what can be stated as explicit propositional knowledge. We could only achieve this understanding by participating to some extent in the language-games of use of the typographical tools. Hence, participation applies not only to users participating in the language-game of design, but perhaps more importantly to designers participating in use. Some consequences of this position for organizing design language-games will be discussed in the following.

Rule Following and Tradition

Now, I turn to the paradox of rule-following behavior. As mentioned, many rules that we follow in practice can scarcely be distinguished from the behavior in which we perform them. We do not know that we have followed a rule until we have done it. The most important rules we follow in skillful performance defy formalization, but we still understand them. As Michael Polanyi (1973),

the philosopher of tacit knowledge, has put it: "It is pathetic to watch the endless efforts—equipped with microscopy and chemistry, with mathematics and electronics—to reproduce a single violin of the kind the half-literate Stradevarius turned out as a matter of routine more than 200 years ago." This is the traditional aspect of human rule-following behavior. Polanyi points out that what may be our most widely recognized, explicit, rule-based system—the practice of Common Law—also uses earlier examples as paradigm cases. Says Polanyi, "[Common Law] recognizes the principle of all traditionalism that practical wisdom is more truly embodied in action than expressed in the rules of action." According to Polanyi this is also true for science, no matter how rationalistic and explicit it claims to be: "While the articulate contents of science are successfully taught all over the world in hundreds of new universities, the unspecifiable art of scientific research has not yet penetrated to many of these." The art of scientific research defies complete formalization; it must be learned partly by examples from a master whose behavior the student trusts.

Involving skilled users in the design of new computer application when their old tools and working habits are redesigned is an excellent illustration of Polanyi's thesis. If activities that have been under such pressure for formalization as Law and Science are so dependent on practical experience and paradigm cases, why should we expect other social institutions that have been under less pressure of formalization to be less based on practical experience, paradigm cases, and tacit knowledge?

Rule Following and Transcendence

If design is rule-following behavior, is it also creative transcendence of traditional behavior. Again, this is what is typical of skillful human behavior, and is exactly what defies precise formalization. *Through mastery of the rules comes the freedom to extend them.* This creativity is based on the open-textured character of rule-following behavior. *To begin with, we learn to follow a rule as a kind of dressage, but in the end we do it as creative activity* (Dreyfus & Dreyfus, 1986). Mastery of the rules puts us in a position to invent new ways of proceeding. As the Wittgenstein commentator Alan Janik has put it: "There is always and ineliminably the possibility that we can follow the rule in a wholly unforeseen way. This could not happen if we had to have an explicit rule to go on from the start . . . the possibility of radical innovation is, however, the logical limit of description. This is what tacit knowledge is all about" (Janik, 1988). This is why we need a strong focus on skill both in design and in the use of computer systems. We focus on existing skills, not as to inhibit creative transcendence, but as a necessary condition for it.

But what is the role of "new" external ideas and experiences in design? How are tradition and transcendence united in a Wittgensteinian approach? It could, I believe, mean utilizing something like Berthold Brecht's theatrical "alienation" effect Verfremdungseffekt to highlight transcendental untried possibilities in the everyday practice by presenting a well-known practice in a new light: "the aspects of things that are most important to us are hidden because of their simplicity and familiarity" (Wittgenstein, 1953). However, as Peter Winch (1958, p. 119) put it, in a Wittgensteinian approach: "the only legitimate use of such a Verfremdungseffekt is to draw attention to the familiar and obvious, not to show that it is dispensable from our understanding."

Design artifacts, linguistic or not, may in a Wittgensteinian approach certainly be used to break down traditional understanding, but they must make sense in the users' ordinary language-games. If the design tools are effective, it is because they help users and designers to see new aspects of an already well-known practice, not because they convey such new ideas. It is I think fair to say that this focus on traditional skill in interplay with design skill may be a hindrance to really revolutionary designs. The development of radically new designs might require leveraging other skills and involving other potential users. Few designs, however, are really revolutionary, and for normal everyday design situations, the participation of traditionally skilled users is critical to the quality of the resulting product.

The tension between tradition and transcendence is fundamental to design. There can be a focus on tradition or transcendence in the systems being created. Should a word processor be designed as an extension of the traditional typewriter or as something totally new? Another dimension is professional competence: Should one design for the "old" skills of typographers or should new knowledge replace those skills in future use? Or again, with the division of labor and cooperation: Should the new design support the traditional organization in a composing room or suggest new ways of cooperation between typographers and journalists? There is also the tension between tradition and transcendence in the goods or services to be produced using the new system: Should the design support the traditional graphical production or completely new services, such as desktop publishing?

Tradition and transcendence, that is the dialectical foundation of design.

Design by Doing: New "Rules of the Game"

What do we as designers have to do to qualify as participants in the language-games of the users? What do users have to learn to qualify as participants in the language-game of design? And what means can we develop in design to facilitate these learning processes?

If designers and users share the same form of life, it should be possible to overcome the gap between the different language-games. It should, at least in principle, be possible to develop the practice of design to the point where there is enough family resemblance between a specific language-game of the users and the language-games in which the designers of the computer application are intervening. A mediation should be possible.

But what are the conditions required to establish this mediation? For Wittgenstein, it would make no sense to ask this question outside a given form of life: "If a lion could talk, we could not understand him" (1953). In the arguments below, I have assumed that the conditions for a common form of life are possible to create,

that the lions and sheep of industrial life, as discussed in the first part of this chapter, can live together. This is more a normative standpoint of how design ought to be, a democratic hope rather than a reflection on current political conditions.

To develop the competence required to participate in a language-game requires a lot of learning within that practice. *But, in the beginning, all one can understand is what one has already understood in another language-game.* If we understand anything at all, it is because of the family resemblance between the two language-games.

What kind of design tools could support this interplay between language-games? I think that what we in the UTOPIA project called design-by-doing methods—prototyping, mockups, and scenarios—are good candidates. Even joint visits to workplaces, especially ones similar to the ones being designed for, served as a kind of design tool through which designers and users bridged their language-games.

The language-games played in design-by-doing can be viewed both from the point of view of the users and of the designers. This kind of design becomes a language-game in which the users learn about possibilities and constraints of new computer tools that may become part of their ordinary language-games. The designers become the teachers that teach the users how to participate in this particular language-game of design. However, to set up these kind of language-games, the designers have to learn from the users.

However, paradoxical as it sounds, users and designers do not have to understand each other fully in playing language-games of design-by-doing together.

Participation in a language-game of design and the use of design artifacts can make constructive but different sense to users and designers. Wittgenstein (1953) notes that "when children play at trains their game is connected with their knowledge of trains. It would nevertheless be possible for the children of a tribe unacquainted with trains to learn this game from others, and to play it without knowing that it was copied from anything. One might say that the game did not make the same sense as to us." As long as the language-game of design is not a nonsense activity to any participant but a shared activity for better understanding and good design, mutual understanding may be desired but not really required.

User Participation and Skill

The users can participate in the language-game of design because the application of the design artifacts gives their design activities a family resemblance with the language-games that they play in ordinary use situations. An example from the UTOPIA project is a typographer sitting at a mockup of a future workstation for page makeup, doing page makeup on the simulated future computer tool.

The family resemblance is only one aspect of the methods. Another aspect involves what can be expressed. In design-by-doing, the user is able to express both propositional knowledge and practical understanding. Not only could, for example, the typographer working at the mockup tell that the screen should be bigger to show a full page spread—something important in page makeup—he could also show what he meant by "cropping a

picture" by actually doing it as he said it. It was thus possible for him to express his practical understanding, his sensuous knowledge by familiarity. He could, while working at the mockup, express the fact that when the system is designed one way he can get a good balanced page, but not when it is designed another way.

Designer Participation and Skill

For us as designers, it was possible to express both propositional knowledge and practical understanding about design and computer systems. Not only could we express propositional knowledge such as "design-by-doing design tools have many advantages as compared with traditional systems descriptions" or "bit-map displays bigger than 22 inches and with a resolution of more than 2000 x 2000 pixels are very expensive," but in the language-game of design-by-doing, we could also express practical understanding of technical constraints and possibilities by "implementing" them in the mockup, prototype, simulation, or experimental situation. Simulations of the user interface were also important in this language-game of design.

As designers, our practical understanding will mainly be expressed in the ability to construct specific language-games of design in such a way that the users can develop their understanding of future use by participating in design processes.

As mentioned above, there is a further important aspect of language-games: We make up the rules as we go along. A skilled designer should be able to assist in such transcendental rule-breaking activities. Perhaps, this is the artistic competence that a good designer needs.

To really learn the language-game of the use activity by fully participating in that language-game is, of course, an even more radical approach for the designer. Less radical but perhaps more practical would be for designers to concentrate design activity on just a few language-games of use, and for us to develop a practical understanding of useful specific language-games of design (Ehn & Kyng, 1987). Finally, there seems to be a new role for the designer as the one who sets the stage for a shared design language-game that makes sense to all participants.

Some Lessons on Design, Skill, and Participation

As in the first practice-oriented part of this paper on designing for democracy at work, I end this second philosophically oriented part on skill-based participatory design with some lessons for work-oriented design.

General lessons on work-oriented design include:

1. Understanding design as a process of creating new language-games that have family resemblance with the language-games of both users and designers gives us an orientation for doing work-oriented design through skill-based participation—a way of doing design that may help us transcend some of the limits of formalization. Setting up these design language-games is a new role for the designer.
2. Traditional "systems descriptions" are not sufficient in a skill-based participatory design approach. Design artifacts should not be seen primarily as means

for creating true "pictures of reality," but as means to help users and designers discuss and experience current situations and envision future ones.
3. "Design-by-doing" design approaches such as the use of mockups and other prototyping design artifacts make it possible for ordinary users to use their practical skill when participating in the design process.

Lessons on skill in the design of computer-based systems include:

1. Participatory design is a learning process in which designers and users learn from each other.
2. Besides propositional knowledge, practical understanding is a type of skill that should be taken seriously in a design language-game since the most important rules we follow in skillful performance are embedded in practice and defy formalization.
3. Creativity depends on the open-textured character of rule-following behavior, hence a focus on traditional skill is not a drawback to creative transcendence but a necessary condition. Supporting the dialectics between tradition and transcendence is the heart of design.

Lessons on participation in design of computer-based systems include:

1. Really participatory design requires a shared form of life—a shared social and cultural background and a shared language. Hence, participatory design means not only users participating in

design but also designers participating in use. The professional designer will try to share practice with the users.

2. To make real user participation possible, a design language-game must be set up in such a way that it has a family resemblance to language-games the users have participated in before. Hence, the creative designer should be concerned with the practice of the users in organizing the design process, and understand that every new design language-game is a unique situated design experience. There is, however paradoxical it may sound, no requirement that the design language-game make the same sense to users and designers. There is only [the] requirement that the designer set the stage for a design language-game in which participation makes sense to all participants.

Beyond the Boredom of Design

Given the Scandinavian societal, historical, and cultural setting, the first part of this chapter focused on the democratic aspect of skill-based participatory design, especially the important role of local trade unions and their strategies for user participation. In the second part, some ideas inspired by Ludwig Wittgenstein's philosophical investigations were applied to the everyday practice of skill-based participatory design. Practical understanding and family resemblance between language-games were presented as fundamental concepts for work-oriented design.

The concept of language-games is associated with playful activity, but what practical conditions are needed for such pleasurable engagement in design? Is the right to democratic participation enough?

In fact, the experiences from the work-oriented design projects indicates that most users find design work boring, sometimes to the point where they stop participating. This problem is not unique to the Scandinavian work-oriented design tradition. It has, for example, been addressed by Russell Ackoff (1974), who concluded that participation in design can be only successful if it meets three conditions: (1) it makes a difference for the participants, (2) implementation of the results is likely, and (3) it is fun.

The first two points concern the political side of participation in design. Users must have a guarantee that their design efforts are taken seriously. The last point concerns the design process. No matter how much influence participation may give, it has to transcend the boredom of traditional design meetings to really make design meaningful and full of involved action. The design work should be playful. In our own later projects, we have tried to take this challenge seriously and have integrated the use of future workshops, metaphorical design, role playing and organizational games into work-oriented design (Ehn & Sjogren, 1991).

Hence, the last lesson from Scandinavian designs is that formal democratic and participatory procedures for designing computer-based systems for democracy at work are not sufficient. Our design language-games must also be organized in a way that makes it possible for ordinary users not only to utilize their practical skill in the design work, but also to have fun while doing so.

. . .

REFLECTIONS ON EHN'S WRITING

Each time I read Ehn's article, I discover that I may be more in debt to his writing than I previously thought. Rereading it just prior to writing this paragraph, I was struck by his use of the Shu-Ha-Ri con-struct, to his attention to "understanding through doing," and his understanding of how people grow new understanding through the act of doing.

I evidently wasn't ready to read very many of his words in 1993 and have grown into them over the years. It makes me wonder how many other concepts he mentions, but which I haven't yet noticed.

I hope you will take the time to reread this article in another year or two.

MUSASHI

Miyamoto Musashi was a 17th-century samurai who never wrote software.

He claimed never to have lost a fight. Losing a fight meant serious body damage, and it was quite an accomplishment to be alive with all limbs in place at the age of 70.

A romantic novel series about Musashi depicts his early life, fights, and mental development. It is a wonderful read and also vividly portrays his fighting approach, which his personal book describes.

His personal book is the *Go Rin No Sho*, in English *The Book of Five Rings* (I have the Thomas Cleary translation, Shambhala, 2000), which he wrote at age 70. That book outlines his approach as clearly as he can make it, describing mental states, specific moves, and the use of large groups. It is short, clear, and wonderfully absent of the usual Zen doubletalk, "Be by not being, fight by not fighting, win by losing," and so on.

I include Musashi here because three characteristics of his fighting style match my software development style, and he describes them so well:

- Do not develop an attachment to any one weapon or any one school of fighting.
- Practice and observe reflectively.
- Win.

The first recommendation is to use any and all schools and techniques, without great attachment.

At the time of his writing, warriors formed schools around particular stances, styles, weapons, and tactics. His view was that each had its merits and weaknesses; one should use the range of them without getting stuck in any one.

The same is true in software design techniques. Don't get stuck in UML, RUP, CMM, SEI, XP, CRC (insert your favorite school's or tool's acronym here). Use whichever you need at the instant you need it. Discover what you need at different moments, so you can develop a tool- and method-attack strategy that will tell you which one to pick up and when to put it down.

The second recommendation is to reflect on what you do and how you do it. Reflective practice has been discussed throughout this book.

The third recommendation is to pay more attention to winning than to looking good.

Winning the software development game is shipping the software. If you can do so without process, do so. My favorite-ever recommendation to a group was:

"What? You have a five-week project, with three developers who have done this before in the same technology? You don't need a development coordinator—just do it and go home."

Musashi said, "Do not do anything useless."

Musashi cared about winning the game, which in his case was life-or-death. I am attached to delivering the software. The prettiness of the dance doesn't matter if the software comes out at the wrong time.

In the following, notice that even in the 17th century, Musashi describes Shu-Ha-Ri and the importance of developing skill.

The "opponent" in software development is the problem to be solved. "Killing the opponent" is delivering the software and winning the game. Here are some of his words (or Cleary's translation of them), presented as individual excerpts.

THE BOOK OF FIVE RINGS

- Now, in composing this book, I have not borrowed the old saying of Buddhism or Confucianism, nor do I make use of old stories from military records or books on military science . . .
- The field of martial arts is particularly rife with flamboyant showmanship, with commercial popularization and profiteering on the part of both those who teach the science and those who study it. The result of this must be, as someone said, that "amateuristic martial arts are a source of serious wounds." . . .
- The master carpenter, knowing the measurements and designs of all sorts of structures, employs people to build houses. In this respect, the master carpenter is the same as the master warrior. . . . As the master carpenter directs the journeymen, he knows their various levels of skill and gives them appropriate tasks. . . . Efficiency and smooth progress, prudence in all matters, recognizing true courage, recognizing different levels of morale, instilling confidence, and realizing what can and cannot be reasonably expected-such are the matters on the mind of the master carpenter. The principle of martial arts is like this. . . .
- Speaking in terms of carpentry, soldiers sharpen their own tools, make various useful implements, and keep them in their utility boxes. . . . An essential habit for carpenters is to have sharp tools and keep them whetted. . . .

- You should observe reflectively, with overall awareness of the large picture as well as precise attention to small details. . . .
- Having attained a principle, one detaches from the principle; thus one has spontaneous independence in the science of martial arts and naturally attains marvels: discerning the rhythm when the time comes, one strikes spontaneously and naturally scores. . . .
- In my individual school, one can win with the long sword, and one can win with the short sword as well. For this reason, the precise size of the sword is not fixed. The way of my school is the spirit of gaining victory by any means. . . .
- When your life is on the line, you want to make use of all your tools. . . . We find that whatever the weapon, there is a time and situation in which it is appropriate. . . . Both the spear and the halberd depend on circumstances; neither is very useful in crowded situations. . . . they should be reserved for use on the battlefield. . . . [the bow] is inadequate for seiging a castle. . . .
- In the present age, not only the bow but also the other arts have more flowers than fruit. Such skills are useless where there is a real need....
- You should not have any particular fondness for a particular weapon, or anything else for that matter. Too much is the same as not enough. . . . Pragmatic thinking is essential. . . .

- Whatever guard you adopt, do not think of it as being on guard; think of it as part of the act of killing. . . .
- Whether you adopt a large or small guard depends on the situation; follow whatever is most advantageous. . . .
- (FIRST TECHNIQUE) . . . your sword now having bounced upward, leave it as it is until the opponent strikes again, whereupon you strike the opponent's hands from below. . . .
- (SECOND TECHNIQUE) . . . If your sword misses the opponent, leave it there for the moment, until the opponent strikes again, whereupon you strike from below, sweeping upwards. . . .
- (THIRD TECHNIQUE) . . . as the opponent strikes, you strike at his hands from below. . . . as he tries to knock your sword down, bring it up in rhythm, then chop off his arms sideways. The point is to strike an opponent down all at once from the lower position just as he strikes. . . .
- Having a position without a position, or a guard without a guard, means that the long sword is not supposed to be kept in a fixed position. . . Where you hold your sword depends on your relationship to the opponent, depends on the place, and must conform to the situation; wherever you hold it, the idea is to hold it so that it will be easy to kill the opponent. . . . Even though you may catch, hit, or block an opponent's slashing sword,

or tie it up or obstruct it, all of these moves are opportunities for cutting the opponent down. This must be understood. . . .

- . . . how to win using the long sword according to the laws of martial arts. This cannot be written down in detail; one must realize how to win by practice.
- . . . the power of knowledge of the art of the sword. This is something that requires thorough examination, with a thousand days of practice for training and ten thousand days of practice for refinement. . . .
- Other schools become theatrical, dressing up and showing off to make a living, commercializing martial arts. . . . Do you think you have realized how to attain victory just by learning to wield a long sword and training your body and your hands? This is not a certain way in any case. . . .
- . . . the views of each school, and the logic of each path, are realized differently, according to the individual person, depending on the mentality. . . .
- Thus in my individual school there is an aversion to a narrow, biased attitude. . . .
- In my school, no consideration is given to anything unreasonable; the heart of the matter is to use the power of the knowledge of martial arts to gain victory any way you can. . . .

APPLYING MUSASHI TO SOFTWARE DEVELOPMENT

I share three views with Musashi. I differ on the fourth.

Appropriate Tool, Appropriate Technique

Know your tools, know what you need at the moment, and you will know how to get value out of the tools at your disposal, even if they aren't perfect. You can even profitably use tools that were not originally constructed for software development.

Here is how I work in two different circumstances.

When given a CASE tool to use, I first exclude from use all of the tool's capabilities that do not lend value to the project at hand. Although this is an underutilization of an expensive tool, my goal is not to use a tool to its maximum, it is to deliver software.

On a different project, we may select as our primary strategy having the CASE tool create the final code. On this project, we plan on extending the tool as we need to so that it performs the job we want it to do.

Know your favorite tools and techniques for key tasks without getting overly attached to any one. Learn to adapt to whatever is available.

Direct Solution

See if you can just "cut off your opponent's arm with a single blow," as in sword fighting. In software terms, see if you can just "do it and go home." Avoid waste.

When you have to feint, block, and parry, understand that you are doing that because there is no alternative. Do just enough of it to win. Avoid flamboyant showmanship, because it does not help deliver the system.

In software development, look for simple solutions to your process problems just as you look for simple solutions to your technical problems. Recall the one-sentence summary of Crystal Clear: "Put the people in a room with printing whiteboards, give them access to user experts, and have them deliver running tested software every two months." If you can do that, then just do that.

Reflection and Skill Development

Continue to develop your skill, and take time to reflect at regular intervals.

Microtouch Intervention

I do part company with Musashi in one area. He was in the business of killing or getting killed. I am in the business of helping people deliver software. There is a dramatic difference.

I like to cut quickly to the heart of the problem but keep the people fully intact. Arm-chopping is not an effective intervention strategy. I am after the smallest possible changes to the people on a project that accomplishes the job: *microtouch intervention*. (Actually, I suspect Musashi would agree with me, if he were in my business.)

Microtouch intervention is based on two ideas:

- With better understanding, smaller interventions are required.
- Many microscopic changes can produce a very large effect in unison.

Better understanding, smaller interventions. Two centuries ago, syphilis patients died. A century ago they underwent near-fatal arsenic treatments. These days they are given antibiotics. Early antibiotics were broad-spectrum bacteria killers; nowadays the antibiotics are targeted to the specific bacteria they are to kill.

Early computers were made with large vacuum tubes. Then, they were made with transistors. Now they are made with only a few thousands of atoms, recently even just single atoms.

Less energy is needed to effect a needed change the better we understand what we are doing. When we understand enough, we need only move molecules small distances, and the consequences will ripple out to produce the macro-effect we are interested in.

In software development, we are still in the amputation stage. As we better understand the forces underlying our profession, we can make smaller and smaller changes to improve a situation. I know that asking people to change their personal habits is a big request, and so I prefer to change team seating or a few job assignments and let the human communications mechanism effect the much larger changes.

Small changes add up. I find it remarkable that just aligning many, microscopically small magnetic domains in a metal converts a nonmagnet to a strong magnet.

Aligning people's purposes has the same effect on a project.

Imagine many people, working to their own value systems, pursuing whatever goals happen to hit them each day. They will sometimes, almost randomly, help each other or thwart each other.

Suppose you ask each person to make a tiny change, one that they find acceptably small. You can arrange the changes so that the people thwart each other less, help each other more. They are oriented in the same direction. With almost no energy change, the project team achieves a resulting power all out of proportion to the changes made (this is shown graphically in Figure 3-17 and Figure 3-18). This is summed up in Kent Arett's statement, "Paint the vision and get motivated people, and it's 'Game Over.'" (see "Fewer and Better" on page 161).

Microtouch intervention has its limits, of course. Sometimes, the correct move is not to continue with microtouch intervention but to replace the entire project structure with a new one. This happened once when we saw that a 30-person, colocated team could deliver the same as the failing 300-person multinational team.

The art, of course, is knowing when to rebuild the project and when microtouch intervention will work. Makes me wonder how Musashi would express that.

APPENDIX C

Books and References

BOOKS BY TITLE

A

Adaptive Software Development, Highsmith, J., Dorset House, New York, NY, 2000.

A Discipline for Software Engineering, Humphrey, W., Addison-Wesley, Reading, MA, 1995.

Agile Competitors and Virtual Organizations, Goldman, S., Nagle, R., Preiss, K., John Wiley & Sons, New York, NY, 1995.

Applying UML and Patterns: An Introduction to Object-Oriented Analysis and Design and the Unified Process, 2nd Ed., Larman, C., Prentice-Hall, Upper Saddle River, NJ, 2002.

B

Be Quick—But Don't Hurry!, Hill, A., Wooden, J., Simon and Schuster, New York, NY, 2001.

Birth of the Chaordic Age, Hock, D., Berret-Koehler, San Francisco, CA 1999.

C

Cleanroom Software Engineering Practices, Becker, S., Whittaker, J., Idea Group Publishing, Hershey, PA, 1996.

Common Knowledge: How Companies Thrive by Sharing What They Know, Dixon, N., Harvard Business School Press, Boston, MA, 2000.

Constantine on Peopleware, Constantine, L., Yourdon Press, Englewood Cliffs, NJ, 1995.

Crystal Clear: A Human-Powered Methodology for Small Teams, Cockburn, A., Addison-Wesley, Reading, MA, in preparation, draft online at http://members.aol.com/humansandt/crystal/clear.

D

Death March: The Complete Software Developer's Guide to Surviving 'Mission Impossible' Projects, Yourdon, E., Prentice-Hall, Upper Saddle River, NJ, 1997.

Deduction, Johnson-Laird, P., Byrne, R., Lawrence Erlbaum Associates, Mahwah, NJ, 1991.

Design Patterns, Gamma, E., Helm, R., Johnson, R., Vlissides, J., Addison-Wesley, Reading, MA, 1995.

Designing Object-Oriented Software, Wirfs-Brock, R., Wilkerson, B., Wiener, L., Prentice-Hall, Upper Saddle River, NJ, 1990.

Developing Object-Oriented Software: An Experience-Based Approach, IBM Object-Oriented Technology Center, Prentice-Hall, Upper Saddle River, NJ, 1997.

DSDM Dynamic Systems Development Method: The Method in Practice, Stapleton, J., Addison-Wesley, Reading, MA, 1997.

Dynamics of Software Development, McCarthy, J., Microsoft Press, Redmond, WA, 1995.

E

Extreme Programming Applied: Playing to Win, Auer, K., Miller, R., Addison-Wesley, Boston, MA, 2002.

Extreme Programming Explained: Embrace Change, Beck, K., Addison-Wesley, Boston, MA, 2000.

Extreme Programming in Practice, Newkirk, J., Martin, R., Addison-Wesley, Boston, MA, 2001.

Extreme Programming Installed, Jeffries, R., Hendrickson, C., Anderson, A., Addison-Wesley, Boston, MA, 2001.

F

Flow: The Psychology of Optimal Experience, Csikszentmihalyi, M., HarperCollins, New York, NY, 1991.

G

GUIs with Glue, Hohmann, L., Addison-Wesley, Boston, MA, in preparation.

I

If Only We Knew What We Know: The Transfer of Internal Knowledge and Best Practice, O'Dell, C., Grayson, C.J. Jr., The Free Press, New York, NY, 1998.

Improving Software Organizations, Mathiassen, L., Pries-Heje, J., Ngwenyama, O., Addison-Wesley, Boston, MA, 2001.

Inevitable Illusions: How Mistakes of Reason Rule Our Minds, Piattelli-Palmarini, M., John Wiley and Sons, New York, NY, 1996.

Introduction to the Personal Software Process, Humphrey, W., Addison-Wesley, Reading, MA, 1997.

J

Java Modeling in Color with UML, Coad, P., Prentice-Hall, Upper Saddle River, NJ, 1999.

Journey of the Software Professional, Hohmann, L. Prentice-Hall, Upper Saddle River, NJ, 1997.

Just for Fun: The Story of an Accidental Revolution, Torvalds, L., Diamond, D., Harperbusiness, New York, NY, 2001.

M

Making Sense of the Organization, Weick, K., Blackwell Business, Oxford, 2001.

Managing the Flow of Technology, Allen, T., MIT Press, Boston, MA, 1984.

Mathematical Theory of Communication, Shannon, C., Weaver, W., U. of Illinois Press, Champaign, IL, 1963.

O

Object-Oriented Analysis & Design with Applications, Booch, G., Benjamin-Cummings, San Francisco, CA, 1994.

Object-Oriented Methods, Pragmatic Considerations, Martin, J., Odell, J., Prentice-Hall, Upper Saddle River, NJ, 1998.

Object Solutions: Managing the Object-Oriented Project, Booch, G., Addison-Wesley, Reading, MA, 1996.

On Numbers and Games, Conway, J., Academic Press, London, 2000.

P

Peopleware: Productive Projects and Teams, 2nd Ed., DeMarco, T., Lister, T., Dorset House, New York, NY, 1999.

Planning Extreme Programming, Beck, K., Fowler, M., Addison-Wesley, Boston, MA, 2001.

Project Retrospectives: A Handbook for Team Reviews, Kerth, N., Dorset House, New York, NY, 2001.

Punished by Rewards: The Trouble with Gold Stars, Incentive Plans, A's, Praise, and Other Bribes, Kohn, A., Houghton Mifflin, Boston, MA, 1999, see also http://www.gnu.org/philosophy/motivation.html.

R

Reengineering the Corporation: A Manifesto for Business Revolution, Hammer, M., Champy, J., Harperbusiness, New York, NY, 1994.

S

Scrum: Agile Software Development, Schwaber, K., Beedle, M., Prentice-Hall, Upper Saddle River, NJ, 2002 (see also http://www.controlchaos.com).

Situated Learning: Legitimate Peripheral Participation, Lave, J., Wenger, E., Cambridge University Press, Cambridge, 1991.

Sketches of Thought, Goel, V., MIT Press, Boston, MA, 1995.

Skunk Works: A Personal Memoir of My Years at Lockheed, Rich, B., Janos, L., Little, Brown and Company, Boston, MA, 1994.

Software Creativity, Glass, R., Prentice-Hall, Upper Saddle River, NJ, 1995.

Software for Use, Constantine, L., Lockwood, L., Addison-Wesley, Reading, MA, 1999.

Surviving Object-Oriented Projects, Cockburn, A., Addison-Wesley, Reading, MA, 1998.

T

The Art of Computer Programming, Vol. 1-3, Knuth, D., Addison-Wesley, Reading, MA, 1997, 1998.

The Art of Systems Architecting, 2nd Edition, Maier, M., Rechtin, E., CRC Press, Boca Raton, FL, 2000.

The Book of Five Rings, Musashi, M., Cleary, T. (translator), Shambhala Publications, Boston, MA, 2000 (see also http://www.samurai.com/5rings/).

The Goal, Goldratt, E., North River Press, Great Barrington, MA, 1992.

The Mythical Man-Month: Essays on Software Engineering, Brooks, F., Addison-Wesley, Reading, MA, 1995.

The OPEN Process Specification, Graham, I., Henderson-Sellers, B., Younessi, H., Addison-Wesley, Reading, MA, 1997.

The Pragmatic Programmer: From Journeyman to Master, Hunt, A., Thomas, D., Addison-Wesley, Reading, MA, 2000.

The Psychology of Computer Programming, Weinberg, G., Silver Edition, Dorset House, New York, NY, 1998.

The Rational Unified Process, Kruchten, P., Addison-Wesley, Reading, MA, 1999.

The Science of Programming, Gries, D., Springer-Verlag, New York, NY, 1987.

The Sciences of the Artificial, Simon, H., MIT Press, Boston, MA, 1987.

The Selfish Gene, Dawkins, R., Oxford University Press, Oxford, 1990.

The Tree of Knowledge: The Biological Roots of Human Understanding, Maturana, H., Varela, F., Shambhala Publications, Boston, MA, 1998.

Theory of Constraints, Goldratt, E., North River Press, Great Barrington, MA, 1990.

U

Using CRC Cards: An Informal Approach to Object-Oriented Development, Wilkinson, N., SIGS Books and Multimedia, New York, NY, 1995.

W

Work-Oriented Development of Software Artifacts, Ehn, P., Arbetslivscentrum, Stockholm, 1988.

Writing Effective Use Cases, Cockburn, A., Addison-Wesley, Reading, MA, 2001.

REFERENCES BY AUTHOR

A

Allen, T., *Managing the Flow of Technology* MIT Press, Boston, MA, 1984.

Auer, K., Miller, R., *Extreme Programming Applied: Playing to Win*, Addison-Wesley, Boston, MA, 2002.

B

Bach, J., www.satisfice.com

Beck, K., Cunningham, W., "A Laboratory for Teaching Object-Oriented Thinking," *ACM SIGLPLAN* 24(10): 1–7, 1989.

Beck, K., *Extreme Programming Explained: Embrace Change*, Addison-Wesley, Boston, MA, 2000.

Beck, K., Fowler, M., *Planning Extreme Programming*, Addison-Wesley, Boston, MA, 2001.

Becker, S., Whittaker, J., *Cleanroom Software Engineering Practices*, Idea Group Publishing, Hershey, PA, 1996.

Booch, G., *Object-Oriented Analysis & Design with Applications*, Benjamin-Cummings, San Francisco, CA, 1994.

Booch, G., *Object Solutions: Managing the Object-Oriented Project*, Addison-Wesley, Reading, MA, 1996.

Bordia, P., Prashant, K., "Face-to-Face versus Computer-Mediated Communications: A Synthesis of the Literature," *The Journal of Business Communication* 34(1), U. of Illinois, Champaign, IL, Jan. 1997, pp. 99–120.

Brooks, F., *The Mythical Man-Month: Essays on Software Engineering*, Addison-Wesley, Reading, MA, 1995.

Brown, K., Klastorin, T. & Valluzzi, J., "Project Performance and the Liability of Group Harmony," *IEEE Transactions on Engineering Management*, 37(2), May 1990, pp. 117–125.

Burns, C., Dishman, E., Verplank, W., Lassiter, B., "Actors, Hairdos & Videotape—Informance Design: Using Performance Techniques in Multi-Disciplinary, Observation-Based Design," *Computer Human Interaction '94 Conference Companion*, Boston, MA, April 24–28, pp. 119–120.

C

The "C3" Team, "Chrysler Goes to 'Extremes,'" in *Distributed Object Computing*, October, 1998, pp. 24–28.

Coad, P., *Java Modeling in Color with UML*, Prentice-Hall, Upper Saddle River, NJ, 1999.

Cockburn, A., *Surviving Object-Oriented Projects*, Addison-Wesley, Reading, MA, 1998.

Cockburn, A., "The Expert-in-Earshot Project Management Pattern," in Succi, G., Marchesi, M., *Extreme Programming Examined*, Addison-Wesley, Reading, MA, 2001, pp. 245–247. (2001a)

Cockburn, A., Williams, L., "The Costs and Benefits of Pair Programming," in Succi, G., Marchesi, M., *Extreme Programming Examined*, Addison-Wesley, Reading, MA, 2001, pp. 223–247. (2001b)

Cockburn, A., *Writing Effective Use Cases*, Addison-Wesley, Reading, MA, 2001. (2001c)

Cockburn, A., *Crystal Clear: A Human-Powered Methodology for Small Teams*, Addison-Wesley, Reading, MA, in preparation, draft online at http://members.aol.com/humansandt/crystal/clear.

Constantine, L., *Constantine on Peopleware*, Yourdon Press, Englewood Cliffs, NJ, 1995.

Constantine, L., Lockwood, L., *Software for Use*, Addison-Wesley, Reading, MA, 1999.

Conway, J., *On Numbers and Games*, Academic Press, London, 2000.

Csikszentmihalyi, M., *Flow: The Psychology of Optimal Experience*, HarperCollins, New York, NY, 1991.

Curtis, P., Dixon, M., Frederick, R., Nichols, D., "The Jupiter Audi/Video Architecture: Secure Multimedia in Network Places," in *Proceedings of ACM Multimedia '95*, San Francisco, CA, pp. 79–90.

D

Dawkins, R., *The Selfish Gene*, Oxford University Press, Oxford, 1990.

DeMarco, T., Lister, T., *Peopleware: Productive Projects and Teams, 2nd Ed.*, Dorset House, New York, NY, 1999.

Dixon, N., *Common Knowledge: How Companies Thrive by Sharing What They Know*, Harvard Business School Press, Boston, MA, 2000.

E

Ehn, P., *Work-Oriented Development of Software Artifacts*, Arbetslivscentrum, Stockholm, 1988.

Ehn, P., "Scandinavian Design: On Participation and Skill," in *Usability: Turning Technologies into Tools*, P. S. Adler and T. A. Winograd, editors, Oxford University Press, New York, NY, 1992, pp. 96–132, online at http://www.ilt.columbia.edu/Publications/papers/Ehn.html.

F

Fox, R., "Shu Ha Ri," *The Iaido Newsletter*, 7(2), #54, Feb 1995, online at http://www.aikidofaq.com/essays/tin/shuhari.html.

Frakes, W., Fox, C., "Sixteen Questions about Software Reuse," *Communications of the ACM*, 38(6):75–87, 1995.

G

Gamma, E., Helm, R., Johnson, R., Vlissides, J., *Design Patterns*, Addison-Wesley, Reading, MA, 1995.

Glass, R., Vessey, I., Conger, S., "Software Tasks: Intellectual or Clerical?" in *Information and Management*, 23(4), Oct., 1992, pp. 183–191.

Glass, R., *Software Creativity*, Prentice-Hall, Upper Saddle River, NJ, 1995.

Goel, V., *Sketches of Thought*, MIT Press, Boston, MA, 1995.

Goldman, S., Nagle, R., Preiss, K., *Agile Competitors and Virtual Organizations*, John Wiley & Sons, New York, NY, 1995.

Goldratt, E., *Theory of Constraints*, North River Press, Great Barrington, MA, 1990.

Goldratt, E., *The Goal*, North River Press, Great Barrington, MA, 1992.

Graham, I., Henderson-Sellers, B., Younessi, H., *The OPEN Process Specification*, Addison-Wesley, Reading, MA, 1997.

Gries, D., *The Science of Programming*, Springer-Verlag, New York, NY, 1987.

Guindon, R., Curtis, B., "Insights from Empirical Studies of the Software Design Process," *Future Generation Computer Systems*, 7(2-3), April, 1992, pp. 139–149.

H

Hammer, M., Champy, J., *Reengineering the Corporation: A Manifesto for Business Revolution*, Harperbusiness, New York, NY, 1994.

Herring, R., Rees, M., "Internet-Based Collaborative Software Development Using Microsoft Tools," in *Proceedings of the 5th World Multiconference on Systemics, Cybernetics and Informatics* (SCI'2001). 22–25 July, 2001. Orlando, Florida. Online at http://erwin.dstc.edu.au/Herring/SoftwareEngineeringOverInternet-SCI2001.pdf.

Highsmith, J., *Adaptive Software Development*, Dorset House, New York, NY, 2000.

Hill, A., Wooden, J., *Be Quick—But Don't Hurry!*, Simon and Schuster, New York, NY, 2001.

Hock, D., *Birth of the Chaordic Age*, Berret-Koehler, San Francisco, CA, 1999.

Hohmann, L. *Journey of the Software Professional*, Prentice-Hall, Upper Saddle River, NJ, 1997.

Hohmann, L., *GUIs with Glue*, Addison-Wesley, in preparation.

Hovenden, F., "A Meeting and A Whiteboard (Describing the Power to Speak)," in *Proceedings of the 4th World Multiconference on Systemics, Cybernetics and Informatics* (SCI'2001). July, 2000. Orlando, Florida.

Humphrey, W., *A Discipline for Software Engineering*, Addison-Wesley, Reading, MA, 1995.

Humphrey, W., *Introduction to the Personal Software Process*, Addison-Wesley, Reading, MA, 1997.

Hunt, A., Thomas, D., *The Pragmatic Programmer: From Journeyman to Master*, Addison-Wesley, Reading, MA, 2000.

I

IBM Object-Oriented Technology Center, *Developing Object-Oriented Software: An Experience-Based Approach*, Prentice-Hall, Upper Saddle River, NJ, 1997.

J

Jeffries, R., Hendrickson, C., Anderson, A., *Extreme Programming Installed*, Addison-Wesley, Boston, MA, 2001.

Johnson-Laird, P., Byrne, R., *Deduction*, Lawrence Erlbaum Associates, Mahwah, NJ, 1991.

K

Kerth, N., *Project Retrospectives: A Handbook for Team Reviews*, Dorset House, New York, NY, 2001.

Knuth, D., *The Art of Computer Programming, Vol. 1-3*, Addison-Wesley, Reading, MA, 1997, 1998.

Kohn, A., *Punished by Rewards: The Trouble with Gold Stars, Incentive Plans, A's, Praise, and Other Bribes*, Houghton Mifflin, Boston, MA, 1999, see also http://www.gnu.org/philosophy/motivation.html.

Kruchten, P., *The Rational Unified Process*, Addison-Wesley, Reading, MA, 1999.

L

Larman, C., *Applying UML and Patterns: An Introduction to Object-Oriented Analysis and Design and the Unified Process, 2nd Ed.*, Prentice-Hall, Upper Saddle River, NJ, 2002.

Laubacher, R., Malone, T., "Retreat of the Firm and Rise of the Guilds: The Employment Relationship in an Age of Virtual Business," MIT Sloan School of Management 21st Century Initiative Working Paper #33, Aug. 2000.

Lave, J., Wenger, E., *Situated Learning: Legitimate Peripheral Participation*, Cambridge University Press, Cambridge, 1991.

M

Maier, M., Rechtin, E., *The Art of Systems Architecting 2nd Edition*, CRC Press, Boca Raton, FL, 2000.

Martin, J., Odell, J., *Object-Oriented Methods, Pragmatic Considerations*, Prentice-Hall, Upper Saddle River, NJ, 1998.

Mathiassen, L., Stage, J., "Informatics as a Multi-Disciplinary Education," in *Scandinavian Journal of Information Systems*, Vol. 11, No. 1, 1999.

Mathiassen, L., Pries-Heje, J., Ngwenyama, O., *Improving Software Organizations*, Addison-Wesley, Boston, MA, 2002.

Maturana, H., Varela, F., *The Tree of Knowledge: The Biological Roots of Human Understanding*, Shambhala Publications, Boston, MA, 1998.

McCarthy, J., Monk, A., "Channels, Conversation, Cooperation and Relevance: All You Wanted to Know about Communication but Were Afraid to Ask," in *Collaborative Computing*, Vol. 1, No. 1, March 1994, pp. 35–61.

McCarthy, J., *Dynamics of Software Development*, Microsoft Press, Redmond, WA, 1995.

Musashi, M., Cleary, T. (translator), *The Book of Five Rings*, Shambhala Publications, Boston, MA, 2000 (see also http://www.samurai.com/5rings/).

N

NASA, "Deorbit Flight Software Lessons Learned," JSC38609, NASA Johnson Space Center, Jan. 19, 1998.

Naur, P., "Programming as Theory Building," pp. 37–48 in *Computing: A Human Activity*, ACM Press, 1992.

Newkirk, J., Martin, R., *Extreme Programming in Practice*, Addison-Wesley, Boston, MA, 2001.

O

O'Dell, C., Grayson, C. J. Jr., *If Only We Knew What We Know: The Transfer of Internal Knowledge and Best Practice*, The Free Press, New York, NY, 1998.

P

Piattelli-Palmarini, M., *Inevitable Illusions: How Mistakes of Reason Rule Our Minds*, John Wiley and Sons, New York, NY, 1996.

R

Raymond, E., "Homesteading the Noosphere," http://tuxedo.org/~esr/writings/cathedral-bazaar/homesteading/.

Rich, B., Janos, L., *Skunk Works: A Personal Memoir of My Years at Lockheed*, Little, Brown and Company, Boston, MA, 1994.

S

Shannon, C., Weaver, W., *Mathematical Theory of Communication*, U. of Illinois Press, Champaign, IL, 1963.

Shrage, M., "The Proto Project," in *Fast Company*, May, 1999, p. 138, online at http://www.fastcompany.com/online/24/schrage.html.

Schwaber, K., Beedle, M., *Scrum: Agile Software Development*, Prentice-Hall, Upper Saddle River, NJ, 2002 (see also http://www.controlchaos.com).

Sillince, J.A., "A Model of Social, Emotional and Symbolic Aspects of Computer-Mediated Communication within Organizations," in *Computer Supported Cooperative Work*, Vol. 4, 1996, pp. 1–31.

Simon, H., *The Sciences of the Artificial*, MIT Press, Boston, MA, 1987.

Stapleton, J., *DSDM Dynamic Systems Development Method: The Method in Practice*, Addison-Wesley, Reading, MA, 1997.

Sullivan, K, Chalasani, P., Jha, S., Sazawal, V., "Software Design as an Investment Activity: A Real Options Perspective," in *Real Options and Business Strategy: Applications to Decision Making*, L. Trigeorgis (Ed.), Risk Books, December, 1999.

Sully, P., "Liveware Matters," *EXE Magazine*, 3(1), June, 1988, pp. 42–46.

T

Torvalds, L., Diamond, D., *Just for Fun: The Story of an Accidental Revolution*, Harperbusiness, New York, NY, 2001.

W

Webb, D., Humphrey, W., "Using TSP on the TaskView Project," in *CrossTalk, The Journal of Defense Software Engineering*, Feb. 1999, pp. 3–10. Online at http://www.stsc.hill.af.mil/crosstalk/1999/feb/webb.asp.7

Weick, K., *Making Sense of the Organization*, Blackwell Business, Oxford, 2001.

Weinberg, G., *The Psychology of Computer Programming*, Silver Edition, Dorset House, New York, NY, 1998.

Wilkinson, N., *Using CRC Cards: An Informal Approach to Object-Oriented Development*, SIGS Books and Multimedia, New York, NY, 1995.

Wirfs-Brock, R., Wilkerson, B., Wiener, L., *Designing Object-Oriented Software*, Prentice-Hall, Upper Saddle River, NJ, 1990.

X

Extreme Programming, http://extremeprogramming.com.

Y

Yourdon, E., *Death March: The Complete Software Developer's Guide to Surviving 'Mission Impossible' Projects*, Prentice-Hall, Upper Saddle River, NJ, 1997.

INDEX